Of a Certain Age

Of a Certain Age

NAIM ATTALLAH

QUARTET BOOKS

First published by Quartet Books Limited 1992
A member of the Namara Group
27/29 Goodge Street
London W1P 1FD

Copyright © by Naim Attallah 1992

A catalogue record for this title is available from the British Library

ISBN 0 7043 7028 X

Typeset by Contour Typesetters, Southall, London
Printed and bound in Great Britain by
Bookcraft Ltd , Midsomer Norton, Avon

In memory
of
Eric Asprey

CONTENTS

SIR HARDY AMIES

Hardy Amies was born in London in 1909. After studying languages in France and Germany he trained as a weighing-machine salesman in Birmingham before entering the world of design. In the 1930s he rose to become one of Britain's leading couturiers. During the war he served as an intelligence officer in the SOE and in 1946 he founded his own fashion house. His salon is one of the few left in Britain to rival the great dress houses of Paris. He is dressmaker by appointment to Queen Elizabeth and he was knighted in 1989.

In your autobiography you record that there was no marked display of affection in your childhood. Was that something you were aware of at the time or did it occur to you only on mature reflection?

I was never aware of it. I have the feeling of having had loving parents who were not demonstrative; I have no feeling of ever having been deprived of affection.

Were they ambitious for you?

Yes, my mother particularly so – and fortunately she lived just long enough to see the glimmering of the first successes.

Yet in your book you make a point of avoiding discussing the relationship with your mother. Why is that?

I don't know. I actually got on better with her than I did with my father, though he was a most affectionate man, and we didn't get on badly by any means, but in the long run he wasn't very bright, and she was brighter. My mother had what is laughingly called taste – of course it was restricted to suburban taste, her life being very circumscribed. She was a village girl, but because of the years that she'd spent in a court dressmaker's she could recognize a real lady, and how she behaved, and she respected that.

Your brother who was Down's Syndrome 'coloured your childhood' as you put it. Did you resent the amount of attention and care he required?

Not in any way whatsoever. It's only looking back that I realize that it must have been a tremendous strain on my mother and on the resources of my father. But I wasn't conscious of that at the time, and I never had any feelings of disappointment. We loved him – Down's Syndrome children are always lovable – and later I inherited responsibility for him when my parents died, but by that time he had been in a home for several years.

You left the family circle at the first opportunity, and though you insist there was nothing 'unpleasant' about your upbringing, one has the impression that yours was not a very happy childhood . . .

3

It was certainly pursued by a lack of money, but although that imposed huge restrictions, we were not on the poverty line. Overall, I think we were happy.

Your mother's death seems to have been a terrible blow. What are your memories of that time?

She had been ill with cancer for so long that there was an element of relief; it was only afterwards I was moved.

Your father remarried within a short time, and both you and your sister seem to have disapproved of his second wife. Why was that?

Although she was a goodhearted woman she was socially very inferior to our standards, which is an awfully snobbish thing to say, but it's true. As in most families the daughter is closer to the father, and so my sister minded more than I did. She was at first jealous of this really hideous woman. She was so ugly apart from anything else.

Then why did he marry her?

I wouldn't care to go into the details. I now realize that my father was a very sexy man, and obviously she had certain tricks which satisifed him.

You are very close to your sister Rosemary . . . is she the most important person in your life?

Yes. I'm six years older than she is, rather bossy, and frankly, much cleverer than she is, something she has always admitted herself. There are strains which are difficult to articulate. I am very conscious of my responsibility towards her, but one of the difficulties is that she is, I think, sexless, in the sense of not really being interested in sex, although she has had sentimental attachments to women. Consequently, she's never really understood my life which perplexes her still. It's difficult for her to accept that I have male friends, though there are some who have always been in my life and with them she has made friends, I'm happy to say.

She hates it when people call you effeminate.

Yes. I am able to laugh at it, because I'm not really effeminate at all. In fact I would loathe to be a woman. Another difficulty is that she accuses me of not liking women; and that is true to an extent. I like them as artistic figures, as a sculptor likes his clay, but on the whole I despise their minds.

So you feel much more comfortable in the presence of men.

Yes. It's not that I don't want women in my life – I'm very happy to have them around. But we're in danger of getting on to sex, which I said we weren't going to talk about.

In the early 1930s when you were in Germany you were a great enthusiast for Hitler – like, of course, a great many other people then, before the direction of his interests became clear. Were you very disillusioned?

The disillusionment came gradually. The family with whom I stayed welcomed Hitler as a saviour of the middle classes and the aristocracy, and I simply went along with them and didn't question their judgement. A much greater influence in my life at that time was the manager of the local factory, a north German, an extremely orderly man who, I now realize, was very attracted to me. He was an intelligent, politically clear-thinking man, who favoured the Nazis to begin with, but changed in the course of events, and by the time I left he was very disillusioned.

Have you ever taken a serious interest in politics since then? Have you ever joined a political party?

No. I'm only interested from the outside. Our local MP is Douglas Hurd, and I go to his meetings out of politeness to him. Also, before the last election I couldn't bear the thought of the socialists winning, so I wanted to give him all the help I could.

I doubt whether it's generally known that you were part of special forces during the last war. That would seem improbable to those with

5

stereotypical ideas of a dress designer. Did you enjoy that period of your life?

Not really. I considered myself lucky to have spent the major part of the war in a branch of the War Office in London. Unless I was on duty, which was about once a month, I had every Sunday and half of Saturday free and was generally home by 6 o'clock. This enabled me to keep my hand in in the dressmaking world. I still suffer from a bad conscience from that time, however, since I think I ought to have resigned because I didn't believe in what I was doing. I didn't think the idea of dropping parachutists into occupied countries was working; I suspected always that we were so infiltrated that we dropped people straight into enemy hands. I considered the whole operation tremendously amateurish and I started to feel quite cynical about things.

Did you always want to be a dressmaker?

No, I never thought about it. It always seemed something so remote from our lives, in spite of my mother. And in those days there were no designers in England; clothes were bought in Paris. It wasn't until I had an offer from the husband of my mother's boss that I suddenly thought, my God, this of course is what I want to do.

I imagine that a lot of people not in the business regard dress design as a frivolous affair. Does that bother you?

No. I am not aware that people do regard it in that way. On the contrary, they are always amazed to hear about how much I earn for the country. At the time I joined the profession it was becoming socially acceptable, so I profited from that development.

How on earth did you manage to set up any sort of business, let alone a fashion house, at a time of such terrible austerity?

The war was a long time starting and it was a long time finishing. Churchill wanted unconditional surrender, which horrified me in view of my German connections. But during the time it dragged on I had the chance to lay down plans. I felt no guilt, since I didn't take any hours off, just my full allowance of free time. Then my darling stepmother gave me a thousand pounds, which was quite a lot of money in those days. I had ten thousand pounds when I started, and we made ten thousand pounds profit during the first year. There was actually no feeling of austerity; everybody wanted new clothes. The Americans were the ones who really encouraged us, because they were on my doorstep before we even had the clothes – in fact they bought them from paper patterns. I opened on 1 February 1946, and by April I was in America at their expense.

In an interview with Richard Rosenfeld you used terms like 'smarty pants' with some affection and talked about the 'gentry'. Did you feel very conscious of social divisions when you began? You appeared to adore the smart set.

Yes, I knew that I had to get on. Looking back, I learned the language of the English upper class just as I'd learned German and French. The London upper class is like a club and I am always amazed that I am admitted as a member. And I'm so very pleased, because one meets much more interesting people. Sometimes I see others in the same business and I think, how naff you are. I'm not naff, but I easily could have been.

You describe yourself as a self-confessed snob. Have you no qualms about that at all?

No. I am a staunch supporter of the class system. I uphold it out of conviction; it's the best of England, no question about it.

Don't you have a commercial incentive to say that?

Of course, the commercial side suits me very well, but there are two more important reasons. Firstly I have a happier life for being a snob because I have a wide circle of friends, and the top people are far more interesting than the bottom people. Secondly, I'm very keen on English history and have an above average knowledge of it, certainly above average for a dressmaker. I have also lived in Germany, and I am perfectly at home in France, and I know how much both of these countries would love to have a queen. The French and German aristocracies are clubs within themselves; they are self-supporting, but there's no top.

So you're a great supporter of the monarchy?

I would die for it. I really would take out a gun and go and shoot people if they ever threatened it. It's one of our most precious assets. To destroy it would be the most wicked thing. I say this not just because I admire the present Queen. I would still support the monarchy even if we had a bad queen, heaven forfend that we did. It's the idea I defend; primogeniture is order – it's God.

You design dresses for the Queen. How important is that for you?

I'm really a supplier, a *fournisseur*, a furnisher of clothing to her. She accepts my advice if it suits her to do so. Her guiding principle in ordering clothes is that they shall be appropriate to the occasion for which she wants them. Not that she has explained all that to me – it's something I sense. She has supremely good manners.

You clearly have great admiration for her.

Enormous, and for many reasons – her politeness, the order of her mind, the way the palace is run, the way she has never failed to keep an appointment.

I suppose there is a sense in which the fashion business depends on a certain sort of snobbery, on the urge to be differently and better dressed than others.

I don't think that's an urge of any consequence. Our customers simply want to be comfortable and correctly dressed for the occasion. There is sometimes a competitive element, most evident when mothers are choosing a wedding dress for their daughter, and want it to be better than the one they saw on their friend's daughter. But the competitiveness is not so strong in their ordinary buying; in many cases they don't want to stand out, they just want to be comfortably acceptable.

You have promoted an 'English style'. What do you think are its characteristics?

The main characteristics of the English style is that it has to have something to do with the country. A well-dressed, well-bred English-woman is at her best when she looks as though she has either just come up from the country or is just going back there. Urban clothes are better made by the French. Another feature is a certain nonchalance – a word invented in my studio. We abhor the dressed-up look, and we're not good at what is called dead chic – *mort chic* – that's not our line of country. There also has to be a curious timelessness about English clothes, because it's not good style to wear a new dress. My favourite duchess gave a very important private ball for which she wore a twenty-five-year-old dress. She had a new dress made by me for the servants' ball which took place the day before so the servants could not say that her grace was wearing an old dress. But for her own proper ball she wore an old dress and she looked marvellous. That is English style at its best.

Do you think of your designs as artworks? After all, they are clearly works of imagination . . .

Absolutely not. I look on them as the work of an artisan. I don't like going to museums where they have collections of garments which have usually been designed for one particular occasion, then put away. My clothes are worn out and do not appear in museums.

I suppose dress designing is so personal a service that you become closely acquainted with some of your customers, a bit like a portrait painter . . .

That's not quite true. I have seen very few of my customers over forty years. Don't forget the structure of the house which dictates that clients are seen by a *vendeuse* who does more than just sell; she serves the customer and waits on her and guides her through all the fittings, and very often becomes her friend. I like to retire and leave it to her. It is also a question of

9

using up time and energy; I love to see my customers, but if my business were based on their always having to see me, I'd have been dead years ago. I don't even see the Queen any more.

I have always wondered quite how it is that fashions change in the way they do. It never seems to be the case that things are suddenly and radically different. Do you think there is some sort of evolutionary law which governs it?

Fashion changes much less than you think. The idea of it changing is one promoted by newspapers which find it a very good way of filling a page. The women I know, not only my own customers but in my life generally, change the length of their skirts by perhaps one inch per season. Good expensive clothes for ladies don't actually date. I recently went to a very high-class wedding in Scotland and saw five different women wearing coats which were ten years old. I felt proud of that.

And they looked smart?

They looked correct. There is a difference. It's a difference the Queen understands; she knows being too smart implies something hard. The Duchess of Windsor on the other hand dressed too smartly.

You said once that you can always tell when a lady's got style – 'You have only to see her in her underclothes to appreciate that.' Perhaps you've been luckier than I have, but how else can you tell . . . I mean, what constitutes style?

I think the word is insouciance. You must never show that you are impressed by your own clothes, or have that 'Don't I look wonderful?' expression. You must never be conquered by your clothes; style is to be master of your clothes. When you see women in their underwear they must be immaculate. I take a rather old-fashioned view since most ladies of great style nowadays wear Marks and Spencer underwear, but I prefer the undergarment to be of beautiful quality, superbly hand-made, and extremely plain. Frilly underclothes constitute extremely bad style.

There are now design schools and indeed art schools with sections devoted to clothes design. Do you think it is actually possible for the industry to sustain the current numbers of designers?

No. A very wise question. Firstly I deplore the fact that there are design departments in art schools; it gives them quite the wrong idea, because clothes design is not art, it's craftsmanship. They even give degrees now which is totally idiotic. In my view a dress is not a dress until it has been sold; before that it's just a rough sketch, a suggestion. There must be the desire for a woman to possess it, to pay money for it, and that philosophy is sadly lacking in the art schools. Secondly there has definitely been a decline in the teaching of craft. There should be more prizes for craftsmanship rather than design. What we lack are trained craftsmen and craftswomen, not designers. There are too many designers.

Fashion will I suppose become more and more international, especially with the advent of the Common Market at the end of this year. Will there be room for distinctive national differences? Indeed, is it possible now to see that a particular dress is French or Italian?

If it looks vulgar it has a good chance of being Italian as distinct from French. But that is an unattractive remark.

You have been outspoken, if not scathing, about women in design. Why is it that there are so few well-known women designers? One would have thought that they were the obvious source for ideas and yet many of the more famous designers seem to be men.

Men are objective, women are not – about clothes, or indeed anything else. The one outstanding exception was Chanel, and it is extraordinary how her influence is still felt today. But she had a man's mind and was very disciplined in her designs. Also a designer of high-class expensive clothes cannot exist alone; he has to have a team with him, and this is what is forgotten by most people, and certainly not appreciated by the press. I am here today at the age of eighty-three because I have support, and in three years' time my house will have been fifty years in existence. I am the boss, and men make better bosses than women do. Because we're more intelligent.

11

Twenty years ago you were saying that the couture business was really finished; it was too labour intensive to make any money. But it still seems to be going. How long do you think such businesses might continue?

Well, we lose money at the moment, but if we are clever enough to earn in other fields, in licensing fees, in design labels, and in using our studio intelligently, then I think we will win through.

Have you ever designed clothes to be provocative?

Not consciously. They are sometimes seductive, but not provocative. If a dress is too sexy it's a bad dress, I've always said.

At one point you sold a considerable share in your business to Debenham's only to buy it back again later on. Why did you feel it was necessary to do that? Did they try to control your creative output?

No, they didn't do that. The disadvantage was essentially in having new bosses, in fact in having bosses at all, since I'd always been totally independent. When they bought us they promised to do two things: one was to help launch a women's ready-to-wear business which would have had the marvellous platform of Debenham's sixty shops; secondly they were going to launch a proper scent business – but they did neither. And in addition we had the aggravation of being bossed by them. There was blatant jealousy towards me, and it was also quite clear to them that they couldn't control me. Though I had no shares in the business most of the contracts were in my name – Japan, for example, would never have given a contract to Debenham's, they would only give it to Hardy Amies. This irked them, but in the end it always comes down to personalities, and the personalities at Debenham's were inferior. When it all came to a head and they wanted me to do something which I wouldn't do, they said – and the words still ring in my ears – 'If you don't do this, Hardy, we'll cut you up into little pieces,' meaning they would destroy me. I thought it was time to part company, so a favourable price was arranged and I bought myself back.

The recession continues to bite despite all the government talk. I imagine that the fashion business must feel the force of that very early . . .

When there is a recession people buy wisely. If a woman is prepared to spend £2,500 on a suit, she knows she is buying the best possible value. So the recession hits shoddier merchandise more than ours. We suffer a little bit, but my retail figures for the last year are down only ten per cent, which is not too bad, and the overseas revenue is up.

You never married. Was that a conscious decision or was it just that the right circumstances never occurred?

It never occurred to me that I would marry. I did once get engaged to a girl, but I cannot think why; it certainly wasn't because I wanted to go to bed with her. I thought perhaps she would make a good wife to me, but she was sensible enough to say no. I have been quite content and self-contained in the way I have lived, and I've never felt lonely for one minute. I have my sister, and I love having friends around. Ken Fleetwood who has been with me for forty-two years and is now the design director of my business comes to my country house fifty weekends out of fifty-two. We are not lovers, but he is like a son to me in the broadest sense.

About three years ago I interviewed Harold Acton who is a confirmed bachelor, but when I asked him if he had ever desired a woman, he said that he had, and indeed had a penchant for oriental women. Have you ever desired a woman?

No. I'm tremendously physical but I can't say I have ever desired a woman. I love flesh, I'm very tactile, very 'MTF' – Must Touch Flesh. I actually love touching women for the pleasure of it, to hold their hands, to stroke their arms, and I love beautiful women. It gives me immense pleasure to dress a woman to perfection. You can't do it to a man because he just looks a pratt, a bloody fool. So curiously enough whilst I am obviously attracted to men more than I am to women, I still think it is idiotic to dress a man. I've always said a man should order his clothes with intelligence, put them on with care and then forget all about them.

You have, I believe, made arrangements to leave your fashion house to your employees. Certainly a very generous gesture, but I wonder if you have ever regretted not having had children to come after you?

It never crossed my mind. In fact I'm very grateful I haven't got children. The children of men in the dress business all seem to want to be lawyers or bankers, they never want to follow their fathers. When I see the troubles and responsibilities that children bring, I don't regret not having had children for one moment.

How would you sum up your recipe for success?

I've worked hard, not desperately hard, but I've always done my duty and I have a conscience about not doing the right thing. I have also had an amazing amount of luck. Perhaps the most significant factor was my three years on the road as a salesman selling weighing machines; it was not a very happy existence, but I did it and created an aura of orderliness and of dutifulness which somehow stood me in good stead. If I hadn't done my duty with that rotten job I would never have got the good one.

I understand Molyneux was your god, why is that?

Firstly because he was an Englishman, secondly he had extremely good taste in clothes. He believed in simplicity, as I do. All good clothes are totally unfussy. The first dress I ever saw of his was the simplest possible garment that just buttoned up the front, but it was absolutely impeccably made in beige linen with black buttons. And I learned that lesson and I follow it to this day. Although I can't draw, I have a gift of being able to see a garment from a piece of cloth. There are glib designers, little boys who can draw, make a little sketch, but they never seriously think of it, as I do. When I'm working on an article I think about it all the time, and then it takes me ten minutes to write it, because it's already written in my head. Although I don't want to compare myself with a genius, this is exactly what Mozart did. On the way to Prague he was thinking about what he was going to write when he got there, and then he sat down and wrote the overture to *Don Giovanni* in ten minutes.

How important is a beautiful face for the success of a dress?

A beautiful face helps tremendously, but the real challenge for the designer is to give a woman grace; it's what I call honouring cloth – you mustn't foul it up. No seam is ever attractive, so you must have a minimum of seams, then you have to achieve a certain skill of disguise. A woman of a certain age does not have an attractive bosom, and anyway to show the bosom too markedly is common; to disguise is very important. Then you indicate the waist by the position of the buttons, rather than by nipping it in – the cloth must not be fucked up.

At the age of eighty-three you seem very fit. What is your secret?

Homoeopathy is very important in my life. I'm not fanatical about it but I will use a homoeopathic remedy if I possibly can. I haven't taken an aspirin for fifty years. And tennis is a very good cosmetic. I play an hour's tennis on Saturday and Sunday, and for the rest of the week people tell me how well I look.

I read somewhere that you're not in the least afraid of death.

No. You're just going into nothing, so why should you be frightened of nothing? I don't believe in an afterlife. I believe in the existence of God, but it could have any other name – nature, for example, or order. I think there's something that was put into our minds, and the question is, why the fuck are we here? I don't know the answer, but there is something we want to order, but the order is gone when you're dead, totally gone. And I don't mind it. I was meant to have a life, not a death.

A lot of people who are not religious in their youth, tend to become more religious with advancing years.

I don't have that feeling at all. My sister, being six years younger, thinks I'm going to die before her, and she would like to have a funeral for me. I quite agree, because I don't know of any other way of doing it. These non-denominational affairs are too awful for words. I'd rather have the whole thing, incense and choir, the lot. But this is nothing to do with fear, nothing to do with getting on the right side of God, not ·remotely.

15

And nothing to do with conviction?

No. It's *toujours la politesse*. It's good manners.

You were knighted in 1989. After the long association with the royal family did you not think this was a somewhat belated honour?

No. It never crossed my mind. I still think it's the biggest stroke of luck. Queen Victoria founded the Royal Victorian Order for services to the sovereign. I don't think she ever intended it for dressmakers.

You've had two books published now. Has that been a rewarding experience?

Publishers have one serious fault and that is that they never read anything. [Laughs.] You just know they haven't read the bloody book. George Weidenfeld is quite an inspiring man to help you make a book, but I don't think he's terribly interested. In any case I think my books are pretty dull in the end because they've got so many tactful omissions. Men should never have women editors because they don't understand how men's minds work. Diana Mosley was so funny when she said apropos of publishers that they all keep a troupe of Nigerians in their cupboards and when they edit a book they bring one out of the cupboard and give her a stub pencil. Women always bring in irrelevancies. They're illogical creatures. Even Mrs Thatcher is a typical example, quite illogical, doesn't follow it through. She also imitates an upper-class voice which is the biggest grating thing that anybody can do. The voice is the key to the class system in England; once a man or woman opens his or her mouth you know what his or her class is. True Scots accents, or Lancashire, or Manchester, they're lovely; what is awful is the whine, the Walthamstow whine.

You're a very emotional man. Have you ever fallen madly in love?

Oh yes . . . every week, mostly with the milkman. [Laughs.]

How would you like to be remembered?

I would like people to say, oh we miss him, he was such fun. I like laughing with people more than anything in the world. Life is a joke, a big joke.

CLAUS VON BULOW

Claus von Bulow was born in Denmark in 1926. He was educated in Switzerland and Denmark and at the age of sixteen he went to Trinity College, Cambridge. He attended l'Ecole des Sciences Politiques at the Sorbonne in Paris, and after a period with Hambros Bank in London he was called to the bar at Middle Temple and was a member of the chambers of Lord Hailsham. Later he served for many years as chief executive assistant to J. Paul Getty. In 1985, after two spectacular trials in the US, he was acquitted of the charge of attempting to murder his wife.

Your parents divorced when you were four years old. Do you have any memories of that time?

No. One is told about that time, and then one thinks it becomes a memory, but it isn't really. I remember a cherry tree outside my bedroom and a very attractive housemaid, but I don't remember my parents living together. One has selected memories.

What happened to you immediately after that? Did you live with your mother?

Yes, my mother was given custody. My father ultimately remarried a nice Norwegian girl, the granddaughter of Ibsen the playwright, and so that gave a new dour atmosphere to my father's household. He was a great charmer, I suppose you would call him a *boulevardier*, a man about town who had endless mistresses and a great many children out of wedlock, here and there. I remember very well an occasion when I was about eight years old, and after lunch my grandfather suggested a walk in the garden. I thought, oh my God, he's going to tell me the facts of life, but no, he was about to tell me who wasn't who; Oscar Wilde said '*Debrett's Peerage* is the best work of fiction in the English language,' and Trevelyan said, 'Nobody who was anybody knew who their father was.' My grandfather was very anxious that I shouldn't end up inadvertently marrying one of my own sisters, or indeed make a gaffe at the dinner table.

But did you have anything to do with your father?

Not much. I'm sure he had access but I don't recall seeing him very much. I was very ill around the age of seven – undoubtedly I had what you would call a tubercular tendency – and so I was sent off to boarding school in Switzerland, and immediately became very healthy. It was the Danish climate that disagreed with me. I suppose there was commercial aviation in 1934, but it was a pretty dicey proposition, so a boy at school in Switzerland stayed until the summer holidays. I didn't come home at Christmas or Easter, it was too much of a hassle.

But can you recall how you viewed your father then?

19

I don't really think I had much of an opinion. My father never paid a penny towards my education or my maintenance. That was left to my maternal grandfather who was a very austere, dignified, Victorian gentleman, whereas my father was a helluva lot of fun, and to a child the question of who pays the bills just doesn't occur. I therefore feel guilty towards my grandfather, but later I made it up to him.

Did you inherit anything from your father, do you think?

I inherited a sort of skill as a raconteur. Some people have even thought of me as a womanizer . . . and all that is from my father.

And a taste for good living?

No, I think my grandfather also enjoyed good living, but it wouldn't have included promiscuity. He was the northern Protestant Lutheran incarnate, and very choleric, and I feel bad that neither his three daughters nor I could get very close to him, because I came to realize that the love and gifts from him were incomparably greater than those from my father. My grandfather of course was very much an establishment figure, whereas my father was a playwright and a drama critic.

Was he successful?

Yes, all his plays were produced at the Royal National Theatre in Copenhagen, and mementoes from those productions are still exhibited in the gallery there. He was indisputably the leading drama critic of his day. He introduced Brecht and others of that ilk to the Scandinavian stage and was for many years the president of the German–Danish Literary Society. This was perhaps his undoing. The German occupation of Denmark differed marginally from that of other European countries. The fighting lasted only a few hours. The king and the government stayed on and repeatedly ordered everyone to carry on normally with their work. There was therefore no collaborationist government, and distinctions were a bit fuzzy. Of course, there were strong feelings; Denmark had often fought German invasions. General Franz von Bülow had commanded the successful battle against a Prussian invasion in 1848, and my maternal grandfather lost five cousins in the 1864 war. My father was more like Furtwängler, whose biography you recently published. They both thought that art was outside politics. My father accepted the Goethe Prize and the Humbolt Prize and allowed his plays to be performed in Berlin and throughout the Nazi empire. Today this sounds pretty innocent, but I did not think so at the time, and nor did the Danish people at the moment of liberation in 1945. However, moods change. A favourable biography of my father was published in Denmark in 1988, entitled *The Price of Vanity*. Not a bad title for both of our lives. It's the old saying about going for a ride on a tiger and ending up inside.

How did you feel when he was accused of collaboration?

It was of course after the war that he was accused of collaboration, and it didn't really occur to me during the war that he was doing just that. I should say that until August 1943 Denmark was occupied by the Wehrmacht without the disagreeable ancillaries like the Gestapo and the SS. My mother had rather powerful and influential friends in England and when Denmark was invaded they suggested that there were ways of getting me out but she decided to wait and see what happened. But by the time I was fifteen all sorts of canards were sent out from England, such as that the second front could be on the west coast of Jutland, which would have given much quicker access to Berlin than the Pas de Calais. She fell for this one, so she flew to Sweden and started communicating with me from there and trying to get me to visit her for Christmas 1942. In fairness to my father, he went to the German ambassador in Copenhagen and asked if his fifteen-year-old schoolboy son could have an exit visa to go to Sweden for Christmas. It all seems extraordinary today but I'm sure he got it because he was *persona grata* there. And so I came to Sweden. What they had not anticipated was that my mother would smuggle me out in the bomb bay of a Mosquito night bomber to England. That illustrates my idealistic schoolboy naïvety: hip hip hooray! England here I come! It never occurred to me that I might cause difficulties for my father.

And did you?

I don't think so, because at that time the particular people in authority in the German occupation would have made more trouble for themselves.

The situation wasn't helped by the BBC who broadcast my escape as a triumph. After the war my father was put into custody, tried and ultimately acquitted because what he had done did not constitute an offence. He had not broadcast German propaganda, he had not written for them, he had not denounced anybody. Had he had dinner with the wrong people? Yes, and that is something that is socially objectionable conduct, but it is not a criminal offence, even in a treason trial. It was giving a good name to a bad cause. It can very easily happen to somebody who is not politically aware.

You did not visit your father when he was in prison and he died the year after he was released. Do you have any regrets in that area now?

Oh no, I offered to go and see him. He didn't want it.

Why not?

How would I know? You must remember we were not very close. There was another wife and there were three children by her, and my father had not paid very much attention to me as a child.

Was your change of name from Borberg to von Bulow solely on account of wishing to dissociate yourself from your father's family name?

No. My name was von Bulow from the age of four. I went to school under that name. My mother took back her maiden name because my grandfather had no male heirs. In order to finalize matters legally I had to wait until the age of eighteen, but in a pragmatic sense I took the name much earlier.

The name von Bulow sounds much more aristocratic, and there are those who have suggested that this was an early sign of your upwardly mobile tendencies.

Then they are crediting me with extraordinary precocity, because it happened when I was four. I could show you the captions under the photographs in my school magazine, and later on the Cresta Run, where I was the youngest rider in 1937, aged ten.

Your childhood seems to have been unsettled and unconventional.

Not at all. I don't think you can call divorce by itself unconventional. Today approximately fifty per cent of people who get married eventually divorce. I had a very privileged childhood, went to the nicest schools, even though going to boarding school aged seven in another country is really being thrown in at the deep end. But I think it's rather good for a child not to be dependent on the affiliations created by his parents. You learn to swim. Obviously boarding school away from parents is a calculated risk, and in the days of severe bullying and punishments I'm sure there were people who were irretrievably damaged. In my case I learned three foreign languages, and more importantly I learned how to adjust in a foreign environment. I am sure this was helpful much later both in the Middle East and the Far East.

Did you cry?

No, I took a little memory image of my mother as she would deposit me at the school at the beginning of term, and I would replay that as a private movie, just as everybody in sexual relationships has a private movie in their mind.

Did you have a good relationship with your mother throughout your adolescence and early manhood?

There was a gap in the first three years of the war, because she was in England and I was not, but I think we had a good relationship. She had a wonderful sense of humour, she was exceedingly eccentric, and very beautiful. I kept hoping that one or other of several admirers would in fact marry her. She was an extraordinary and wonderful human being who totally immersed herself in my future. She made great sacrifices, and during rationing she fed this growing young male to her own deprivation. It may have suited her, of course. Women are much more fortunate than men in that they really have that sense of sacrifice and devotion. Of course, somebody else is the materialistic beneficiary of that, but it is the gift that makes your richer. And I have, because of the tragedy much later in life, been given something of the same opportunity with my daughter.

The circumstances surrounding your mother's death seem shrouded in mystery, with even a hint of scandal. Some people have even accused you of murdering your own mother. What exactly happened?

My mother died of a heart attack. She had had a heart condition for some time, and she died aged fifty-nine, which of course is young. But there's absolutely no mystery. She simply died in the night. I was not living there at the time with her. There was nothing strange about it. Whenever the spotlight is on anybody, there are always people who want to show that they know the celebrity in question – or in my case the notoriety – and so they will start inventing stories as if they were intimates. They can then bask in the reflected glory of this morning's news. As we well know, and this goes for the media in general, good news is no news.

One of the suggestions was that you reported her death four days after it happened.

But that is not true. That came in the Hollywood film and they were forced to take it out. What do you do when somebody for whom you are responsible has died, or you think she has died? It is immediately *reported* to the doctor who, depending on circumstances, reports it to the proper authorities. There are certain formalities which it is the doctor's duty to perform. There was nothing odd about it, it was not a motor car accident, not a suicide, not a murder. The doctor then issues his certificate, and then you, the bereaved, the next of kin, go to – in my case – the Westminster records office and *record* the demise. There is a delay, especially as in this case a weekend came in between, but it's a purely bureaucratic one. The Hollywood scriptwriter changed the word 'recorded' to 'reported' in order to create an artificial box-office mystery. They knew the official files proved them wrong, but they refused to change the word and the insunuation until their lawyers told them to change the worldwide film prints!

Nothing else?

Nothing else. You have to remember that Hollywood on a multi-million-dollar project does not make unintentional errors. They have fact finders, and they knew perfectly well that there was no mystery, but if there's no mystery, there's no box office, and so they invent what is conceptually a libel in order to sell tickets.

You studied at Cambridge. Was that a significant period in your life?

Yes, I was at university at an age when most people are still at high school. I was extraordinarily fortunate – I'm damned if I know why – but I was picked up by a lot of people who were much older than I, and who, I am sure, needed an audience. For instance, I became a wheelchair-pusher to a man called John Hayward, who shared digs with T.S. Eliot at a house called Merton Hall which belonged to Victor Rothschild. Even after going down from Cambridge, I would push John Hayward's wheelchair to the theatre, to the films, to restaurants, and he probably taught me more about the use of the English language than any curriculum ever did. Eliot was a very shy man who didn't give much to an undergraduate, but enough. There were others like E.M. Forster, who was a don at King's, and Bertrand Russell, who was a fellow at my college, Trinity. I don't know whether it was because of the war and the fact that I was a young foreigner, but I also got quite close to Trevelyan who was master of Trinity.

Did you ever come across Evelyn Waugh?

Yes, indeed. I remember a luncheon with Evelyn and Christopher Sykes. Waugh had been treated for depression at the time. He had grown a moustache, and Christopher said that he'd never seen him with a moustache before. 'Oh,' said Evelyn, 'I've had three moustaches: the first one was in a fit of enthusiasm on achieving the age of puberty, the second one was when through a clerical error in the War Office I was commissioned in the Household Cavalry, and this third one is in direct competition with Lady Pamela Berry.' Later I got to know Cocteau well. He was one of these people who have no unexhausted potential. He had been a poet, a dramatist, a film maker, a draughtsman, a ballet writer – he had done everything. He was greatest perhaps as a conversationalist, because he was not one of the great intellects of this century, but when you listened to him, and you didn't just listen to his voice, you watched the movements of his hands as he was talking, you had never had a better conversation in your life. I also came across André Gide. There was a wonderful story about André Gide having buggered a little boy in Morocco. Afterwards he said to the boy, 'You have just had intimate relations with the greatest living French author', and the boy replied, 'Who? François Mauriac?'

And after Cambridge you were called to the bar?

No, I was too young to go to the bar. I went to Paris and attended the Sorbonne – l'Ecole des Sciences Politiques – and after that I did a year as a trainee in Hambros Bank. By that time I was old enough 'to eat my dinners' and to be called to the bar.

And you worked with Quintin Hogg, now Lord Hailsham?

Yes, but before that I was a pupil to a man called Jack Ashworth, who was the treasury counsel and later became a high court judge as they always do – that was my privilege. I only mention this because it required security clearance since you have government papers going across your desk the whole time, and it had never occurred to me at any time since I left Denmark to change my nationality. Denmark was still a free country after World War II and there was no earthly reason for changing one's passport. Much later, in America, it counted very much against me during my trial. I remember the judge in Newport saying, 'I'm not so naïve as not to realize that there are tax advantages', which was total boloney. In America, a resident in the United States pays all the same taxes as the US citizen. Coming back to Quintin Hogg, it is too pretentious or presumptious to say I worked with him. I simply went into chambers, and they were Quintin Hogg's chambers.

Was he a significant influence in your early life?

I'd like to think that anybody who is somewhat bigger than the norm is an influence in your life. Quintin is a very remarkable classical scholar and intellect and – he would hate my saying this – almost more French than English. The French had the first great egalitarian revolution, and promptly went ahead and invented the most élitist educational system in the world. Quintin won every prize you could win at Eton and Oxford. There's no doubt that he is intellectually superior to most of his colleagues at the bar or in politics. That is not altogether a lovable thing, but it is a totally admirable thing for a young man; you're very much inspired. When I was with him he suddenly went off and became first lord of the admiralty at the time of the Suez Crisis; he had to hand over a very big case he was conducting to another QC, and when his notes were sent over they were all in classical Greek!

When you lived in London you were friends with Lord Lucan among others. What is your view of the mystery surrounding Lord Lucan?

I certainly knew Johnnie Lucan because I was a friend of John Aspinall's, and so was he. It so happened that Johnnie Lucan hit the headlines, whereas thirty other people in the same environment did not. He came and had lunch with my wife and me in New York, I can't remember the exact date, but it was two or three years before his disappearance. One day after he had disappeared two policemen called – Johnnie Lucan's address book had been taken by the English police – and I still remember my stepchildren's total delight that the police had come to talk to me. I have to say that Johnnie Lucan was a man out of his era. He was absolutely a 'central casting' 1914 trenches officer, a man of great courage, great loyalty and integrity, but a man who should have died in the war, as opposed to getting the adrenalin from gambling. He was just typical of 1916 or 1940, the young men who died . . .

But were you shocked by his disappearance?

No. I am informed that in his custody case for the children, his wife's mother and his wife's brother testified in favour of Johnnie Lucan and against their own kin, and the court in its infinite wisdom decided that they were wrong. When he was really up against it, he would have had no confidence in justice. Now that doesn't answer all sorts of other questions, but he clearly decided not to face that test. I personally think he drove a motorboat out into the Irish Channel and sank with it.

Claus von Bulow

You don't think he's alive?

Oh God, no. Johnnie Lucan must have been six foot five or six, and the idea of hiding him is absurd.

After that you served for many years as chief executive to Paul Getty which seems a slightly curious diversion in your legal career. What was the attraction of the job?

First I should say that I was a young man in what could reasonably be described as one of the three or four most powerful sets of chambers in the Temple, but one day Hailsham went back into the government and Kenneth Diplock became a high court judge, so from having had wheelbarrows of work coming pouring in, suddenly there were ten under-employed young men in what were really dormant chambers. I was made an offer I couldn't refuse. It was very financially attractive.

But there is a rumour that you were paid twenty thousand dollars per annum.

It's not a rumour, it's the truth. But we're talking about salary only, and about the year 1959. I was paid three quarters of what the chairman of British Petroleum was paid, I was paid more than the prime minister of England. But when, later on, the Connolly PR Agency in New York is paid to make Claus von Bulow look bad, they take 1959 figures and transfer them to America, and no plumber would work for twenty thousand dollars in 1992. I had a great many responsibilities. I was vice-president of Getty Oil International, in charge of crude oil sales – that's where the money is. I was a member of the executive committee with responsibility, *inter alia*, for regular negotiations with Saudi Arabia, our host country. And, most importantly, I was Mr Getty's chief lieutenant, which covered almost everything. Do you really think that anyone would work for a company which is ultimately sold for over $12 billion if his *only* reward is the salary you quoted, and he is expected to fly over 100,000 miles a year round the globe to do some of the work I have just outlined? Of course not.

*Were you very admiring of the opulent, colourful lifestyle of Paul Getty?
Was he a kind of role model for you at any time?*

Quite frankly I think in many respects I lived rather better than he. I had a
large flat in Belgrave Square, one of the ten best flats in London, and I lived
very well.

How did you pay for it?

My mother bought it, and I paid five hundred and fifty pounds a year for
what was called ground rent and rates. My manservant, who did
everything – cooking, pressing, etc. – cost me, including his food, ten
pounds a week. It seems incredible today. Inflation starts after 1966.

Did you enjoy working with Paul Getty?

I adored him. He was absolutely marvellous. He had a great sense of
humour and humour is always improved by the physiognomy of the person
who presents it. He always looked as if he were at his own funeral, which
made the jokes extra funny. He wasn't in fact miserable, he had a very nice
time. People have even assumed that because he was married five times, he
had bad relations with women, but it wasn't so. His father had made a lot
of money, and when he died he left fourteen and a half million dollars to
his widow, and half a million to his only son in what the Americans call a
spendthrift trust. Paul spent the rest of his life proving that he was no
spendthrift, and dad was going to eat his words. And when that is your
attitude it becomes an obsession. But I never found him parsimonious in
the way that people have described. If he invited you for dinner he paid the
bill and it never occurred to him to do otherwise. But if you were to invite
him to have dinner round the corner, he didn't see why he should pay the
bill, just because he was richer than you. This gave him a bad name. Elsa
Maxwell, for example, invited him to dine with thirty other people at
Maxim's and then sent him the bill when he declined to pay. Now that was
a great mistake on his part, because when you have been to a whorehouse
and the girl has clap, you pay the bill and get out.

You married when you were thirty-nine years old, by which time you had done a great deal of living. Had you consciously avoided marital ties till then, or was marriage something you stumbled into?

I think both men and women consciously avoid a great many involvements. We are all at some point in our lives on the defensive and avoiding entanglements. Sunny was the most wonderful and beautiful girl, but you have to be climatically attuned to falling in love. I was ready and fell totally in love. At other times in my life I might have met somebody and not been ready.

Most men when they marry and have a child settle down to some extent; they have an increased sense of stability and responsibility which fatherhood brings to them. You seemed quite unable to settle . . .

I don't think that's remotely true. I married in 1966 and I settled down. The tragedy was in 1981. I was a normal loyal husband. I have said it before and I don't want to go over everything, but there was only one issue of substance between my wife and myself and that was the issue of working. Nothing else. I am an extrovert, champagne-charlie character, but we became more or less recluses, and I was prepared to live with that.

In what sense?

This has to be put in perspective. If we had lived on a farm in Virginia or in Yorkshire, we wouldn't have qualified as recluses, but living on Fifth Avenue and on Bellevue Avenue in Newport, we did. Those are places where people put on a black tie and go out for dinner or go out to the theatre; they're not places where people choose to lock the door and not see anyone. But I had had enough gallivanting by then, so that was not the issue. Sunny was an extremely fair human being who perfectly understood that a man should work, but emotionally she felt rejected when the work involved absence. That was the dichotomy that created a potential tragedy.

Your wife, unlike you, was not particularly well-educated. Was the intellectual disparity a major difficulty?

Not at all. Sunny was an outstanding autodidact. She read extensively and intensively in literature, anthropology and comparative religion. It is perfectly true that when her contemporaries were going off to college in America her mother took her off to the couturiers in Paris, but she was very interested, very bright. I don't for a moment want this interpreted as if there was an Eliza Doolittle/Henry Higgins situation, but it is always exciting when you are allowed to be a mentor to somebody you love.

The von Bulow saga was one which seems to epitomize the 1980s. It had all the ingredients – sex, scandal, drugs and above all, money. How did you cope with being at the centre of that drama?

There is a scene in *Bonfire of the Vanities* where the main character is coming out of the police court in the south Bronx and is faced by a hundred paparazzi, and he says to himself, 'I am dead and therefore nothing matters.' And that is one way you survive. You're dead, therefore infinitely greater questions arise in your mind than this particular problem. Unfortunately this kind of placid, philosophical approach is also very dangerous – fatal, in my case – because it meant that I simply saw a lawyer and asked him to get on with the job. But this was not a case for a lawyer alone; this was a case for a team of top-ranking endocrinological experts. The issue was one of medicine. It wasn't had I done it, or had somebody else; it was, had *anything* been done. Anyway, I opted out of the first trial until it was all over. I just paid no attention at all, I couldn't believe that this had happened, it was such a shock.

Did you ever feel that you might crack up?

No, because I had a child. That's what kept me going. It was out of the question that I could leave her to face the music alone. After all it was a question of a fifty-three-, fifty-four-year-old man who had had a good life. Do you remember Lincoln's story about the man in America who was tarred and feathered and ridden through town, and when people asked him how he felt about it he said, 'Well, if it wasn't for the honour of the thing, I'd much rather walk.' If you're the only person who is stained, then so what, you've had your life; but with a child you just can't do that.

Ten years ago the broadcasting of courtroom proceedings was quite new in America. Was it an added strain for you to have the intimate details of your domestic life beamed into the living rooms of millions of Americans?

No. The legal system is intended to give a defendant a fair trial. If for any reason at all ideal justice does not prevail the system provides for appeal, but it is not balanced in favour of allowing an appeal. My appeal was also televised live. That entails two or three hours of lawyers arguing points of law in front of nine judges; there could be no drier subject for television, but the fact that it was televised live meant that the state of Rhode Island had to show the entire United States that they were doing it right. I couldn't be shoved under the carpet. There's been a great deal of publicity about how I won the appeal on technical grounds, but there are no ways of winning appeals *other* than on technical grounds; appeals are not supposed to work on the merits of guilt or innocence. The system would break down. Again the second trial was televised live by CNN from 10 o'clock in the morning to 4 o'clock in the afternoon. There was an editor, somebody who would intervene from time to time to explain to the public what had happened. They stopped it after three days because people telephoned and wrote in saying, 'For God's sake, tell that man to shut his mouth, we want to hear what is going on . . .' When I was at the nadir of my fortunes – tried and convicted – I went with my daughter to a parents' outing at her boarding school, and three or four parents with umpteen children went to Macdonalds where the cashier was extraordinarily nice to me. I turned to one of the other parents, walking out, and remarked how nice it had been of the woman to be that way with me, and he said, 'You've got it all wrong, she thinks you are an actor. She's wondering what programme you're going to do next year.' You become a celebrity, the world becomes a stage, you are just fodder for entertainment, fodder for Mr Andrew Neil to make a buck and for you and me to read about it.

At your first trial when you were condemned to prison for thirty years, were you surprised by the verdict?

Most certainly not. I heard the evidence in court and if I had been a member of the jury I would have convicted. No hesitation about it whatsoever. This was particularly a medical issue, and the medical evidence at the first trial was one hundred per cent one way. I had no chance. In other words there was, in the juror's mind, no doubt whatsoever that there had been an administration of insulin. Who did it, the victim or the accused? If you then load that with sex and money on one side, you've got a conviction. I wasn't remotely surprised. I also happen to be of Nordic extraction with an English educational background, so I'm not just stiff upper lip, I'm frozen rigid upper lip. Some people of a warmer temperament might have yelled, 'I'm innocent!' That's not me.

The spotlight was on you and your family for a very long time, and Americans are notoriously voyeuristic. But people from the outside never ever know the whole story – there are always things missed out from the picture. Do you feel that significant parts of the story remain untold, and will they forever remain untold?

First of all I don't think that in 1992 the Americans are more voyeuristic than the rest of the developed world. Would you really say that the *Sun* and *News of the World* are any better? As for parts of the story that were never told, yes there are, but they will not be told by me. In December 1987 the family made a peace treaty which enabled my daughter to get her equitable share of her grandmother's inheritance, and one of the conditions was that I would not myself tell my story, or assist anyone in telling my story, and obviously when one says my story, one is talking about the crux of the accusation. In other words when you asked me if there was any mystery about my mother's death, I'm entitled to say no, because that really has nothing to do with Newport. I'm always entitled to respond to a falsehood, but I'm not allowed to volunteer an apologia.

When you were sentenced to thirty years were you always confident that the verdict could be reversed?

No. There have been a thousand years and more of church dogma as opposed to religious faith, and today that cloak of infallibility has been inherited by the scientists, the Reverend Stephen Hawking and co. All the time they're discovering that yesterday's scientific finding was wrong, but in certain tragic circumstances you can't run the test again, you can't reproduce the circumstances in which the original test was taken.

There are many people who remain convinced of your guilt. Does that bother you?

33

No. It doesn't bother me. I have lived a great deal in France, and I have noted that in the Faubourg St Germain there are people who will get red in the face when the name of Dreyfus is mentioned. And I've heard it said by a darling beloved friend of mine that Dreyfus was a serving officer in the French army during a period of forty years of cold war, 1871–1914, and all right, so the man's innocent, but why did he, as a loyal patriotic French officer, have to go and scream about his innocence as opposed to dying honourably on Devil's Island as hundreds of thousands of his fellow officers would die in 1914–18? By the same token there are lots of people who resent the fact that I survived. People – and I happen to be one of them – read something in the newspapers and adopt it as gospel. The jurors, thank God, listened to the medical testimony. The world listens to the media.

You have been described as very cool and nonchalant, almost to the point of indifference. After the trial some people thought you must have nerves of steel to be able to drive off with Andrea Reynolds to the apartment which, as your critics pointed out, had been bought with Sunny's money. How do you react to that sort of criticism?

I think that's a silly and provocative question. My daughter at that age could hardly have stayed in her childhood home alone. The last trial I won. Once I'm innocent, where is the problem? I don't think I should dignify the critics with a response. As far as Andrea Reynolds is concerned she would not have lasted from March 82 to June 85 if it had not been for the warmth of her personality, her basic human values, and the sense of sanity she was able to create for my daughter. Andrea was quite extraordinary in being an adult woman advising a young girl in very formative and hard years about how to become a woman. The publicity is misleading and beside the point. Andrea and I had different views on publicity. The ghastly *Vanity Fair* business was in appalling taste. Henry Ford said, never apologize. Well, I will apologize for that series of photographs which were taken in the middle of the trial when I was letting my hair down and making a total clown of myself. I was a zombie and a little tipsy. I am quite sure that people under constant bombardment in the trenches would from time to time lose their cool. In any case, I flipped, and Dominick Dunne was there to see it, and to pick it up and publish some of the photographs which were to have been off the record. I have attracted a great deal of hostility from certain homosexuals because I'm not one. They have disliked me intensely and this was a case in point. I noted Tina Brown, when she left *Vanity Fair*, said, 'It's become too gay, and needs to go straight.'

Are you still friends with Andrea Reynolds?

Absolutely. There were many other loyal friends, and that was wonderful, but nevertheless from the point of view of sharing my life on a daily basis there wasn't a queue of women forming to the left; Andrea came, and she was fantastic. In the long run we were very different and had a different approach to life. I suppose I am generally somewhat retiring; I don't expose myself willingly to the searchlights and flashbulbs.

When the film came to be made, Schroeder the director said, 'What drew me to the film was that von Bulow relishes keeping alive the possibility of his guilt.' What do you say to that?

That's just a Hollywood film director with his sales pitch. What he's doing is selling tickets for the film. Guilt or innocence was determined by a jury on the medical evidence, but if you accept that then there's no suspense and there's no box office. What else would you expect him to say? That's box-office talk.

He goes on to say, 'He wants us to believe he's innocent, yet he casts doubt as well.'

He's just trying to sell the film. Hollywood makes no factual errors, except intentionally, because once you spend twenty million bucks there's plenty of time to check. The one thing the entire family has agreed about was that we deplored this film. It was unkind about Sunny. It was vulgar. It went off speculating in deliberate disregard of the evidence which disproved the storyline. Dershowitz's book was OK, but the film producers just bought the book so as to give credibility to a script which was concocted for box-office appeal. I refused to see the film, but I know the script.

35

You have become a great celebrity for the wrong reasons; do you ever feel sometimes that you relish this publicity?

No. Have you ever been best man at a wedding? Have you been a guest at a function where you are expected to speak? If you are on your feet it is your duty to perform; you respond to the situation. Do you respond willingly? No.

But once you're there you've got to survive.

Yes, you have to survive. I don't think, with the solitary exception of *Vanity Fair*, that there is anything in the public domain, in interviews on television or to the press about which I am sorry. Of course, there is only one interview that is safe, and that's live on radio or television.

Your legal fees were paid by J. Paul Getty Jr, I understand.

My first trial was paid for entirely by me, and then Paul volunteered; he was not asked, he was not responding to a plea, he offered with extraordinary spontaneous generosity. As things progressed from appeal to criminal trial, to the civil litigation, to my daughter's civil litigation, the money just flowed. He wanted me and Cosima to have no worries other than the ones that were inevitably there. Fortunately, because of the settlement of the civil litigation, I was able to repay him in full. Even then he did not ask to be reimbursed, but obviously we felt that he had many worthy charities and we were no longer a charity case.

The human element in the whole saga seems to be that your daughter stood by you.

I actually urged Cosma to continue as normal a relationship with the rest of the family as was possible.

I didn't suggest otherwise.

During the first trial, I was going to be stuck in Newport, Rhode Island,

and she was a child at school in New York. No one offered her hospitality or chaperoning except some loving schoolfriends. Little by little a number of things happened to her which had nothing to do with me . . . her disinheritance, for example, and this undoubtedly influenced her.

Do you think adversity brought you closer together?

Adversity is the one factor that brings what matters in life to the forefront. Surely the success of the Christian religion is the Crucifixion and Resurrection; that is what makes people understand their own sorrows and sufferings. It's unique for mankind to have embraced a religion of apparent defeat. Life does not consist of a three-car garage and a family with five television sets and a deep freeze.

Do you think your belief in God helped you in your trials? Did you seek his help at all?

The answer must be yes to both but I don't think I sought help in praying for an acquittal; that's too simplistic. I would pray for Sunny and for Cosima and for my mother, and I was convinced that what was being sent to me was not being sent inadvertently or haphazardly. I had been a hard-working stiff in London, I had become a Newport beach bum, I had somehow or other been living a life that did not face the issues; and I had been given here, in a way I would not ever have wished for, an opportunity of changing course.

Do you still think of Sunny sometimes?

I have over ten photographs of her in my small London flat. Of course I think of her, of course I think of her.

Do you think that people to a large extent weave their own destiny, or is it in the lap of the gods?

I think it's both. It is curious that my father, my grandfather and I all met with a major crisis in our fifties. We have already dealt with my father. My grandfather's crisis was different and it never tainted his reputation for integrity. After World War I the largest commercial bank in Denmark crashed. It held large loans and bonds from the pre-war governments of Russia and Germany, and they defaulted. My grandfather was chief legal adviser to this bank. He also served as chairman of the Danish National Bank who were asked to give assistance to the failing bank, and he was chairman of the upper house of parliament, which would have to approve such government support. Finally he was vice-chairman of the all-powerful East Asiatic Company, whose founder chairman was scheming against the solvency of the threatened commercial bank. My grandfather was wearing altogether too many hats for his own comfort. Come to think of it, I suppose that, as a former minister of justice, he was also put in a quandary when he had to advise the bank after its managing director was indicted. The bank failed, was reconstituted, and, under the name of Den Danske Bank, is still the largest in Denmark. Many books have been written about this bankruptcy and my grandfather was one of the few principal players to come out of it as clean as a whistle and with his career and honour intact. Coming back to your question, we know there are people who follow astrological advice in the daily newspapers; that's total rot. Nevertheless, I do think that people under a certain sign have certain characteristics. Yours are different from mine, provided your sign is different from mine. There are times in life when you should stay in bed, because if you get up you're likely to break your leg going downstairs, and there are other times when the gold is lying in the gutter and all you have to do is bend and pick it up. Do I believe in predetermination? No, I believe that man has a choice between good and evil. Men, for instance, often think that indiscriminate fornication is a right they have been given. It's not true; you damage yourself with any action that cheapens you. You pay for whatever prostitution you commit, whether it is financial or sexual or social or whatever. To that extent you are responsible.

But do you believe that you have prostituted yourself in any way?

But of course. I think we all do. We all keep cutting corners in integrity. Look at what happened in Wall Street and even the City of London. I have a theory about that. I have always thought that there is not a single law or disciplinary rule within a professional body or field of endeavour that is as strong as peer pressure. Your fear of your friends not having dinner with you ever again is incomparably stronger than any penalty under the law, and this has been the trouble with the New York Stock Exchange. These people who have been prosecuted went wrong because those who led the markets, the Pierpont Morgans of former days, were no longer around. Then it was not a question of whether the US government might catch you being dishonest, but would your friends and colleagues cease to deal with you if you didn't behave? Does any young man get out of the trenches just because the sergeant says so? No, he gets out of the trenches to get killed because his friends in his village back home will not speak to him if he doesn't.

Jeremy Irons who played von Bulow in the film said, 'What is fascinating about this man is people's perception of him. It is very much a puzzle for me as it will be for the audience.' Do you agree that you produce an extraordinary multiplicity of reactions in people?

Yes. Once something is in the media – it could be a new pair of shoes, it could be a person – you will have a multiplicity of reactions, because they are no longer given to the public directly, they're given through the perceptions of those conveying the news.

But people either love you and support you or they hate you and think you should be behind bars. What do you think promotes this divergence of opinion?

Once you are in the public domain you are fair game, and the kind of people who will be assigned to cover your story are the ones to whom assassination comes naturally. In the case of Dominick Dunne, the man has the natural venom of his confused proclivities and that makes him a highly successful and highly paid journalist. They're not hired to say nice things.

Russell Aitken, your father-in-law, said you were a very dangerous man.

May I please, for Sunny's sake, make clear that he was my stepfather-in-law. I never knew my father-in-law but he was a very remarkable and wonderful human being who died when Sunny was four.

Well, your stepfather-in-law said: 'He's an extremely dangerous man because he's a Cambridge-educated con man with legal training, totally amoral.'

I can't be expected to respond to that. Have you been told what people think about him?

Do you have a wish ever to visit Sunny? Do you miss her ever?

I visited Sunny regularly when I still lived in the States. And yes, I miss moments of our life. Suddenly images come back, especially when I travel. And she's the mother of my daughter. That is one of the most tragic aspects, that she did not see what became of Cosima. I think she would have been very proud of her.

Have you any ambitions left?

No. I want to reap the benefits of advanced age, and I'm absolutely loving it. When you're young, you go to cocktail parties because you never know whom you may meet who may be interesting. By the time you reach my age you've got your slateful, there isn't room for more intimate friends; I have enough of those who have remained loyal. I keep an eye on my daughter who lives within a hundred yards of me, but not to the point of being possessive . . . she's twenty-five now. I never feel lonely. And I can stand my own company a great deal more easily than I can stand a lot of other people's.

As we get older, we still desire women obviously but there isn't the same intensity. Do you miss that intensity, or do you prefer the serenity that somehow comes with old age?

I have to say, Naim, I have no idea what you're talking about. I remember many years ago arriving with a young woman at Beaverbrook's house in the South of France, and I was rather pleased with myself and my girlfriend. Beaverbrook mumbled to me after lunch, 'You seem very happy with your situation, but you don't know the real beauty of reaching my age' – he was about seventy-five by then – 'when you know you can only do it once a month, and there's only six days to go . . .'

Looking back on your life, what lessons would you say you have learned?

I think you have to care enough about those whom you love. My grandmother had a little poem – of course, poems should not be quoted if they originate in another language – but basically what it says is: Fight for everything you hold dear, die if necessary, then living is not so hard, and nor is death. I knew that as a child, and then somehow I forgot it; later, through certain circumstances, it came back and I found myself having to fight for my own child. For my own life I really didn't care two hoots.

MOLLIE BUTLER

In 1932 Mollie Montgomerie married her childhood friend, the Arctic explorer August Courtauld, who in 1930 had gone missing for nearly a year in Greenland and returned to England a national hero. In the war years she raised six children while her husband served in Naval Intelligence. Afflicted by multiple sclerosis, he died in 1959. At the age of forty-seven she fell in love with the politician and statesman Rab Butler, one of the architects of post-war Britain. They married, and embarked on twenty years of rare happiness during which Mollie Butler was the mainstay of her husband's career until his death in 1982.

In your book you call your parents 'most unworldly people', a description which does not seem to be meant unkindly. Is this unworldliness something you feel you have inherited to any degree?

I think so. I grew up very late. It was only when I grew much older that I began to realize things I had never understood before, which I think must mean I'm unworldly.

Your first visit to Covent Garden was to see Die Meistersinger *which left an 'ineradicable impression'. Did Wagner's music continue to move you?*

No, it did not. I think that particular opera impressed me because I was with a particular young man and the atmosphere of Convent Garden in those days was very heady with everyone in full evening dress and *décolleté*, very different from now when people wear jeans. Of course Wagner is a genius, and it's my fault that I don't love his music. I realize that, and I miss something by not loving it, but on the other hand I love music to such an extent that I don't mind not loving Wagner because I get so much pleasure from others. Bernard Levin would be very shocked to hear me say it, but Mozart, Beethoven and Bach are my top people.

You described the 'almost superhuman' qualities which your first husband August showed when he was stranded in Greenland, and indeed one has the impression that you lived your life in awe of him in some measure. Do you think that's true?

Yes. I never had brothers and, although I knew lots of men before I married August, in those days we were quite formal with young men. We never progressed very far in our relationships; it was all very modest and proper. August was a remarkable man whom I loved dearly, but there was something deep in him that was very hard . . . you couldn't influence him. We used to argue constantly but I never ever won an argument, never got the better of him. We even argued about Hitler when Hitler first came to power – August thought Hitler was doing a good job. When our children were going to be christened, we argued as far as the font, but he always got his way with the name he wanted.

But your marriage to him was a happy one?

Very happy. He was a genius in a way, and it's so sad that his splendid qualities were never really used. He hated authority, and therefore in the navy he didn't get on as fast as he should have done. He was extremely disciplined, however. Imagine the self-discipline required to survive five months solitary on the ice cap and be none the worse for it in any way! He was descended from the Huguenots who have very strong puritan blood; it showed itself in August. He was devoted to me so there was no need for me to be in awe, but even Rab, my second husband, said he used to find August quite frightening.

You said that the agony of waiting when August was trapped had scarred you for life. Are you still anxious now when people are overdue?

Worse, much worse since I've become older. I'm like a hen, clucking. My family are very good about it; they know how worried I get so they do telephone when they get home. People say, oh you shouldn't worry, but if you're made that way you can't help it.

When you went off to Tobermory to sail the Cariad, *did you not resent the idea that you were being tested to see if you would come up to scratch? It seems a bit like being 'on approval'.*

I didn't know at the time that I was being tested. August just said he'd love to take me sailing, and I didn't know that the purpose of the visit was to test me. I thought it would be amusing. My mother insisted that we have an older lady as a chaperone – things were very different in those days.

Life has changed a good deal since then. Do you think young people are better off nowadays because they are more free?

I don't think they're better off in every way. They are far more aware of what's going on in the world and therefore they are far better at trying to help. In my day there was not the media information about the ghastly things that might be happening all over the world, and so we were much more irresponsible and selfish in a way. I often think young people nowadays are far nicer than we were. They do of course tend to shack up together in a way that we would never have thought of, and although there's no harm in that, it seems to me it's a pity because they don't perhaps meet the person they would most want to live with forever. I have had two very happy marriages, which is perhaps rare, but I remember saying to my children, when you marry it isn't a question of can I live with this person; it's a question of can I live without this person? Love in marriage is the most wonderful experience, so in a way it's a pity not to wait for that. If you fall into bed with the first man who comes along, then you may miss what you would have found later on. I don't think it's a question of morals any more. People used to be very moralistic about children being born out of marriage, but the arrival of the pill virtually put a stop to all that, and we realized it was more a question of manners than of morals. It was the unwanted child that made the whole thing amoral or immoral.

Are you a very religious person?

I wish I were more religious. I try to pray, but I think prayer's very difficult. I can't believe we're put on this earth for no reason, but it's all a great mystery. I would love to have the marvellous faith Rab had; to him it was all so simple – he *believed* – and his life was lived entirely according to his religious principles.

When you went to Greenland with August, you recorded your return like this: 'I had a feeling that we had returned from another world.' Are you a romantic at heart, do you think?

Frightfully romantic, much too romantic. What impressed me so much about Greenland were the Eskimos who were the kindest people on earth; they all loved each other, and a sort of brotherhood of man existed there. And then there was the beauty of the place, the startling glittering white snow and ice and the purity of the sky and the mountains. It was completely different from anything that I'd ever seen before.

When you spoke about the war you said you had a sense at least of comprehension, a sense of purpose, as opposed to the seemingly irrational violence which characterizes the present time. Do you think it was really different or is it that our reporting of violence is so much more comprehensive, so that it seems worse?

I think many of the ghastly things that happened in the war were not reported in the papers, but all the same there was this feeling that we were all in it together. People were much more friendly to each other, much more understanding of each other, much more ready to enter into each other's feelings than they are now, and we were bound together by our general desire to win the war. The same community spirit no longer exists. Long ago the people in the big house cared for those in the village and tried to help them. It was called *noblesse oblige*, it was their duty and they did it. Then the state moved in and now everybody thinks they have a right to this and that, and if the state doesn't give it them, then it's a rotten government.

You also said that 'the quality of life seemed more solid, less fragile, than today'. Do you think that this sentiment is based on fact or is it something akin to nostalgia, something which inevitably comes to us all as we look back on times past?

I think as one gets older life becomes so much more precious and we realize how fragile it is because there isn't so much of it left. I hate even to kill bluebottles now, odious though they are. In the past I wouldn't have thought anything of it.

In your book you rather tended to blame the socialist government for the privations which occurred after the war, but surely no one could have really done anything at the time, the whole nation was exhausted. It was not a matter of ideology was it?

No, I agree. I think it was wrong of me to take that line. They had not been in office, so they were inexperienced, which was hardly their fault. They also had very bad luck; they had that frightfully cold winter and there was very little fuel, and the fact that the trains couldn't run and the shops had to shut were the consequences of war. Everybody was exhausted, everything had run out and everything was run down.

There must have been many practical changes in your life when August became more and more ill with multiple sclerosis over the years from 1953 . . . what other changes occurred in you, or is it too painful to recall?

Well, he wasn't really my husband any longer; he was another man. Already in January 1955, the neurologist told me that a third of his brain had gone, so the man I'd loved and respected had left me and a stranger had taken his place. It's a most terrible disease when that happens. One can cope with any physical illness, but when the personality goes, one is left with someone else. That's why I was so lucky that Rab came into my life. I might have died before August if it hadn't been for Rab. My children certainly thought I would because the agony of watching him was so terrible.

You write very movingly about your involvement with Rab Butler. You say: 'Much is written about young love, but love in middle life is like a renaissance and is as strong as anything I have ever known.' Can you put into words how it differs from young love?

Love is a mystery, so you can't really put it into words. What I can say is that when you're young you take things much more for granted; but when you're older, more mature, that maturity has an effect on your feelings, and they're that much stronger. Anyway that's how I found it. I was forty-seven when I fell in love with Rab, I was crazy about him and remained utterly devoted to him always. I remember him saying to me a few days before he died, 'I think we love each other more than we did before.' I was rather cross and wondered how he could say that since I'd always loved him as much as I could.

You did quite a lot of politicizing from time to time. Did you ever have a political ambition of your own?

Never. I was so thrilled to be with Rab, to hear him speak, to do things for him in the constituency and to be part of his set up that I wouldn't ever have wanted to be a politician myself. We did differ politically on certain issues, for example, over the death penalty. I was a convinced abolitionist from the time when my first husband was high sheriff and I had to sit through two murder trials. Rab came to share my view but he was not an abolitionist to start with. I also wanted him to do something about homosexuality, but he said, 'I don't see why I should, I don't like it.' [Laughs.]

I suppose that all political parties are faction-ridden. They are almost by definition full of strong-willed people. Did you find it difficult to cope with that?

In our day, the Labour Party loved Rab. When he was going to speak in the House the labour benches filled up. There wasn't this awful polarization that there is now in politics. There were exceptions – for example, Hugh Gaitskell used to have a go at Rab, and I remember feeling very bitter towards Hugh on one occasion, although afterwards I discovered the reason why he had spoken so intemperately about Rab. He had just come from a memorial service for a great friend of his in St Margaret's, Westminister, and when he arrived in the House Rab had just been making a speech about his budget. Hugh was so full of emotion that he let his own feelings fly in an attack on Rab. Both the *Manchester Guardian* and *The Times* the next day said that Gaitskell had spoken in a way that a former chancellor of the exchequer should never have done.

Did Rab get on with Aneurin Bevan?

He loved him. He thought he was wonderful, the greatest orator in the House. Churchill's speeches may have been impressive, but they were all prepared down to the last comma, whereas with Aneurin Bevan, it just came pouring out.

When you spoke of the period before your second marriage you said that at the time (1945–51), when the conservatives were in opposition, Mr Butler, as he was then, was forging a new conservatism.

Everybody is agreed that Rab brought the Conservative Party into the twentieth century with those charters that he wrote. He had enormous influence, and I'm sure that when the history books come to be written Rab will be seen as the great architect of the Conservative Party. He had a terrific intellect, and what was so sweet was that when you met him, you'd never know it. He was such fun, though the sad part is that a lot of people didn't know about this side of Rab. He made me laugh all day long. He was sweet with the children, he loved animals, he was unique. Philip Zeigler rather mocked me in his charming review of my book, when he wrote that it was obvious when reading between the lines that I thought Rab was perfect; but then I did think he was perfect. Philip Zeigler wasn't in love with him, so how could he know? [Laughs.]

Do you think the Conservative Party nowadays, in the post-Thatcher era, is animated by very different concerns from the conservatism of your day?

That's an awfully difficult one to answer because the people in the Conservative Party now are very different from the people of my day. People then said what they thought was right, not what they thought would get them votes. I don't think the calibre of politicians is the same nowadays. Where is a Churchill, where is a Macmillan (though I hated the man), a Gaitskell, a Bevan, a Macleod? They were giants. I may be wrong but I think Mr Major may yet turn into a great man. The way he has come from his background without a single chip, without a grumble, a whinge of any kind, is miraculous. That he should belong to the Conservative Party after what he suffered as a child and as a youth, I think is amazing.

In 1957 when Eden resigned you took it for granted that Rab would be prime minister, and were fearful that what you called your 'happy relationship' would be disturbed. When he was passed over, was a feeling of relief uppermost, or had it been overtaken by a sense of disappointment for Rab?

The latter. I was terribly upset for him. After all everybody thought he would be the next prime minister, except Mr Macmillan who had organized it so that he himself would succeed. Rab was so marvellous; he overcame his initial disappointment and got on with the next job. He was wonderful that way; he never bore a grudge and was always such a generous spirit.

Rab's leadership qualities were never in doubt, and you say in your book: 'One is left sadly wondering at the decision to ignore these qualities.' What private conclusion did you come to?

51

I came to the conclusion that the Conservative Party as a whole preferred some conventional person that they understood. I'm not speaking personally of Alec Home, but they preferred someone like that. Rab was a frightfully complex, complicated man, and a lot of people didn't understand him, because he often made slightly oblique remarks which they couldn't follow. Rab's brain was always ahead of everybody he was talking to, and because he was so bright himself, he thought everyone would understand what he meant; but a lot of the time they didn't, and they thought – wrongly – that he was indecisive. I believe history took a wrong turning; we missed a wonderful prime minister.

You write with barely concealed contempt for Macmillan and clearly did not trust him. Your dislike seems to have been almost intuitive – you speak of 'the coolness of his eyes', and 'the insincerity of his old-world courtesy'. Were these things you felt from the first, or were they applied retrospectively so to speak.

No, from the first. He was such a jealous man. As Macleod said in his article in the *Spectator*, Macmillan was determined, from the first day of his premiership to the last, that he was not going to be succeeded by Butler. Why? Because Butler was a better man, and he was not going to have a better man succeed him. You may have heard some of Macmillan's broadcasts in which he said that he gave Rab every chance, but he couldn't take it. That was absolute rubbish, and also a disgusting way to talk, but people were unfortunately taken in. The man who's written his life, Alistair Horne, was absolutely brainwashed by Macmillan's version of history.

Given the tension that there must have been between Macmillan and Rab, how on earth did they manage to work together? How was it actually possible to sit round the same table and make important political decisions without letting those personal feelings interfere?

The truth is that Rab did not have this feeling about Macmillan that I had. Rab was generous; I was not. I saw the coldness in Macmillan, and I hated him, but Rab genuinely did not realize that Macmillan was always trying to do him down. He admired his intellect, and they got on well because they were clever men.

But didn't he realize he was passed over because Macmillan planned it?

I think in 1963 he finally did. But by then Macmillan was an old, ill man and I think perhaps Rab's ambition was blunted by then. I can only tell you that I minded far more than Rab did in 1963. I minded for him passionately, because he was only 61, he was at the height of his powers, and he would have been superb.

In 1963 when it looked again as if Rab might be prime minister, Enoch Powell tried to influence matters by saying that he would not accept office if Home became PM, and indeed in the event Powell declined office. People also tried to dissuade Rab from serving, which would have resulted in Home being unable to form a government. Eventually, as you seemed to know in your heart he would, Rab agreed to serve. Why?

He explained it all himself afterwards. He said that it wasn't as if he and Alec had very different ideas about everything; Alec was a friend and Rab didn't believe he could have lived with himself afterwards if he had let his own ambition split the party, which it would have done if he had stood out against him. He and Alec had been friends from the year dot, and Rab felt it would have been an act of disloyalty which would have ended in dividing the party. Bill Deedes, gave a wonderful description of Rab's decision not to stand, something like 'some lonely call of duty, very rare in politics'. Rab was indeed a very rare character.

But when he agreed to serve under Home, did they get on very well?

No. I hate to say this, because I love Alec Home and I loved his wife, Elizabeth, but I think they felt in their innermost hearts that Rab really should have been prime minister. Often if you do something to someone that you feel is not right, you never forgive that someone. And I think Alec and Elizabeth felt that.

There were those, Powell's biographer for example, Andrew Roth, who thought it ludicrous that Powell should have gone out on such a limb for Rab when Rab himself was prepared to saw off that limb. Was Rab ever conscious of letting Powell down in that sense?

I don't think he was. Rab was essentially pragmatic and though he had lost the premiership, he had been made foreign secretary, and his inclination was to get on with that job. I think it was wonderful of Enoch to do what he did. Of course he's such a romantic – you perhaps remember that awful broadcast he made when he says of Rab: 'We gave him the pistol and he wouldn't fire the shot.' He knew Rab was the right man, and he was so angry that he was unable to influence him. But Enoch's such a darling: I'm sure he's forgiven him now.

General opinion afterwards, and even today, was that Macmillan rigged the results of his investigation into whom the Party wanted as his successor. Indeed, Enoch Powell wrote an article entitled 'How Macmillan Lied to the Queen.' Do you think that period was an all time low in political morality, or do you think such events commonplace in what might be called the cut and thrust of political life?

If you read history you'll find that sort of thing happened in the eighteenth and nineteenth centuries. It was of course deeply dishonest, but I'm afraid that there's nothing new in politics. A totally honest politician like Rab is a rarity.

You recall that Rab never succumbed to bitterness. Did you?

No, I don't think so. Bitterness is counterproductive. It was more a feeling of sadness that England had lost a great prime minister who like Hamlet would have performed wonderfully had he been put on. Other people don't agree with me, but then they didn't know Rab as well as I knew him.

Your account of life with Rab reads like a love story, moving but dignified. One can understand perfectly why you admired him so much. Did you ever come to understand why he so admired you?

No. Why should I? All I know is he fell in love with me and he said it was so lovely to be spoilt.

Did you spoil him?

I suppose I did. I loved him so much, perhaps I did. But we were very close, we found each other late in life, and it was the most wonderful thing to happen.

How was he as a father? Did his children love him as much as you did?

He was an extremely good father but while they were growing up he didn't see an awful lot of them because he was so involved with his work. They loved him and admired him but they were not close to him in the way that my children, dare I say it, were close to him. My children adored him, as did his own, but I found when I married that there wasn't the same closeness in that family that I had experienced in my own family. It may have been that they had a different way of showing it.

When Rab decided to take up the appointment as master of Trinity College, Cambridge, you recalled that your heart sank. Did you ever have cause to regret his decision?

I did, because I think he might have lived longer if he had not become master of Trinity. Being master is a very sedentary job and Rab put on an awful lot of weight while he was there. He was a tall man, six foot two, and when he went to Cambridge he weighed fourteen stone; when he left he weighed seventeen stone, which was too much for his heart. Then he developed a condition which would have been perfectly operable if his heart had been all right, but in his case they couldn't risk it. I have a feeling that if Alec Home had offered him an earldom, he could have remained in the House of Lords as an *éminence grise*, and he might well have lived longer. There's no doubt that he loved Trinity College – we both did – and we had the happiest thirteen years there.

Are you relieved that you did not have to cope with taking women into college at Cambridge.

I think they have made very little difference. I sometimes go back there and they now have a charming woman chaplain whom the undergraduates adore. I'm not a feminist, but I'm certainly not against women doing these things. They make very good doctors; why shouldn't they be priests?

Mollie Butler

When you look back on your life do you feel that by being a woman you were disadvantaged ?

I was disadvantaged because my parents had no money, not because I was a woman. The idea of feminism is ludicrous; women have quite enough power if they know how to use it. There's no need for all this fuss and militancy in my view.

Do you think women make good prime ministers?

I feel ambivalent about Mrs Thatcher. She did some wonderful things when she first came in; but she stayed too long, and that was her tragedy. Rab always found her rather lacking in humour, and I doubt if he would have approved of all the things she did during her term of office. I didn't like her style. I thought her too *de haut en bas*, too dismissive of people, too right-wing in her views. One had the feeling that her views were so cut and dried that she wasn't going to act on what anyone else said. She was around when Rab was in politics, and I used to meet her. In those days she had no conversation at all, no small talk, and I think probably to this day she remains the same. She seemed to me not to have the idea that you could learn anything from gossip. I had the feeling with her that life was hard and earnest, and the fact that you could sit down at a dinner party and relax and tell stories and learn about people was utterly foreign to her.

Have your views on religion changed since Rab died?

As I get older and I'm so much more alone, I think much more about it. When you're in your eighties you can't help it. I feel terribly lonely now. Even if I go out twice a week to dinner, it still leaves five nights on my own. I love music, but then you have to be quite stable to listen to music. For three years after Rab died I couldn't listen to music, because whatever your feeling, music makes it more so. But I am lucky in that I have wonderful children whom I see often. They are my six best friends.

Do you believe you will see Rab again?

Sometimes I have the feeling I never shall, and it's desperate, because I love him so much still. It's something we can't know, we can only hope, and I have to try and cling to the times when I have the positive feelings.

Did you ever get angry with Rab?

Yes. But you *must* if you love someone. A relationship where you don't get angry with each other is not really alive. I once shocked someone by telling him I'd taken Rab by the throat, and I said, 'Well, you have to love a man very much before you can take him by the throat,' and he replied, 'I'm afraid I've never been loved very much then.' [Laughs.]

Did you ever have doubts about Rab's love for you?

Although Rab loved women, he was totally faithful; I never met a man more so. It wouldn't have occurred to him to look at anyone else, just me. I was not jealous about anything except my husband's love – people can have beauty, brains, whatever they like, but all I wanted was my husband's love. If Rab had looked at another woman, I would have torn her eyes out. I said to him once that I didn't like the way he was looking at a particular woman. 'Oh darling,' he said, 'don't worry me like that. All my eggs are in one basket, and I'm not interested in other baskets.' Wasn't that sweet?

LORD DACRE

Hugh Trevor-Roper was born in 1914 and educated at Charterhouse and Christ Church, Oxford. In 1947 he won international recognition for his book *The Last Days of Hitler*, a reconstruction based on research on behalf of British forces in occupied Germany. He was regius professor of modern history and fellow of Oriel College, Oxford (1957–80) and has published on a wide range of topics, including medieval Christendom, European witch-hunting, the Kennedy assassination, the Kim Philby affair and the Scottish Enlightenment. In a rare misjudgement he championed the authenticity of the so-called Hitler diaries until their fraudulence was revealed. He was a director of Times Newspapers between 1974 and 1988 and he was made a life peer in 1979.

Why exactly did you choose the title Dacre? I gather it upset the wife of William Douglas-Home who already had the title Lady Dacre and is a baroness in her own right.

That is right. I chose it after consulting the Garter King of Arms. It was a title which had been in my family, so Garter considered it was reasonable for me to take it, provided it was differentiated by being *of* something. And so it became Lord Dacre of Glanton.

Did you predict that you would upset Lady Dacre by choosing that title?

No. Time was short but I rang her up and asked her if she had any objections. She said she had none, so I went ahead. Parliament was going into recess and it therefore had to go through at once, so once she had agreed I told the Garter, and it was duly registered. By the time she expressed second thoughts it was too late. When I reminded her that she had had no objection, she said that she had been suffering from mussel poisoning at the time and hadn't really been herself. We had a correspondence afterwards which was at times animated, but in the end she wrote me a very charming letter and peace was restored.

You have spent most of your life in the universities. There is quite a lot of talk at present about grading universities in such a way that only some of them do research. To an outsider the whole idea of research in, say, Greek noun phrases or the negative in Middle English seems a strange one. What is it for *in your view?*

Knowledge does not advance on any front without research. A university without a research side to it is like a hospital which has no teaching branch to it; it tends to stay put. You make a legitimate point in that some subjects are not worth researching into; research can become a fetish and like all professional subjects it is in danger of over-professionalization, with academics writing for other academics on smaller and smaller topics. That is an inherent danger in any research unless it is carefully controlled. People build empires out of research and sometimes the conquests are not worth making. But research is the basis of a university; otherwise it is simply a school.

61

What sort of duties did you undertake during the war? I know that you were with the security service, but what did that entail?

You must know I'm subject to the new official secrets act. However, I can say that I came to be in the security service by accident, that is to say I came to work on the activities of the German secret service, which was not what was intended for me. My superior officer and I discovered and identified the radio communications of the German secret service which created a great convulsion in the intelligence world. We were then moved into the secret service proper, and from then on we became an essential part of the business of reading and working out the organization of the German intelligence services.

Among your colleagues in the security service was Kim Philby. It rather undermines one's confidence to discover that our security service not only catches spies but recruits them. How were people recruited in those days? To an outsider it all has the air of 'there's this chap I know', and so many turned out to be duds.

I think it is true that at the beginning of the war and before, the secret intelligence service, MI6, was recruited on a personal basis by people of rather limited experience. They couldn't advertise of course, and the people chosen were not always ideal. Accidents happened.

In your own case, how were you recruited?

I was recruited because of the work which we had already done. The secret service judged it essential to keep control of this work which had been done outside the secret service, and therefore I was moved as part of an organizational change. I was not chosen personally.

But how did this work start in the first place?

Accidentally. I was drafted at first and had a territorial commission. We were given a task which had nothing whatever to do with intelligence but by chance we made a huge discovery. To begin with no one would take it seriously, and consequently my superior officer and I worked on it in the evenings privately in our flat which we shared, and we deciphered the messages. It was a very simple cipher and I'm not claiming any great achievement, but once it was realized that we had discovered the operations of the German secret service, there was quite a storm. We were severely rebuked for making the discovery, and even more so for having deciphered it.

How do you think people ought to be recruited for such services? Is there, do you think, any way of ensuring loyalty, or at any rate of limiting the damage of disloyalty?

I don't know of any infallible test which would exclude the wrong people. I myself was astonished when Philby joined SIS. I was already there and was surprised to hear people talk with great enthusiasm about his appointment. I knew that Philby had been a communist.

You knew then?

Yes, but I was as wrong as everybody else, only in a different way. Lots of people, my friends included, had been communists at university, but it was not taken seriously. It was a passing phase, and it all evaporated at the time of the Russo-German pact. I considered that our superior officers in the security service were often unreasonable, seeing reds under the bed all the time, and turning down clever people on the grounds that they had left-wing views. When Philby joined I was rather glad that someone had got through the net. It never occurred to me that he was a communist still, even less that he would be a communist spy. So we were all mistaken on this. Recruiting policy, however, was not the only thing that kept able people out. It wasn't a job in the usual sense, in that you couldn't talk about your work, not even to your wife, it was not well paid because the budget was small, you disappeared in the morning, came back in the afternoon, and it led nowhere. It was not a very glamorous job unless you lived in a world of fantasy, in the Bulldog Drummond, Philip Oppenheim kind of world, which of course some of them did. People were therefore chosen out of a rather limited pool; they generally had some money of their own and they often lacked normal ambition. I was pretty censorious about them at the time, though I came to perceive the difficulties inherent in the situation. Nowadays of course recruitment is on a different basis; it's no longer done in clubs.

If money was not the motivating factor, did people join for a sense of adventure?

I suppose it was adventure of a kind, at least for people who joined in peacetime. In wartime we didn't so much join as end up there. I made a distinction between the amateurs and the professionals. The amateurs thought, and were blamed for thinking, in short terms; we wanted to win the war and we had no long-term aims, but the grandees of the service tended to regard the war as an inconvenient interruption and were determined not to allow the amateurs to burst the system. Philby was obviously determined to stay a professional, and he played the professional game. We made nuisances of ourselves since we didn't care if we were kicked out, but Philby didn't cause trouble; he was ingratiating and very competent. I don't think he did us any harm during the war. He did afterwards, but if he did pass information to the Russians during the war, they either had it anyway, or they didn't use it. I doubt if he actually did anything dangerous or contrary to British policy or aims during the war.

Setting aside the war, how much harm do you think Philby, Blunt and company actually did?

It's difficult to be sure in concrete terms. One can of course say that they gave a bad name to their service, they spread distrust and suspicion and did a great deal of harm within their own world, the society to which they belonged. They certainly damaged the aims and interests of the British government and the West as they were at that time. It is possible, for example, that Albania would not have fallen so completely into the communist grip if it hadn't been for Philby revealing the operations of the SIS or the CIA. Equally, you can look back on it and say, well, perhaps it wasn't decisive after all, perhaps the CIA and SIS operations were rather madcap. Some people were killed, but then Philby would have said that the secret service involves everybody taking risks, and it's the luck of the game. Another thing Philby did quite early on was to prevent the exposure of the Russian espionage system in Britain. There was a Russian defector to Istanbul called Ivanov who offered to provide the British government with the names of the Russian agents operating in the British intelligence world.

If that information had reached the right people it would have exposed Blunt, Philby, Burgess and Maclean at an early date, but Philby had got himself into the position of being able to take charge of the matter. He obviously informed the Russians, who kidnapped Ivanov and he's never been heard of since. There's no doubt that he was shot. In this way Philby protected himself and the others from exposure.

When you reflected on why it should have been Cambridge rather than Oxford that produced communist spies in the 1930s you blamed a certain puritan high-mindness, but in itself that is surely no bad thing. What was it that narrowed that outlook to the point of treason?

I don't know. Supposing there had been a high-powered Russian recruiter operating in Oxford, can I be sure that he wouldn't have found Philbys there? I honestly can't answer that. That puritanism, however, that extraordinary self-satisfaction which I do ascribe to Cambridge is lacking in Oxford. People don't take themselves so seriously at Oxford. Cambridge people issue writs against each other inside the university, which I find laughable. There is a world in Cambridge which takes itself extremely seriously, and if you do that, it's a stage nearer deciding that your conscience is more imperative than convention, humanity and loyalty to the government. It's that kind of high-mindedness which I ascribe to Cambridge.

The present government's determination to maintain secrecy at every level appears to many people to be perverse. Do you think it right that the defence of national interests should be barred in that anyone who had gone through 'the proper channels' with suspicions about Philby or Maclean or Blunt would have got nowhere?

Many people have found their way round these restrictions; sometimes they do it by going through the proper channels and sometimes they do it by knowing how to create interest in the right quarters. For all I know it may sometimes be done with official encouragement. I hold the view that most secrets are in print if you know where to look for them, and half the time the secrecy rules are merely a means of preventing the public knowing what is already known to the foreign governments from which ostensibly it is being concealed. For instance, during the war, and indeed until recently, one couldn't even name the head of the British secret service, nor could people say that anyone was in it, yet the entire professional staff of the secret service was known by name in Germany and had been published in the German press in October 1939. I have seen it for myself and they were all named.

Were they accurate?

Absolutely accurate, and I know exactly how they came by the names. Right at the beginning of the war agents from the German secret service lured two British secret-service officers in the Netherlands to the frontier under the pretence of being the representatives of an anti-Hitler group. They then kidnapped them by force and carried them off to Berlin. The British officers were kept prisoner throughout the war, and under interrogation they revealed all the facts. When I was in Berlin in 1945 I found in the ruins of the Gestapo headquarters a secret document which set out the structure of the British intelligence services and ascribed its knowledge, some of which was coloured by German fantasy, to these two men. But MI6 knew perfectly well that all their names had been blown because Himmler, after the seizure of these two officers, had made a public speech about information received, and this was then reported in the German press.

Of course I can see that one doesn't want to encourage too much curiosity into the operations of the secret service which, whatever one says about it, does have its useful functions – we live in a world of terrorism after all – but I do think it's carried too far and that the secret services tend to breed within themselves a separation from reality. I've known several cases of people who have simply become *fantasistes*, and Peter Wright of course is an instance. A kind of mania can develop, a paranoia, a sort of mini-McCarthyism which feeds on itself.

Why do you think the government went to such lengths to ban Wright's book?

I cannot say. I think it was mad, but I don't know where the move came from. I suppose it grew gradually and was probably a question of pride. They started by thinking they could stop it at a lower level without any fuss, and then when that failed, they had to stop it at a slightly higher level.

But it was absurd, because he lived outside the jurisdiction and he could publish outside the jurisdiction.

Do you think fascism has really been put behind us? The neo-Nazi movement seems to be gaining ground in an alarming way now.

People are misled by words. What is meant by fascism? Fascism and Nazism were quite different, although fascism was taken prisoner by Nazism in the course of the war. Mussolini's regime was not anti-Semitic until it fell under German control, yet anti-Semitism was absolutely central to German Nazism. They are different movements with different origins, and yet we call them both fascism. Since I'm something of a pedant, I like words to be used so that one can argue on the basis of them, and therefore they must be used accurately. I believe that the movements we knew in the 1930s which reached their head in the war are dead, because they were inseparable from a particular political conjuncture which is now over and which will never be repeated in the same form. If by fascism we mean the Italian fascism of Mussolini, and if by Nazism we mean the German Nazism of Hitler with its total philosophy and aims, they cannot happen again. But if we use the terms in a vulgar way, meaning thuggery, right-wing xenophobia, brutality, stamping on the lower classes and so on, that is a far more generalized thing, and it is liable to break out at any time.

At present there are some historians, such as David Irving, suggesting that Nazi atrocities were either the result of Allied propaganda or were grossly exaggerated. Will it ever be possible, do you think, to rewrite history, given the pressures for European unity?

Assuming that Europe, whether united or disunited, remains liberal, and that we have free press and free exchange of information, I don't think that historical revisionism of that kind is possible. History is always being revised, but it's revised from within rational norms; when we have more evidence, and different documents are produced, we see things from a slightly different point of view, but assuming a certain honesty in the historical profession, that is not a sign of perversity, it's just a sign of what is always happening.

Lord Dacre

But isn't history largely a matter of interpretation?

Yes, but what historians call historical revision is reinterpretation of agreed objective evidence, whereas what people like David Irving are trying to do is to rewrite history in defiance of the evidence. They thereby exploit legitimate revisionism in order to argue a political thesis, which in my opinion is unarguable. Their interpretations are scandalous, not honest.

Do you think the atrocities perpetrated by the Nazis during the war could have been exaggerated?

In the First World War there had been atrocity-mongering which afterwards was proved to have been false, and therefore there were people during the Second World War who did not believe all the talk of atrocities which they fully expected to be disproved afterwards. But one of the advantages of the Nuremberg trials was that it put the evidence on the record in a way in which it couldn't be contested. After the First World War the victorious allies didn't occupy Germany, they didn't change the government of Germany, they didn't confiscate or even have access to German secret documents, and therefore the Germans were able to build up the theory of the stab in the back, the myths on which Nazism afterwards fed. In 1945 it was different: Germany was totally defeated and occupied, documents were seized and trials were held, and whatever one may say about the trials, the fact is that all the documents that were produced were put to the court and could be ruled illegitimate or irrelevant. The defence had lawyers whose business it was to disprove allegations if they could, and no German historian has suggested that the documents used at Nuremberg were not valid documents. The evidence is public and has been agreed and cannot be contested, and that is the great difference between the post-1945 position in relation to history and the post-1918 position. So I don't think that revisionism which exploits the mood of incredulity or the desire for European unity, or the wish to forget the past to the extent of negating well-established and undeniable facts, I don't think that is a possibility now.

I gather you read Mein Kampf *in the original when you worked for intelligence. What sort of impression did it make on you at the time?*

That's not quite true. I read *Mein Kampf* in German in 1938 as a consequence of an article by Ensor, a very able historian, who had been prophesying that there would be a major international crisis resolved either by European war or by a climbdown by the West in the autumn of 1938. One thing he said was that the beginning of wisdom in international affairs was to read *Mein Kampf*, and that it had to be read in German because it was not fully translated. People at that time tended to regard Hitler as a mere froth-blowing demagogue, nasty, but slightly comic, whereas Ensor was claiming he was very dangerous. That article decided me to read *Mein Kampf* in the original. I could see it was the work of a man with a powerful mind who had already achieved much of what he had threatened to achieve and showed no signs of weakness of any kind. It was a coherent ideology, a horrible one but nevertheless coherent, and I decided that it was serious. And I became rather serious myself in consequence; I'd led rather a frivolous life up to that time, but I reckoned then that we were in for a war. I did not believe as many others did that Hitler was a clown, a mere adventurer. He was a gangster, though not only a gangster; he was a dangerous and effective political force.

How do you view someone like Lady Diana Mosley who admired Hitler and believes that many of the atrocities attributed to him are not possible?

She is one of those people who think that because somebody is polite and considerate to her personally, he can't possibly be a criminal. The world is full of people who are conned by confidence tricksters, ladies who listen to honeyed words and can't imagine such a nice person having another side to him. I once wrote a review of an article about Goebbels, and she wrote a letter of protest, saying how monstrously I had misrepresented Goebbels. She said she had often dined with Goebbels and his wife who were such kind hosts and conversation was so agreeable and they lived in quite modest style. It was the same thing with Hitler. I'm afraid she's just a gull, as was her sister Unity.

Do you think the last war was the inevitable outcome of the Versailles Treaty?

The Treaty of Versailles provided the excuse. The real reason was that the Germans did not believe that they were defeated. They were of course defeated, but there's a difference between defeat and recognizing defeat. The ruling classes maintained that they had been deprived of victory; and in the spring of 1918, just as in 1940, they considered they had won the war, and couldn't understand why everyone didn't then surrender. And then suddenly at the end of 1918, they were totally defeated, which came as a great shock. The entire organization of propaganda, the doctoring of documents, even before Hitler, shows that they were determined that this be rectified. They needn't have done it by war; they could have tried to build up German power and negotiate from strength. But Hitler wanted war; he was an all-or-nothing man, and he was determined that it could be done only in his lifetime. It was the same argument used in 1914, that Russia was going to be too powerful and that the social basis of Germany had to be changed. This is where anti-Semitism comes in. Hitler's complaint in *Mein Kampf* is that the Kaiser's Germany was a Byzantine Judaized aristocratically-run incompetent Germany; it had all the German virtues of racial and military strength, if only it had been properly led. In order to be sure of victory this useless aristocracy had to be eliminated and replaced by an organization based on blood. He really believed in race and blood, and elimination of the Jews. According to Hitler the social structure had to be changed in order to liberate the full energies of Germany and then, led by him, they could win. That was the real cause of the war, in my opinion.

What do you consider the origin of anti-Semitism to be. Is there a definitive historical explanation, or is it specifically religious and cultural?

I've thought a good deal about this, and I'm sure that it is not religious. In the Middle Ages there was anti-Semitism in Germany and in Spain, and it was religiously based. The Jews were the people who had crucified Christ and had refused to accept Christianity, and were consequently public enemy no. 1. But in the eighteenth century this sectarian attitude dissolved with the weakening of religion and religious persecution; and yet anti-Semitism didn't disappear. In the nineteenth century it revived with a vengeance and adapted to an industrial society, this time not for religious reasons at all, but on the basis of blood. This was equally irrational, because there is no such thing as Jewish blood. The only way you can define a Jew is by religion. Hitler had no interest in religion, Jewish or Christian. His problem was how to identify Jews among German lawyers or German police, or indeed Germans in general. It was simple when Jews had come in from Poland, for example, and were called Moses or Abraham, but among Germans how could you distinguish who was a Jew and who wasn't? The only way to distinguish them was by religion; and in this way we have the phenomenon that anti-Semitism survives its particular explanations. Different rationalizations are produced at different times, but one has to ask, what is the real basis of it? My own theory is that it is the determination inherent in the human race to find a scapegoat for one's misfortunes, particularly in an unassimilable group in society. They may be religious dissenters, they may be as in the witch craze of the sixteenth and seventeenth centuries, people who just don't mix, who don't fit in, who make their neighbours uncomfortable, who seem to belong to a different world. Any minority group is liable to persecution, even genocide. Often the unassimilable group is relatively prosperous, like the Armenians, or the Parsees in India, or the Ismailis in East Africa, or even the Quakers in England; they're shut in on themselves, perhaps they don't even try to become assimilated, so they concentrate on business and they become rich, and in turn they become envied. The Jews single themselves out, and they fit into all these categories, and that is my explanation.

I believe you covered the Eichmann trial for the Sunday Times. *Did you undertake the work as a historian, or was it primarily a journalistic assignment?*

I was asked to go by the *Sunday Times* and was glad to do so for my own education. (I had attended the Nuremberg Trials, and I afterwards attended the Auschwitz Trials in Frankfurt.) I was interested both in the revelations in the evidence, and in the procedure. I had been in Israel before and was interested to see the way in which the Israelis would handle the trial.

Your historical researches have covered a number of periods. Which has given you the most satisfaction?

Although I have studied and written about Nazi Germany, it does not give me satisfaction. I find it in some ways a repulsive subject and I have not allowed myself to be tied to it. If I'm an expert in anything I suppose it is in sixteenth-and seventeeth-century history, but I don't really think in 'periods'. I came to the conclusion at one time that political history is really rather small beer; seeing people digging deeper and deeper into a petty cabinet crisis in eighteenth-century English politics – I found that poor stuff. Humanity does not live for this, I thought, and I gradually found myself more drawn to intellectual history. So rather than being interested in a particular period, I'm interested in a particular side of history, the intellect of man rather than the politics. I consider that intellectual history is not separable from its context in practical history; that is to say, ideas do not develop out of previous ideas. This is falsely maintained by professional intellectual historians who, as it were, follow an idea from one generation to another as if people read the books of their predecessors but didn't live in the context of the present. I'm Marxist to the extent that I would allow that ideas are conditioned by the context, which means that one must study the terrible experience of this century if one is going to understand the intellectual views of this century, and the same is true of any other century.

I understand that your political antennae were developed in the thirties but gradually your imagination was captured more by academic rather than political intrigue. How did this come about?

I find this a rather offensive question. It implies that I am only interested in 'intrigue' and merely changed direction within that constant. I am not interested in intrigue. If I have occasionally found myself in controversy it has always been open – perhaps too open for my own good (but that, in my opinion, is because I am a victim of the media!) My answer to the substantive question – how did I come to prefer academic to political *life* (*not* intrigue) is quite simple. I was an undergraduate at a very political college – several of my friends and several of the dons went into politics – and I did at one time think of a political career. Munich made politics very actual to me. But then came the war; and during the war I decided that my real interest was in literature and the study of history. I also valued my independence, or perhaps my ease. The thought of constituents, 'surgeries', public meetings, party conferences, whips (not to say scorpions) repelled me. I also loved country life and shrank from smoke-filled rooms in London. I'm afraid I was rather indolent in those days.

You are a distinguished historian, so I ask this question rather diffidently.

Why does history matter? I can see that chemistry, physics, medicine, computer technology, agriculture, even perhaps psychology, have real consequences, but history seems to fall into a different category. By the time we meditate on the past it's all over. The study of literature may make us aware of the way language is used to manipulate, but it sometimes seems as if the clashing opinions of historians only catalogue possible past mistakes . . .

I agree with Gibbon who says that history is little else than the register of the crimes, follies and misfortunes of mankind. I nevertheless think that it is worth studying because I think that nations are conditioned even though they may not recognize this by their history. If one cuts oneself off from one's history, one is losing a capacity to understand the present, or indeed perhaps the future, not that anyone can understand the future but at least you can speculate. I also think that the study of history enriches the study of thought and art and literature. If somebody totally ignorant of his history goes round a picture gallery, let us say, and relies entirely on his aesthetic sense, his appreciation is entirely different. I'm not saying that paintings should be studied solely as historical documents, because obviously they have an aesthetic quality which transcends that context, but I do think that appreciation is deepened and made intelligent and articulate by an understanding of history.

Historians are constrained by facts, but even in the selection of which facts to highlight, there is a degree of interpretation involved. Since interpretation is necessarily subjective, do you think there can be such a thing as a correct perspective in history?

No, and indeed I don't want there to be. Interest in history really depends to a large extent on the problems which it raises, and the idea that it can be reduced to a science as people thought about 1900 (and the Marxists continue to maintain) is very perverse in my opinion. The attempts to reduce it to a science have all failed and now look very ridiculous. History is made up of continued pressures and options and mistakes. At every point in history there are decisions to be made; decisions can be wrong in a technical sense, I will allow this, if they are simply impossible in the context of the times, but one cannot say that there are no alternatives, that there is a course scientifically plotted, because there is no such course. And

73

indeed that is the interest of it; that is what makes it a living subject, not a dead subject.

What is your view of the relationship between history and biography. Are they very different animals, or can they be 'cross bred'?

I think they can be cross bred. A biography reduced to mere biography would be a very jejune affair. Of course I can envisage a biography of some unimportant shoemaker in Nottingham simply describing his life in shoemaking, but that's not of great moment. He may be a very worthy person but it's not of very much interest. But the greatness of an intellectual or artistic figure depends on his response to his times. You can't detach the biography altogether from the context.

There has been rather disturbing work done in France in recent years which seems to undermine the legitimacy of history. I'm thinking of the views of men like Jacques Derrida and Foucault. Is there any answer to the charge that we make history in our own image?

I think this is a defeatist view. We write history in a more social way than that, we test our arguments against other people's arguments, whether in books or in discussion. Obviously there are subjective interpretations, but honest historians try to check those against rival opinions which might also be subjective and try to discover an objectivity. I'm afraid I'm not in love with Derrida and Foucault.

It would not be too far from the truth to say that you are anti-clerical. Is it that you think priests hypocrites or fools?

I'd have you know that I'm a doctor of divinity. I don't think I'm particularly anti-clerical, but I've long ago given up thinking what I am. People say that I'm so many different things that I've decided to let them say it. It's true I don't like folly combined with persecution, and I can't take theological doctrine very seriously. I regard it as at best legitimate myth to which one pays lip service but one doesn't engage one's mind with it. I find it rather absurd when the clergy involve themselves with abstruse doctrines, when they give themselves airs and try to dictate to us or to persecute us or to persecute each other; then I'm anti-clerical I daresay, but I don't feel anti-clerical.

Are you a believer?

I think the answer is no. If you mean, do I believe the content of the Athanasian Creed, no I certainly don't. Do I believe in the Virgin Birth, certainly not.

Do you believe in God?

I'm a sort of eighteenth-century deist really. I would adopt the position of Voltaire and Gibbon.

My research would seem to indicate you are anti-Catholic ... and that you reserve a particular dislike for converts to Catholicism.

The great Lord Halifax, George Savile, said at the end of the seventeenth century that the impudence of a bawd is modesty compared with that of a convert. I often think of this when I meet certain converts. They also tend to revile the church from which they have been converted, which is a form of intolerance I dislike. I was fairly anti-Catholic at the time when the Catholic Church was ruled by Pope Pius XI, whom I regard as one of the more disastrous figures of this century. The Papacy was responsible for the dictatorship of both Mussolini and Hitler. I know that is a very serious charge, but it is one I can document. If it hadn't been for the activity of Pope Pius XI in suddenly forbidding priests to take part in politics, thereby wrecking the Christian Democrat Party, Mussolini would not have been able to take power in Italy. And if it hadn't been for his persuading the Centre Party in Germany to vote for the Enabling Act which gave Hitler his dictatorial powers, he could not have become a legitimate dictator. The Papacy wanted to get a concordat with Italy and Germany which it would never have achieved if it had had to operate through a liberal government dependent on a parliament containing agnostics, protestants and so on; but it could do a bargain with a dictator. Of course Hitler and Mussolini both broke the concordats, but the Papacy was silly in making them; it should have realized it was dealing with crooks.

But do you see a role for the church in politics nowadays?

I think the church's intervention in day-to-day politics is generally disastrous. I sometimes listen in the House of Lords to bishops making speeches on subjects about which they seem to me to know very little. I draw a veil over that; there's quite enough for the church to do outside politics.

They should be saving souls, you mean . . .

Precisely, though saving souls is a metaphor. I don't mean that they should be forcing their particular doctrines on people.

There have surely been good men and women who drew their strength from their faith. Why do you think so many people turn to religion? The Soviet Union tried to suppress it for seventy years without success.

People come to the conclusion, which is a legitimate one, that the purpose of life is not political orthodoxy, not even political success, that politics and public life contain a great deal of ambition and hypocrisy, and that if we have a purpose in life it should be rather higher. We have at times to think of what are vulgarly called higher things, and religion is a kind of distillation of one's loftier aspirations; the trouble is that it is distilled into such an extraordinary crystallized form that it is difficult to take, or it becomes sectarianism, or a sort of conventional sanctimonious church-going. To put it bluntly, I think that one needs an awareness of a metaphysical dimension in order not to be absorbed in what may be at best dreary and at worst dishonourable courses.

Do you think that your attitudes towards religion ever put you at a disadvantage professionally? I am thinking of occasions such as attendance at conferences like the proposed one at the Vatican on Eastern Europe.

It has never occurred to me that my views on religion were objectionable or even very eccentric. I am not irreligious. I do not believe, with Freud, that religion is an 'illusion' which can be 'ended' by psychoanalysis. Rather, I regard psychoanalysis as a superstitious illusion. I consider that a sense of religion is necessary to a complete man: it is a framework giving metaphysical coherence to the natural and moral world, the primitive myths which it retains having been converted into metaphor. Of course I do not believe these myths – who does? – but I am happy to accept them as metaphors representing the mysteries of nature and the human condition, insoluble as intellectual problems. I regard theology – the attempt to create a system out of these myths – as absurd: an absolute historical curiosity; but I get on perfectly well with (sensible) clergy, whom I regard with respect as a useful body of men – provided they don't pontificate or persecute.

You're a conservative, but of what sort? Are you an old Macmillan conservative with what one might call a sense of obligation, or one of the newer Thatcherite type?

I can't quite answer that. I approve of Mrs Thatcher in as much as I think she saw that a moment had come when consensus had been turned into a continuing slide of appeasement; it was no longer a consensus from a position of rationality and strength. I was therefore in favour of her strong measures. On the other hand, I think there is an unacceptable side of Thatcherism, a kind of ruthlessness which I find unattractive.

So you're more of a Macmillan conservative?

I am, but Harold Macmillan did sell the pass in a way. He believed, or behaved as if he believed, that one could always go on yielding a bit more for the sake of consensus, but consensus is a game at which two have to play, otherwise it loses its reality. If the trade unions on one side believe in pursuit of power at the expense of consensus, then it's got to stop. I was a director of *The Times* when it was losing millions and faced ruin. The unions were totally unappeasable, and what were described euphemistically as 'old Spanish practices' were rife – people drawing salaries under false names for no work, and so on. They thought they had the management in their hands and that somehow this gravy train would go on for ever, on the grounds that the Thomson Organisation which was then in charge was so rich from its other activities that it would go on paying this Danegeld for ever. Rupert Murdoch turned that round by being as rough to the unions as the unions had been rough to the Thomson Organisation. I think a consensus has to depend on a willingness of both sides to consent, and that had been sacrificed in the Macmillan period.

You have a reputation for being something of a dandy . . .

Oh really? My wife would be very surprised to hear me described as a dandy. I did read somewhere that I gave a tutorial in hunting clothes, but it is a complete myth.

Is it fair to say you are a social climber?

I don't think so. I like intelligent people really. I have moved in bits of the *beau monde*, that I admit.

Would you consider yourself a snob?

Yes, I am in a way. Except that I don't take it seriously. I think snobbism is a harmless affectation. To say that somebody is a snob *tout court* is not an offensive thing; it's rather like saying that somebody is interested in going to race meetings. I'm interested in the diversity of humankind, but yes, I quite like sophisticated parties.

Well, that's no sin. In 1957 when you gave your inaugural lecture as regius professor of History, I understand that a notice appeared on the board to the effect that your lecture was cancelled and that A.J.P. Taylor was lecturing in your place. This was presumably symptomatic of the animosity and rivalry between you . . . what was the origin of those feelings?

First of all, it isn't true. It was entirely invented by the press, and Alan Taylor objected to it as much as I did. We were always friends and we differed only on the thesis of his book *The Origins of the Second World*

War. The book became a *succès de scandale* and because I'd reviewed it critically I had to appear on television with him and the whole thing was blown up by the press. Alan and I both got very bored by it. There was an issue about which we dissented, as scholars are entitled to dissent from each other, but the rest is a myth.

But was he expected to be appointed at the time instead of you?

Well, yes. It is true that Alan was tipped, and, being a vain man, he believed he was really entitled to it. This was what surprised me about Alan: generally speaking he adopted a tolerant attitude towards history, he accepted that everything is chance, anything can happen, there is no directing purpose in it, that things always turn out differently from what is expected – this was really his basic, rather nihilist philosophy. But the one point where he failed to apply it was to his own history. Deducing from his general historical attitudes I would have expected Alan to say, well I expected to be made regius professor, but the right person is never appointed, things never turn out as we expect, well, that's how things go . . . but he never applied this attitude to himself. He considered that he was entitled to the chair, that he was the most distinguished person in the running and that it was a miscarriage of justice. But he never blamed me for this; he blamed Harold Macmillan. Later he said he would not have accepted it from this hand stained with the blood of Suez.

Talking of Harold Macmillan, what prompted you to promote him as candidate for the chancellorship of Oxford in opposition to Lord Franks? Did you not feel that it would be interpreted as a quid pro quo? *After all he had appointed you.*

I don't really care about what people say, but I certainly didn't like the way Maurice Bowra had pushed through the nomination of Franks (whom I respect). After Lord Halifax died, the vice chancellor took ill, and Maurice became acting vice chancellor. Maurice was a bully, quite an agreeable bully, but a bully nevertheless, and he always fought to win. He summoned a meeting of the heads of houses who were all very feeble, and he simply railroaded Franks through. I wasn't there, of course, but I had full accounts, and Maurice was so determined to get his candidate appointed that he simply vetoed other names in his brutal way. When Lord

Salisbury was mentioned, for example, Maurice said, 'He's no friend to this university,' and moved on to the next man. Harold Macmillan, who after all was prime minister, a distinguished man and a scholar, a man of intellectual interests who would have been very suitable, was never even mentioned. I thought that this was improper. I had means of communicating with Harold who was in South Africa at the time, and I asked him if he would be willing to stand. He sent back a message to me, saying, 'Nothing would give me greater pleasure. I shall not shrink from the contest.' Those were his very words. It was a very enjoyable contest.

Was it a real battle?

It was rather a good battle because Harold won, yet it was not humiliating for Franks. And Maurice Bowra was furious. There was no nonsense about a secret ballot, and he sat there receiving the votes, examining each one, and either scowling or beaming.

Do you ever regret going to Peterhouse?

That's a difficult question. On the whole I value experience by what I learn from it. I learned something at Peterhouse, and I made many friends there, especially among the scientists, but I'd rather not say too much about Peterhouse.

Peterhouse is well known for reaffirming the importance of high politics and intellectual movement against the fashionable concentration on the grass roots and the masses. Is this something you applaud?

No. I think it's a perfectly reasonable point of view, but in Peterhouse it was combined with politics so reactionary that I found them both ridiculous and rather offensive.

People have said of you that in the background of your life and career there lurks a book, the magnum opus *that you didn't write. Is that something that worries you?*

Not greatly. I would like to have written a great work . . . who wouldn't . . . but when I consider historical writing I see that it very quickly perishes and if it's any good it is boiled down into an article. Students of history have not read the books that they talk about; they've only read concentrations of the argument.

You were, I believe, the author of the wonderfully funny series in the Spectator *under the pseudonym Mercurious Oxoniensis.*

I know nothing about Mercurious.

You weren't involved in it at all?

I've heard people suggest I was involved, but I've never acknowledged it.

But you were the author?

Well, you've said so. I haven't. I don't contest whatever people say about me.

Do you deny that you are the author of it?

[Laughs.] Yes.

Is that a half-hearted denial?

No. *Toto animo.*

You are of course a member of the House of Lords. Do you think it proper in the late twentieth century that there should be an unelected body of legislators, however distinguished, in parliament?

I see nothing wrong in an unelected body. The hereditary principle I admit is very difficult to defend. But it's irreformable in a way, and any replacement would, of course, be liable to different objections. The House of Lords carries some fat, if one may use the phrase, but then so does the House of Commons. The Lords is much more of a real debating chamber than the Commons, because there's not so much of a party side to it.

Do you think it will ever be possible to forge a real federal state in Europe out of the animosities of the last thousand years?

Neither possible nor desirable. I am very much a pluralist and I consider that the pluralism of Europe is what has been the essential feature, if not cause, of its superiority. The various states have distinct identities, irreconcilable attitudes, which compete against each other and these have been the main factors in Europe's effervescence and efflorescence, and I don't wish to see it all homogenized. I support the idea of a free trade area in order that Europe may pull its weight in the world, but that does not mean that it should be ruled by an unelected bureaucracy in Brussels, establishing identical norms everywhere.

You must sometimes reflect ironically on the forged Hitler diaries when you recall your own work on Backhaus. In the appendix of your book you list 'three learned forgers'. Is that something which made matters worse for you?

No, I didn't think about it. What was traumatic was my inability to prevent extracts being published, which was due to complicated muddles at *The Times*. I couldn't stop the process which was forced by a series of episodes outside my control. When the business blew up I decided the only honourable thing to do was to state publicly that I had made a mistake, although I had tried to remedy the mistake and had been prevented from doing so. The mistake wasn't the one I was accused of making, but still, I said I had made a mistake, and I thought naïvely that the other people whose responsibility had been far greater than mine would admit their part in it. But not at all; they all turned on me and kept completely silent about their own involvement, and regarded me as a sort of expendable scapegoat. All the media persecution was concentrated on me, and the rest sat smugly behind their barriers. That was a shock. It lowered my opinion of human behaviour. One likes to feel that people are honourable, and it's painful to find that they aren't.

Your enemies of course delighted in your mistake. You have always maintained that other people's opinions of you were of little importance. Is that really the case, or have you put a brave front on it?

No. Long before that episode I decided that other people's opinions, within limits, are not of interest to me. I'm afraid it's a rather arrogant thing to say, but I don't really respect the opinions of people whom I don't know. I think it's as simple as that. If a trusted friend were to say harsh things about me, that would upset me, but if a journalist whom I've never met makes statements about me I'm quite indifferent to it. I have a kind of proud stoic attitude in this; I just say a man is himself, not what strangers say of him. To thine own self be true, that's my philosophy.

What was your feeling when you learned that a TV series was to be made of the Hitler diaries saga?

I paid no attention at all. I neither saw the film nor read the book. And I declined to write to the papers about it. I simply treated it as non-existent.

A.J. Ayer once said of you: 'Some may think him lacking in charity', and it is true that over the years you have joined battle with a number of enemies, often distinguished people, such as Lawrence Stone, Evelyn Waugh and Arthur Toynbee. The last of these you demolished in an article in Encounter. *Some people, while admiring the scholarship of that article, detected a streak of cruelty. Is that something you are conscious of?*

No. I may say it was Evelyn Waugh who declared war on me, not I on him. Lawrence Stone also asked for it. He borrowed transcripts which I had made from documents in the Records Office, and that was the basis of this half-baked article which he wrote and which I criticized. He behaved very badly. I don't think I've ever severely criticized any young scholar; it's when people give themselves great airs and are taken seriously, that's what arouses me.

I have also heard it said that in your eagerness to win battles you do not shrink from making personal attacks on colleagues. Do you accept that charge?

83

I am not aware of having made personal attacks on colleagues. If I have engaged in controversy, it has always been because I thought at the time that a serious issue was at stake. I wonder what colleague I am said to have attacked personally?

Richard Cobb has spoken of your love of combat, your readiness to jump into the fray over public issues. Is this something you have ever had cause to regret?

I don't think I love combat: it's true I enjoyed the election for the chancellorship of Oxford, but it was a genial, good-tempered affair, and there was a serious issue involved. Maurice Bowra, by bouncing a single gathering of heads of houses, had effectively disfranchized the university. This was widely felt (hence the strong support I received). Of course once the battle was on, Maurice was determined to win, and so was I. Have I ever regretted a controversy? I regret them all in so far as they were extended (largely by the media) beyond their original terms. I regret having been involved with Evelyn Waugh, whose writing I admired. But he opened fire on me in 1947, both publicly (in the *Tablet*) and privately (in an abusive letter to me), and continued the one-sided vendetta for nine years before I finally took notice of him in the article which provoked his onslaught on my historical scholarship; to which I felt that I had to reply.

The controversy whose extension I most regretted was with A.J.P. Taylor. I criticized his book *The Origins of the Second World War* because I thought his thesis wrong, indeed irresponsible. But then the press took over; and from then on I was always represented as the constant adversary of A.J.P. Taylor. In fact I never criticized any other work of his. I minded this, as did he. In 1979 he wrote, in the *London Review of Books*: 'I often read that Trevor-Roper and I are rivals or even antagonists. On my side, and I can confidently say on Hugh's, this is totally untrue. We have always been good friends and no cross word has ever passed between us.' And he wrote to me in 1983: 'I can assure you that my feelings towards you have always been those of friendly affection.' It was the repeated (and successful) attempts of the press to persuade the world that Taylor and I were permanent adversaries that bred in me that distaste for the media which, I'm afraid, is now ingrained in me. (Of course, the affair of the Hitler diaries strengthened it.)

Another controversy was my critique of Toynbee. I admit that I was nauseated by the pretensions and sanctimonious *humbug* of Toynbee, and (especially) his message, which was defeatist and obscurantist; disgusted too by the idiot sycophancy towards him of the American academia and media. But effectively all I did was to quote his own words, which none of his sycophants had read – they had only read Somervell's potted one-volume abridgement of his first six volumes, whereas the real revelation of his purpose, and his vanity, was in volumes seven to ten, published later. I do *not* regret this episode! Toynbee's recent biographer, William McNeill, says that Toynbee's reputation never recovered from my essay. That *pleases* me!

But neither here nor in any other controversy was I drawn in merely by 'love of combat'; there was always a real issue on which, at the time, I felt strongly: Stone's total misrepresentation of historical documents which he pretended he had discovered (when in fact he had borrowed my transcripts and had not tried to understand them); Bowra's contempt for the Oxford electorate and its rights; Taylor's special pleading for Hitler; Toynbee's hatred of reason and the Enlightenment . . . As I don't think I was wrong, intellectually, in any of these encounters (or in my critique of E.H. Carr), I don't regret them – only the personalization of them, or some of them. Perhaps it is all the fault of my style: not enough emollient, shock-absorbing pulp, sawdust, stuffing, etc. . . . .

LORD DEEDES

William Deedes was born in 1913 and educated at Harrow before becoming a journalist with the *Morning Post* (1931–7). During the war he served with the Queen's Westminsters and from 1950 until 1974 he was conservative MP for Ashford. Between 1962 and 1964 he was minister without portfolio. He has long been associated with the *Daily Telegraph* which he edited from 1974–86. He was made a life peer in 1986.

How do you recall your childhood . . . was it a happy time for you?

Not altogether because when I was six my father, who was living peacefully on £900 a year with five servants, suddenly inherited a large shattered castle. From then on life became exiguous and if you're young, even if you're only six or seven, you feel the anxieties of your parents. Living as we were on a tumbledown estate after the First World War, when farming was bringing in nothing, many acres had to be sold off to make ends meet. Therefore I remember my childhood as being privately happy, because I had the land to roam over, but anxious also because I sensed that the foundations of life were shaky as a result of father's predicament in taking on for family reasons more than he could cope with.

Yours was quite a large family . . . five children I believe. Did you see that as an advantage at the time?

Yes, because I think there is a lot to be said for boys being bullied by sisters. I'm the only boy and I owe a great deal to my sisters who prodded me at certain times when I needed it. I have always felt that my sisters had more ambition for me than I had for myself. People nowadays who go in for much smaller families lose an ingredient which bigger families enjoyed. It's difficult to define, but you build up a certain inner relationship which lasts all your life. It's not an essential dimension, but it's a useful one. I'm grateful for it anyway.

I wonder which of your parents now seems to you to have been most influential in your life? Perhaps that kind of question seems too overtly psychological. Do you think parents really have the strong influence that is always attributed to them?

I was aware of tension between my parents because my mother, who was Protestant Irish, born in Dublin and conservative in her outlook, greatly desired that I should go to Winchester and follow her brothers there, which I proved too stupid to do. My father, on the other hand, had a great many newfangled ideas which he alternated rather rapidly with his political views. He had had a curious background. He had gone to the Boer War at the age of seventeen, which did his health no good and he was really an invalid most of his life. He was ostensibly a landowner, but he was also a socialist. In fact he was greatly attached to the Labour Party in those days and stood for parliament once as a labour candidate, then as an independent candidate. About that time – it was around the birth of the Labour Party – he shared a feeling that society was unequal and there was too big a gap between the well-to-do and the rest. He had what you might call the Edwardian, old Etonian conscience, and I look back on him as a very respected Christian socialist. He was left of centre for what might be described as inner reasons rather than ideology. There was one period, for example, when he bought every book he could lay his hands on about Mussolini. There was an endearing enthusiasm about my father's political beliefs and in the early stages he even thought Hitler might do Germany a bit of good. My mother, however, was a staunch conservative and found all this rather difficult. So as a child I remember my mind being pulled between my mother's innate conservativeness and my father's rather dashing radicalism; but this may have done me no harm at all. I didn't follow one or the other, I just realized there was a difference. As it happened, however, I did follow my mother eventually.

Do you think your relationship with your own son was very different from your father's with you?

No. I'm ashamed to this day by the fact that my relationship with my son, who was born during the last war, was more like my father's with me. In other words, I was almost the last of that generation of men who did not feel that a great intimacy with his children was part of a father's duty. Today I find that my own children share the lives of their children in a way that never occurred to me. If my children enjoy modest successes now I am always the first to attribute this to my wife because my own contribution was minimal. Frankly I was neglectful and I treated my children as my father treated me. And, of course, there were nurses and governesses to look after them.

I suppose there will be people to whom your life will seem to have been remarkably privileged: a childhood household with five servants, school-days at Harrow, your own son sent to Eton. Has it been as enviable as it seems?

Not a bit. I actually left Harrow a year early. My housemaster sent for me one day and said: 'I'm very sorry . . . we had a letter from your father to say that he has been seriously affected by the Wall Street Crash.' Everyone was very sympathetic; the housemaster even gave me a couple of quid to pay my fare home. But I suppose there was a bit of privilege in my getting my first job on the *Morning Post* since the paper's managing editor had just got a gun in Uncle Wyndham's shoot in Hampshire and as a *quid pro quo* I got a job on the paper, but I still had to work my way.

You are obviously a very political animal. Was that interest the result of family background or was it something that developed out of your career as a journalist?

It was more family background. I think the Deedes family have had a member of parliament in every century since 1600. A year as a lobby correspondent in 1936–7 certainly gave me a taste for politics and so when an opening arose after the war I wasn't unfamiliar with what the work would entail, but I suspect it's mainly heredity.

You have been both a cabinet minister and a distinguished journalist. Which do you think is the most influential position in the end? What I had in mind is that while a cabinet minister has a good deal of authority he must be constrained by government policy, so I wonder just how much room there is for manoeuvre?

There's never been any doubt about this. A politician is by far the stronger figure for this reason; he is a decision-making figure. Journalists can advocate, campaign, attack, and though they can make themselves immensely influential, they can't make decisions. Only a member of parliament, and even more so a minister, can actually do that, and therefore the two are not really comparable. In terms of power the politician has always got it over the journalist. The journalist might look at times to be more powerful, particularly if you have a figure like Northcliffe or Maxwell or Murdoch, who decides to attack politicians and possibly appears even to change a government; in reality, however, the politician always has the stronger position.

Was Beaverbrook powerful because he was a journalist baron or because he was a politician?

Beaverbrook had another value altogether. Beaverbrook was a major contributor to the social revolution in Britain. I remember my pre-war *Daily Express* very well, and that newspaper was revolutionary in saying to the reader: 'You're as good as any other man.' Beaverbrook was a great believer in making his readers feel the equal of royalty, plutocracy or the aristocracy. He did more to make the reader feel that he was on the up and up than any proprietor I've every known. His huge empire and all his political convictions appeared to be very strong and influential but the real revolution he brought about – though he may not have known what he was doing – was to tell his readers that their daughters would look as good at Ascot as anybody else's. It was immensely influential journalism. I didn't like him, but he had a great instinct.

You spent your entire career as a journalist on a right-wing paper, or one which is certainly thought to be so. Have you ever had any doubts about that political allegiance?

I think I can truthfully say no. I would be regarded in Mrs Thatcher's terms as a wet, and I *am* wet, though I'm dry on a number of subjects, South Africa, for example. I'm more of a wet on social issues – possibly I owe something to my father and my uncle, both of whom were in the other camp. I've shifted here and there, I've had minor changes of opinion, but I've never regretted being on the right or having to write for a right-wing newspaper.

In the hard times in the 1930s there was, it is always said, some sense of community, but now in the 1990s even that is disappearing; a political philosophy has emerged which seems content to place more emphasis on the individual. Do you think this is a healthy trend?

I used to go to the distressed areas as a reporter before the war, and one of the things that struck me was that even in places like South Wales, Newcastle upon Tyne or West Cumberland, where there was real poverty and a shortage of food, there was a definite social empathy; they clung together. If one week you literally couldn't afford a loaf of bread you relied upon your neighbour to give you half a loaf of bread. It was a very different social pattern from what we have now when neighbours are almost strangers one to another. I don't understand the reasons. All I know is that there is a great contrast between (shall we say) the society I found in Newcastle when I went up there in the thirties and the society that has just been uncorked by recent events and reported in the press. Society has become more self-contained, much more cellular. I use that word because modern living is like a beehive in which everybody is in a cell rather than in human association. The other day I went to Moscow and I was very struck by how much more socially interdependent the Russians are. I rather envied them. I talked to countless people on the streets, and I saw almost a throwback to the years before we had home entertainments and distractions which kept us apart. The Russians are very dependent on human association, and it's something that we have – I won't say sacrificed – but it's something we've let slip.

Do you ever have a feeling that politicians have misjudged the degree to which rhetoric can be substituted for reality? I have in mind the way figures, for example, can be manipulated; even if bad they are presented as reasonably good. Doesn't that sort of thing damage the trust needed between government and governed?

That is a difficult question. There is far less direct connection between the people and those who govern them than there was in the past. When I began in politics, public meetings were *de rigeur*; they're very rare today. In my view there is no better recording of where the shoe pinches than at a public meeting of not more than say eighty to a hundred people; even thirty to forty will do. I don't know any better way of discovering what lies inside people's minds and hearts. I am astonished at what you get out of people if you give yourself the time to talk to them for more than ten minutes. It's something that's irreplaceable; it's not something you can read in the papers, or something you can guess. In the great public meetings of the past, politicians did have the advantage of learning from people directly what hurt them. Indeed in very distant days this is what the sovereign did until the whole thing became too burdensome. This is something missing now in our modern democracy and it may in the end prove to be its undoing. One form of redress is for ministers to appear at public meetings where public feeling will make itself felt. I have been to meetings that have been broken up and the minister left in no doubt as to what people thought. There were times in the 1920s when Lloyd George's 'Land Fit for Heroes' produced massive demonstrations. Today, unless you get some extravagant demonstration by young people as in Newcastle, there is no outlet for public feeling, no forum. It's no good telling me that *Any Questions* or *Question Time* or any rubbish on Thursday night is going to replace that, because it doesn't. It may be good entertainment but it doesn't get the *vox pop*.

You were once minister of information. That must have been an ironic situation for a journalist. Wasn't there a danger in that position of suppressing exactly the information that as a journalist you would have been trying to reveal?

Absolutely. As a journalist I have always supposed that the cabinet had countless secrets which I've never been lucky enough to find out. As a minister without portfolio, I could not think of anything the cabinet had decided which the press had not already got hold of. From the outside you appear to be attacking a fortress when you're a journalist. From the inside you appear to be in a mud castle, the walls of which are rapidly being eroded. In other words, you've got no protection. The cabinet ministers for their own reasons talk to their cronies in the press over lunch and then the ministry of information becomes redundant. I'm bound to say towards the end of my two years in that job a sense of superfluity overwhelmed me [laughter]. I was most grateful for the experience, but for future prime ministers, it's not a job that ought ever to be included in any cabinet of sensible men.

Why is there such distaste among British politicians for allowing the people who elect and pay them to have information about the way they are to be governed? The Americans are infinitely less secretive but their government remains intact.

I'm not a great subscriber to this school of thought. First of all I think that countries fundamentally have differences and it's a mistake to think that the system in one country is going to work in another. I understand the American freedom of information; I understand their First Amendment, I also look without much envy at their libel laws. I have been in America and seen public figures completely destroyed by the freedom with which the

Americans are allowed to attack or investigate and expose, and I am therefore not starry-eyed about their system. Nor am I absolutely convinced that the so called blanket of secrecy which the press feel is kept over everything here really exists. Having seen it from both ends, I can assure the press that far less is covered over with secrecy than they believe. I don't believe you can run any business, let alone a government, without a degree of confidentiality. Good government does depend to a certain extent on trusting that colleagues will not, for their own purposes, blow government business to the press or to the public. Of course, the public have a right to know what is being done in their name, but there's a balance to be struck. I was on the Franks Official Secrets Committee. With Oliver Franks, probably the best chairman I've ever served under in my life, we spent fifteen months going through this whole problem of what should be said to the public and what should not. In the end, as you know, we fenced off defence, some fiscal treasury matters and certain foreign affairs matters. I am powerfully persuaded that good government has a right to a degree of secrecy. What that degree is will never be agreed between the press and government. I'll accept your point that we are more secretive here than we need to be; I don't accept that the Americn system would be the better one.

But would you support a kind of freedom of information – not the same as the Americans', but one which would enable the public to get more information? The present state of affairs is surely not very satisfactory.

Experience shows that in Canada and in America where there is a right of the public to discover certain information, they don't always look for what you think they would look for. They look for your income tax return; they look for detail which is frankly not relevant to the public weal. All right, there may well be a case, if it increases public confidence, for giving more access to what government is doing, but don't be disappointed if having granted them that access, you find it's not used to a very high purpose.

There is now, and has been for some time, pressure for an act guaranteeing a right to privacy. Do you think that it is a sensible thing or are the private lives of public figures of legitimate public interest?

I've thought about this a lot. I have to say that I think the lives of public figures are of public interest and legitimate areas for press enquiry. I regret the fact that we should find it interesting that a cabinet minister has a liaison with a woman other than his wife, and I think we should not confuse public interest and prurience. There's a distinction between the two, but we shall never agree on what the distinction is. And so I accept that the private affairs of a public man may become a matter of public interest. However, I draw the line where children are concerned. Very few people in the press ever calculate the effect upon a child at school of an accusation (on possibly not very solid grounds) against its father or it may be the mother. Of course if it is proved that a man has indulged in criminal activity, then too bad if the child suffers, but I've seen tittle tattle about public figures which has made children at school terribly miserable. When there was a brief interest in my own private life, the only newspapers I really despised were those who encouraged my children to talk on the telephone. That is not a form of journalism that I think is acceptable; but I'm liberal and I have to accept that if you go into public life your private misdemeanours become public property. In a democracy you must go along with the public mood and people today are very sensitive about any affectation of superiority. The most potent word in the English language today is 'inferior' and any politician who may have delivered a homily on the subject of one-parent families and is then found to have a mistress in Rome, Paris and Vancouver should be exposed. The public are entitled to know and to draw their conclusions.

You were minister without portfolio in 1963 when the Profumo scandal broke which led eventually to Macmillan's downfall. Did you see that as inevitable at the time? Would it be different now?

In retrospect I think there were a number of errors made in addition to the original error, that is to say I think there was a certain amount of press hype, and I'm not speaking now as one who was a minister at the time. The whole tale became almost a satire of the British in their moral suit of clothes. This is reinforced with hindsight by the fact that Jack, with whom I was at school and have known all my life and am still very fond of, has in the intervening twenty-five years reclaimed his status and his right to be regarded as a good man in a way which none of us can emulate. I regard this as a very interesting moral tale. Those who would be the first to condemn Jack and would still be saying, 'Oh, but didn't he tell a lie to the

House of Commons and so on . . .', very few of them can hold a candle to what he has done since in Toynbee Hall. I have a secret respect for people who have a tumble and recover, and this includes Jack, it includes Nixon, and it even includes Bob Maxwell. I respect the people I've know who have taken a big fall and recovered. I doubt my own capacity to do so.

But would you condemn Profumo for his sexual morality, or for telling a lie to parliament? Which was the more serious?

The falsehood to parliament was the serious aspect of the case, no question about that, but the circumstances in which he was induced to make that unwise statement have always mitigated what he did in my view.

When I interviewed leading women in France for my book, it was suggested to me that indiscretions were considered to be among the perks of being a politician. Do you think the British are simply more hypocritical or is it rather a matter of competition between newspapers, the need to sell?

I think we must respect national differences which have historical backgrounds. The French have a view about sex, the British have a view about sex, and that is just one problem we're going to run into when we start a federal Europe. I am not prepared to make invidious comparisons, but I do think that we have developed a class of newspaper in this country now which knows that the published peccadilloes of public figures sell like hot cakes. I think possibly we sell more hot cakes in this country than the French do in theirs. Indiscretions in Paris would simply not produce the fuss they produce here. I've never found a word to describe the British attitude towards sex. It's still really schoolboys' lavatory-wall stuff and this is what the newspapers cash in on. I'm not devoted to the French, I don't find myself naturally attached to them, but I do deeply admire their more adult and mature attitude towards sex, and the more I look at what our tabloids breakfast on, the more I envy the French. It's going to take a very long time to get this silliness out of the British system.

When Lord Lambton left politics he remarked that there was a world of difference between doing a thing and being found out. That remark was seen by some as being a sophisticated response, by others as cynical indifference. How do you see it?

Lambton was a minister at the time, and I do think that ministers have a certain duty to keep their private affairs from exciting the *News of the World*. Lambton was making a philsopher's point, but the fact is that he was a disgraced minister and I do not think that any amount of satire or humour can really rationalize what he did. I'm quite consistent about this. If you're in public office, you have a duty to your colleagues and to your government to live in the context of your times. It's no good saying, 'If I were in Paris nobody would take any notice of my going to bed with a black woman and a white woman.' The fact is if you're in the UK and you have the *News of the World* looking over your shoulder, then you must take that into account.

Do you ever think that journalism is bound to be constantly concerned with the trivial because of its ephemeral nature? There's nothing quite so dead as yesterday's newspaper. Perhaps the serious papers are just entertaining a different set of people from the tabloids. Or would you argue that there is a difference?

The answer to that is to make a comparison between today's newspapers and the newspapers of the thirties or even the fifties. I've just had to look through the newspapers of the fifties and I am mildly alarmed, as a professional journalist, to discover the extent to which, especially in popular newspapers, the content of serious news has gone down and the amount of trivia has gone up. Assuming that newspapers are guided by men who know where public taste lies, this is a disturbing commentary on public education. I don't want to be too tendentious, but when people abuse the *Star* or the *Sun* or the *News of the World*, I ask myself whether they're picking the right target. Let's take the old *Daily Mirror* of Cudlip's day, or the old *Daily Herald* of Southwood's. I look back on them and, alas, I fear public tastes are not what they were at one time. The appetite for serious news has virtually vanished. I think the attention span is much shorter than it was . . . television has something to do with this . . . and there are many children now who find it almost impossible to read through a whole book. But this is something outside the realm of journalism.

Journalists often like to present themselves as opinion makers. They certainly give opinions but do you think they actually change minds or do they rather bolster prejudices?

The irony here is that in the old days when they knew what was news and what was opinion, and the editorial columns of the papers were strictly confined to the opinion, then I think they did influence people. I'm thinking of something like *The Times* editorial which recommended that Czechoslovakia should yield to Hitler and save Europe a grave embarrassement; or of some of the leading articles even in the *Daily Mail* during the First World War about the shell scandal, the shortage of shells on the Western Front. Now the irony is this: that newspapers have rather self-indulgently enlarged the realm of opinion, and they no longer separate news from editorial. Most news is presented in a way to persuade you of this or that. For example, news about Mr Kinnock in the right-wing newspapers is designed to persuade you that he's in a mess. Nowadays you have far more columnists than before, opinionated fellows (like myself, I suppose I have to add) who write weekly or daily columns and who are expressing views all the time. It follows that the influence of newspapers has greatly diminished because their spread of rather subjective material is such that the public has become almost inoculated against it. People are very careful today about accepting what any newspaper says, so the newspapers have defeated themselves.

Before the war the unemployed were, I suppose, relatively unaware of what one might call the context of their poverty. There was a social cordon sanitaire around them, but the situation is now very different. Put bluntly, they can see what they are missing. Is that not bound to produce great social unrest and a see-saw of repression and resistance?

I think about this. Before the war, the problem for many people was literally getting enough to eat. Today it's rather different. Poverty today relates to what other people have in relation to what you yourself have. We're dealing with comparative standards of living. You're asking me if I think that this is more inflammatory than the old hunger standard, and I'm not sure. There are manifestations amongst young people that they are prepared to show their discontent in a way which the old poor were not – car nicking, and so on. In theory a different standard of life shouldn't lead to a revolution, yet in a way I think it does. I've just been in the Sudan where people are almost at the end of their tether through lack of food, but there is no mood of revolution there, no rising up against the government. You have to remind yourself that when people are denied the necessities of life they go very quiet, but when they're denied the so-called good things of life which they see widely advertised in our consumer society, there is probably a more inflammatory situation.

I recall you writing about Tyneside and drawing attention among other things to the prevalence of one-parent families there. What do you think can be done about that? Is it a sign of social disintegration?

We've learned recently that about a third of the children in this country are born outside wedlock. I do not doubt that there are many lone mothers devoted to their children, but there is no question that more children are in some way handicapped, and therefore the state has to concern itself. It's not a matter of morality, it's a matter of public welfare. Furthermore, a degree of public cost is involved in this. If you look at the figures you will discover that the number of children born outside wedlock creates quite a heavy bill for a government. My philosophy about this is really lamentable because I am a great believer in a self-correcting mechanism. I do not ever think that politicians can alter human behaviour.

If the government feels it a duty to make sure that the parents of those children suffer in no way at all and are treated through public funds, then in my view you will delay the working of a self-correcting mechanism which I deeply believe in. One generation learns from the previous generation. If the government neglects the problem and allows the public to see that a one-parent family suffers in a way which is unacceptable in our sort of democracy, then it is my belief that the self-correcting mechanism would work sooner. But we have to compromise; we have to do the minimum to prevent the children being handicapped and at the same time be aware as politicians that our powers are limited – we cannot correct the situation.

Very soon now we shall be in Europe . . . how do you think it will develop? Is it going to be a federal organization in the end?

On certain terms we can as readily share the culture, history and economy of Europe as any other nation. My principal anxiety is this: that if the architects of Europe with every good intention move too fast, become too enthusiastic, work towards a federal Europe too quickly, they will sow the seeds of conflict. If they overstress conformity then they could produce a reaction against the whole concept of Europe and defeat their own best endeavours. That is the centre of my European belief. I am pro-European as anyone who can remember both world wars has to be. Even Mr Delors is preferable to Marshal Foch. However, you must have proportion, historical proportion. I do not want to see Europe defeated and undermined by excessive zeal, and I think that could happen. There's a limit to the notion whereby European cultures, beliefs, civilization and peoples can be pulled into what some imaginatively regard as being akin to the United States of America, which had totally different origins.

Do you think that Mrs Thatcher is right in her views on Europe?

I think she's right in her views, and wrong on how she expressed them. Her instinct was that there would be a public revulsion against a demand for excessive conformity. It's an instinct I share. She was perhaps clumsy, perhaps over-forceful in the way in which she expressed her opposition to all this, but I know and you know that many in Europe were secretly rather grateful for the things she was saying. She lacked finesse, she could have harnessed people's anxieties, but instead she antagonized them. That was her mistake.

You have served as a cabinet minister so I suppose you must approve of the centrality of 'market forces', but won't an attempt to emulate America in that way produce the same large underclass with all its attendant problems? There are already riots in the streets of Cardiff and in Oxford for whatever reason . . .

In Russia the underclass is incomparably larger than the underclass in the United States or in the UK. If you go to the food markets you discover that at one end the poor relations are scrabbling for government food at government prices and at the other end there is Californian food for those who can afford it. I've never seen a country with greater distinctions between the poor and the privileged. So before we say that the market economy leads to impoverishment as indeed it does for a proportion of the population, let's say that we've got something built in here which is difficult to avoid. To some extent a degree of human poverty is unavoidable in almost any society. I can't think of any formula by which you can avoid a certain number of people going to the wall. But ours is better than anything they've got in Africa, or Latin America, or the Soviet Union. What I think the wealthier societies have to do is to find a means, without crippling themselves, of tempering the wind to the shorn lamb. I'm a great believer in Keith Joseph's philosophy – that the real advantage of a market economy is that you can afford to do more for the impoverished people than by any other means. That is the only solution to what you're postulating.

From time to time you have complained in the context of the newspaper world of the way accountants now rule the roost. Is that not the inevitable outcome of the political faith you have espoused?

I do think that newspapers are at risk of becoming too prone to the advice of the marketing man, and I have seen in my time a very big shift from the authority of an editor to the authority of those who have to sell the newspaper. Editors are now more and more persuaded by marketing people to cater for a certain class of public that they say is necessary for the health of the newspaper. The irony about newspapers today is that we're now employing some of the best minds that come out of the universities. I've never known a period in which we've recruited abler people to journalism, incomparably abler than the people we had a generation ago or in my early days, yet this is not reflected in the quality of the newspaper. Journalists are now much better qualified; they can actually write English and do joined-up writing, yet we have on the whole a more trivialized, a brasher, perhaps less informative set of newspapers. I've only ever had one view about the press: it is there to offer people the basis for making their decisions. And that function has not actually improved under all the better minds from Oxbridge and other universities. That is one of the sadnesses.

With the demise of communism and the triumph of capitalism, are we not going to have a world which simply dances to the tunes played by the United States?

We're between acts at the moment, the curtain is down, and I'm not sure what's going to happen next. But I'm quite sure of this: that the human race, being born to trouble as the sparks fly upwards, has problems which are not going to be cured by the death of communism. I don't know that we're going to live a tranquil and easy-going life and I am doubtful whether in the end we're going to see this rather simplistic solution of the United States prevailing over all. One of the things I worry about with the United States is whether behind all the wealth and the dollars, it is actually a nation in decline. My impression of Eastern European countries, by contrast, is that they are going to evolve some compromises between the failure of Marxism and the falsehood of capitalism, and I think we may find some new formulas developing which will be of great interest. A country like Hungary, for example, may well produce something which is better than anything we've yet attained.

You have spoken of 'capitalism in the service of humanity', but that is surely a utopian idea. Most liberals would disagree and argue that in the first instance capitalism is necessarily at the service of capitalists. Isn't it the 'overflow' which serves the rest?

We're talking about the most efficient way of dealing with human resources which must in the end provide more of the means which every nation has to find for dealing with the unfortunate section of the population which has to be – to put it bluntly – subsidized. Communism did not work, though many had high hopes of it, nor did fascism, so we have this imperfect mechanism, the market economy. It may be a very bad system, but we're now learning that nobody yet has produced anything better. In so far as it can provide enough to enable a country to look after those below the line, then it is a good system. What else can we do? If you say to me that you doubt whether capitalists ever wished to help, and that most of them are out for what they can get for themselves, then I say that is where government has a role to play. It is for government to decide what capitalists should keep to themselves and what governments should lay their hands on for the benefit of the unfortunates.

You sent your own son to Eton. If those who can afford private education do that, does it not dilute the pool of talent available to teach the vast majority of our children?

When I was in the army I was sharing a room with a man who was going to have a house at Eton. We agreed that we ought to put faith in the future – it was just before D-Day – and my son had just been born. My friend said, 'There are preferential terms for penitent old Harrovians, so would you like to put your son's name in my book?' and so I did. We both survived and so my son went to Eton. That's the story there. I accept that the English private education system is now becoming exorbitantly expensive, and I think it's just possible for this reason that there is a limited future for it. I also accept that we are internationally almost singular in our public schools. But I have never believed that their existence damages the national system. The national system is not in a very healthy state, but that does not in my view relate to the public schools. I don't accept the theory that if parents of children who go the private sector were required to use the state schools they would exert enormous influence. I don't see any harm in the public schools continuing. They are enjoyed by labour supporters as well as conservative supporters, so let's have no humbug about that. I myself set a very high value on them. There is a great inclination to reduce standards in education generally, to make exams easier, to reduce the rigours of the academic world. And it seems to me absolutely imperative, however noxious or class conscious it might appear, to keep a sort of yardstick against which you can measure quality. I know this is a very aggressive thing to say, but I feel this very strongly. I do think state education has gone through a very bad patch, that it is on the slide, but if you abolish the only comparative standard you've got, not only in terms of academic results, but in terms of discipline and what you turn out, then I don't think you're doing society any good.

But aren't you maintaining the class system? That's the danger that I see.

I think the class system in this country, compared with the twenties and thirties, has altered far more than anybody can believe. The speed at which we have reduced the enormous differences in class since the First World War is barely recognized today. I would wish in many ways that we had rather more of a pyramid, that all the old grammar schools were still there, rather than this uneven structure of public schools, one or two grant-aided schools and the rest comprehensives. The distinctions are too great. But I don't think there's any need for public-school masters to beat their breasts with guilt and say (as they often do) that they barely have the right to exist. I think the class thing can be exaggerated. It's unimportant compared to standards, which are immensely important.

I imagine you were an admirer of Mrs Thatcher.

Yes.

What was your feeling when she was obliged to resign?

I felt very worried about the way in which it was done, and wrongly thought that it would have a very bad effect on the Conservative Party. I underrated its resilience and the ability of Tories to gloss over what I regarded as a rather doubtful episode historically. The sacking of a conservative leader on a ballot is an unusual occurrence, and it's not in my view in the tradition of the Conservative Party. I never approved of the Humphry Berkeley rules in the first place. My initial feelings lasted for about three months and then to my surprise I realized I was wrong. Judging from the most recent meetings I've conducted, the conservative public have accepted the outcome with far less bitterness than I expected. Some credit for this is due to John Major who has conducted himself well for a man who had very little chance to think out what he was going to do before he had to do it. Some credit is also due to Mrs Thatcher who, notwithstanding the efforts of the press to involve her in bitterness, has in fact, like her husband, stepped outside any sort of controversy. The Conservative Party constantly surprises me.

Had Mrs Thatcher remained would we have fared better?

The action was unfortunate, but I think that it was ultimately for the benefit of the Conservative Party. I'm not revealing anything I shouldn't, but I have a feeling that retirement had been uppermost in her mind for some time and but for the recession all this might have come about in another way. The most difficult decision any prime minister has to make is not when to call a general election, but when to go. For historical reasons no prime minister wants to go on a low, and I think Mrs Thatcher of her own nature might have called it a day a little bit sooner had it not been for the fact that the recession left her with a sense of 'I'd better see this through.' As it was she was not allowed to make her own decision and was forced out through a concatenation of circumstances – the Rome summit, the Howe speech, the Heseltine challenge and then the denouement. I'll sum it up by saying that the Tory Party has had rather more luck than it deserves.

I can readily understand that as the editor of a national newspaper you must have been extremely frustrated by the practices and demands of the print unions, but what view do you take of the idea of trade unions, do you think they are necessary to ensure that employees are not exploited?

The fact of the matter is that those print unions so overplayed their hand as to make life unsupportable, and in so doing they did their fellows a bad turn. One of the great ironies of modern times is that the dockers behaved in such a way as to empty the docks of London, and the printers of Fleet Street who came from much the same background behaved in such a way as to make Fleet Street untenable. Now the newspapers have moved into the vacancies in the docks left by the dockers. It's true, there's a lot of management today which needs superintendence by vigilant trade unions, I've no doubt about that. As part of our meritocracy, there is a standard of modern management which looks awfully like the steel masters and the iron masters and the cotton masters who rose in Victorian times and who treated their work forces very badly. I am totally convinced of the need for a vigilant trade union to keep management from exploitation, but it's unfortunate that excessive zeal by the printers and some other unions have led to this state of affairs. I don't think Mrs Thatcher emasculated the unions, but there is a balance to be struck between leaving trade unions to fulfil their role, and at the same time not enabling them to cripple the economy for reasons which are irrelevant.

Who made the deepest impression on you in your role as a politician?

Though he was dead before I became an active politician, the man I've always followed more closely than anybody else was Stanley Baldwin. I have all his speeches, I constantly refer to him, and I've always regarded him as a thoroughly underrated member of the Conservative Party for several reasons. Firstly he understood the doctrine of one society. We talk about a classless society, but look up some of Baldwin's speeches and you will see that he was the first man to realize that if this country was going to get anywhere we would have to get there together. The General Strike conflicted with Baldwin's philosophy, but with all the criticism that is levelled at him, it has to be said that against all predictions through the thirties he got us into the Second World War more or less as one people; this is not a thing that I underrate at all. Similarly, I've thought often that Alec Home represented something which is missing in British politics now, namely the figure who has better things to do but goes in out of a sense of something which is not ambition, not a desire to better himself, not a desire to win. There is an element of public service about Alec Home which is an essential ingredient of English public life. Think of the way in which when he surrendered the premiership he was perfectly happy to continue as foreign secretary. There was a degree of selflessness about that which I think the modern Tory Party, which has become rather self-regarding, would do well to take up.

You served under several prime ministers. How did you assess them?

I've always had a theory that every prime minister has one special historical function in his time. In Winston's case it was obviously the war. With Alec it was rather different. Just when the Tory party was becoming very inward looking and material Alec reminded us of other values; he set a certain example. Macmillan's primary function was to speed up the process of independence for the colonies. He knew that after India there was no alternative but to dismantle. The wind of change was essentially his business. Eden was really too shortlived to have any particular function except to remind us perhaps through Suez that – as Kipling called it – our dominion over palm and pine had diminished, had in fact finished. Eden was a historical reminder that we were not where we thought we were (I'm thinking of Suez).

What about Thatcher?

The most important thing about her was that in an age in which women sought equality her example was of greater value than all the equal opportunities acts put together. She came at a critical moment for women and was a huge encouragement to them. I'm pro woman and anti feminist in a funny way, if you know what I mean. I think it's stupid not to make more use of the abundant talents of so many women, but I'm not in favour of all these artificial arrangements to make certain that every woman has a position she doesn't necessarily want. And Thatcher embodied all that.

She also broke down a whole lot of adhesions in the Tory Party which had become a slightly clublike organization. As a Tory MP for twenty-five years I knew there were certain understandings, but she would have none of it. She had her own idea of how to go about things and she changed the whole way of thinking in the party. She never felt herself handicapped by anybody who looked down on her; she never felt handicapped by any minister who opposed her.

When the war came, do you think you were more aware than other people of fascism and what it meant because of your background as a journalist?

I wish I had been. It's one of my laments that although the politicians of the 1930s have been roundly abused for failure to know what Nazi Germany was doing, a great amount of unapportioned blame lies with the journalists of those years. As journalists in the thirties we failed lamentably to produce as we should have done a loud enough warning note of what was happening in Germany. There were reasons for this. Proprietors and editors were too much in the pocket of those in the Foreign Office who always wanted to give Hitler the benefit of the doubt. The great thing was not to rock the boat, not to write something that was going to infuriate Hitler. There was a certain element of responsibility attached to this but it was fatally misconceived. As a result the British up to 1938 did not get the warning that they should have had from the free press.

At present there is a bill going through parliament designed to provide people with the right to reply to incorrect information. I know you feel it is an awkward way to deal with the problem and that it would be exploited. But is it not a problem which has to be tackled? How would you do it?

It ought to be done by the editor and if the editor fails to give the reader a fair right of reply, then I am quite clear in my mind that we have to go to a statutory right of reply which will land us in a most unholy mess. We shall have to entertain not only a right of reply on fact, but on opinion, and once you've started to do that it will run and run and there will never be an end to it. I only hope every editor understands what the penalty will be. Mind you, I'm very sceptical, more sceptical than Lord MacGregor, about any parliamentary move against the press. I know my political parties on this score. No party before, or even after a general election is willingly going to antagonize the newspapers by taking a step such as the statutory right of reply. It is a perfectly reasonable sword of Damocles for people like Lord MacGregor to hold over the editors' heads but my political instinct tells me that there is not the slightest possible prospect of either a conservative or even a government under Mr Kinnock doing it. Politicians know which side their bread is buttered.

Is there any effective way of reconciling the freedom of the press with the protection of the individual, or for that matter of minorities? There are already restrictions about inciting racial hatred, for example. On the face of it, it seems very proper, but all governments love to restrict the press – think of the D notices . . .

I don't myself regard the press as unduly threatened by the Official Secrets Act or by D notices. I worked as an editor for nine years before I even had to refer to a D notice, and I think the newspapers for their own reasons tend to exaggerate the extent to which their ability to tell the public what they ought to know is impeded by D notices or fear of official secrets, or, to go wider, fear of defamation or libel. I think the balance in this country is just about right. Every now and again we get huge libel damages and people say the law is an ass. I think we went through a rather exceptional period in which juries lacked guidance from the judge, but that probably will be corrected. In terms of the Temple Court, I'm rather old fashioned; I think that newspapers should not be free to ridicule judges and to attack them in public and say that their sentences lead one to suppose they ought to be in lunatic asylums. Furthermore, the prejudicing of a trial of an individual by pre-press trial as happens in America is, to my mind, obnoxious. To hell with the First Amendment on that score. Let's not have the illusion of loosening the law of secrecy which is simply going to lead to a raising of the levels at which documents are marked confidential or secret. You can take the horse to water but you've got to make the horse drink, and no system with which the civil service will not cooperate is workable or of any value at all, whatever politicians say. If the civil service considers that the law of secrecy is not inimical to the public good then the law will remain what it was, regardless of what parliament says. So I don't want to get into that situation. For the moment we've got something which everybody cooperates with. I can't remember in twelve years of editing the *Daily Telegraph* feeling impeded about telling my readers something they should know; other editors may have different experiences, but I'm afraid I'm individual, I'm odd man out on this.

Would you ever have prevented publication of something on moral grounds, as it were, or because you yourself held strong views on a particular subject?

No. I'm entirely beholden to the tradition of the paper. As you well know the *Daily Telegraph* carries a page 3 which is the envy of some of the tabloids. As the old *News of the World* used to say, all human life is there on our page 3. There are very few known sins that aren't at some point recounted on the *Daily Telegraph*'s page 3, and I would regard it as obnoxious if on subjective grounds I prevented something from being printed. If it is within the tradition of the paper, my personal views on the matter are irrelevant.

Do you believe in censorship at any level?

Don't let's mix up censorship and editorial judgement. The latter, whether it is in broadcasting, in television or in newspapers, has to be exercised. I absolutely hold to that. But that is not censorship. A lot of modern authors regard any failure to publish what they've done as an act of censorship, but it is not, though it is sometimes an act of editorial judgement.

When you decided to stand for parliament, did you have an ambition to reach high office or to implement some particular scheme? What was it that prompted you to take up so different a career?

There were about eight members of my family who had been in parliament before me and they had all chugged along quite cheerfully. There's a wonderful passage in Henri Leroi's *Life of Disraeli* in which there is described an encounter in the Carlton Club during the fall of the coalition. Somebody rushes in and says to the chief whip: 'There's no need for the coalition to fall. There are good men waiting . . . such as Deedes, Snoops and Swift' . . . to which the chief whip replies, 'These are not names that I can lay before the Queen.' I don't think any of my relatives held high office; they just felt quite content, as I did, to represent a constituency. So I entered parliament with the idea that I was perfectly happy to follow in the footsteps of my ancestors and if anything came of it, it came. But I wasn't very keen, truth to tell, because all my life the *Daily Telegraph* has been a very generous host to my small talents and I didn't particularly want my connections with the paper to be interrupted by politics. I could work for the *Daily Telegraph* as a member of parliament but it would have been difficult as a minister. So I can honestly say that I went in hoping to chug along happily as a backbencher.

Working as a politician must have been very different from being a newspaper man or a soldier. Did you find it a congenial environment?

Absolutely not. It's as different as you can imagine. A journalist has to live on his initiative; if he gets an idea, he can pursue it. Provided he gets his bosses' countenance he can get on with it. In Whitehall it's a totally different world because everything you do is subject to scrutiny. You're part of an enormous chain, and the processes through which your bright idea has to travel are unimaginably sick, and so you get rather discouraged, unless you're a very powerful figure which I never pretended to be. It was the contrast between journalism and ministerial life that made me think that I preferred journalism.

As an MP you were once concerned with the drug problem. Some people such as Judge Pickles take the radical view that their use should be legalized. Taking drugs might then become a habit like social drinking and they could be taxed. What view did you take?

I worked chiefly in this field with people like Barbara Wootton who took a more radical view than I did. I swotted up the subject and was helped by doctors, and I must first of all say that it is not a moral position I hold on this. But I do take the view that there are enough health hazards – and other hazards – strewn about the feet of young people today without adding one more. I know that it may be said that if you legalize cannabis or even harder drugs you avoid damage to the law which is being made a mockery of at the moment by people, often well-connected people, who smoke cannabis around the clock. All right, that is a fact. But the higher priority in my view is not to add to hazards that already exist in the way of alcohol, and so on. I've also had it argued to me that fewer young people would smoke cannabis if it was legalized, since it's the illegality which appeals. This is all very beguiling but I simply don't accept it.

Which side were you on in the great poll-tax debate? Is it true, do you think, that its demise represented the triumph of political expediency over principle – its fairness was much trumpeted by government ministers at the time?

I've always accepted that a mistake was made here. What threw ministers off their balance was the misconduct of a minority of councils who proved extremely difficult to bring to account; they were overspending, and they were doing it in such a way that there was no chance of their electorate throwing them out. The government was driven to the poll tax by a desire to produce the mechanism which would make a small minority of councils more accountable. Now, if you produce a large law fundamentally to deal with a minority problem you embark on a very dangerous course. The result was of course that they trapped both the good and the bad; everybody got it wrong. It was a brilliant idea on paper, but they failed to apply to it that acid test of practicality. If a law is not enforceable it is a bad law.

You were for many years part of the Peterborough column – really a high-class gossip column. Do you think you could have been a gossip columnist in the mould of Nigel Dempster, for example?

I'm an admirer certainly. It really consists of knowing a tremendous number of people, and what is more it satisfies a tremendous human want. Provided it's not malicious or libellous, there's no great harm in tittle-tattle about people; it's a service to journalism. I'm not prepared to be tendentious about Nigel Dempster or any of the other columns. I would be ill suited to them, partly because I prefer writing about things rather than people, and it's not quite my cup of tea. But I wouldn't be ashamed to do it.

Five years ago you accepted a peerage. There is some disquiet about the honours system in this country: so often such things seem rewards for political loyalty. Do you think this is fair in a democracy such as ours?

I've had doubts about all prefixes in honours, that is to say anything that goes in front of somebody's name. I think that suffixes, however, are rather different. I also believe that this country with a social revolution which has travelled much faster than most of us appreciate, is growing out of the honours system. The system as it's now constructed has a limited life, but I would prefer to see the country grow out of it than have a swift termination. I find certain difficulties about the House of Lords because, for reasons I can only surmise, the temperature of the House of Lords is kept at the level of an intensive-care ward, and I find it very hard to concentrate my mind when I'm there. The heating arrangements are excessive, but that's a purely personal problem.

I recall that you wrote somewhere that politics kept you apart from your son when he was young, and indeed he explained that he has avoided politics as a career partly because of the effect it might have on his own family. Have you ever regretted this side of things?

I have in a way. Had I not had an admirable wife my children would have suffered. A great many children suffer through the excessive zeal of their families in public life, so I would think more carefully about it given my time again. In reality, and far beyond my deserts, my children do not seem to have been adversely affected by my preoccupation with public affairs. As for my son, he has made a considerably greater success of his life in journalism than I ever did and in fact is now in a position of responsibility in which politics are ruled out anyway.

Laurence Marks in a profile of you spoke of your 'determination to keep the Telegraph *independent of the Tory government it supports'. What does it mean to be independent in that context?*

Not to find yourself in the pocket of any minister, including the prime minister, of whom I was personally very fond but whose company I avoided in relation to anything to do with the *Daily Telegraph*. If I learned one thing before the war, apropos of the relationship between the foreign secretary and *The Times* at the time of Munich and relations between proprietors and ministers in the thirties, it was that there were great dangers in editors getting themselves too close to people in office. Once you are made a repository of a confidence, an invisible mechanism starts to work; you play it the way he would like to see it played and not the way you should play it. So I found as an editor it was imperative to be perfectly friendly with all ministers, to accept invitations, to go and talk to them, to be briefed by them, but it was important to keep a certain distance; that seemed to me as editor to be the most important thing. I'm sure my successor, Max Hastings, does exactly the same thing so that editorial judgements are totally independent. It doesn't matter what arises, you have made no commitment; you have no agreement, and you have no understanding with any minister, and you are therefore free to say 'this is rubbish'.

Every decade has its own conflict. The sixties saw the evolution of so-called free love and student power – in England we had Tariq Ali and in France we had Daniel Cohn-Bendit; the seventies saw the emergence of feminism; the eighties saw Thatcherism at full throttle. The nineties bear witness to the beginning of the end of communism . . . where do you see the next conflict?

Just when we think that the communist world has ended and the threat to our existence is diminished, we begin to worry ourselves – and rightly so – about certain faults and crevices which are beginning to appear in Western civilization. The big issue for us in the next decade is how to tackle very rapid and not altogether beneficial changes in our society. It's almost impossible for ministers to interfere with certain courses which society takes, and in the ethical and moral field, I wonder how far we can depend on what Reginald Maudling when he was home secretary called the self-correcting mechanism. The really important political issue in the West is going to be to what extent government has a responsibility to interfere, and to what extent we are prepared to wait and see how far learning from our own mistakes will work. I put full confidence in the second, not much confidence in the ministers.

In my interview with Prime Minister Edith Cresson, which was published recently in the Observer, *she caused a bit of a stir by suggesting that a large proportion of Anglo-Saxons are homosexuals. Although her claims are not based on any scientific research, would you not say it's true that most Englishmen are not comfortable in the presence of women?*

Well, a proportion are certainly not. I can perhaps best answer by relating an experience when I was chairman of our home affairs committee. Mr Butler who was then shadow home secretary said to me: 'Bill, I hope that you will be able to persuade our party to oppose the Abse bill' (the legalizing of homosexuality). I think it's the only time in my life I was perhaps right and Mr Butler, who had a magnificent intellect, wrong. I said, 'Rab, bear in mind that altering the law will not be enough. People being what they are, this will be followed by a long and continuous campaign of self-justification.' To be told that you are legal is not enough; you must also feel that you are socially acceptable. And indeed I think I have been proved right in this, for you will observe that the law as it stands is not enough and pressure is going to be put on the prime minister to alter it yet again. People are not content with finding themselves within the law, they are insistent upon a form of social equality. The homosexual today desires and indeed insists not only on equality in employment but in all departments, that he should be regarded as – in Mrs Thatcher's well known phrase – one of us.

But why do you think it is that many Englishmen are not very comfortable in the presence of women?

In this country there has always been a sort of shyness between the two sexes. When I went to my first deb dances in London, there was always a certain reserve, but I don't relate this to homosexuality about which my views are complex. I was in San Francisco not long ago and watched one of these gigantic marches of homosexuals protesting about the failure of the government to deal with their problems. It is jolly difficult at my age to avoid drawing conclusions from certain phenomena. I fight against this very hard. If you are going to remain in active journalism, you don't want to regard every symptom that you don't like as a process of degeneration, but I do find this new phenomenon gives me pause, and I think that a world in which virtually everything has become socially acceptable is a world in which standards, frankly, have slipped. There is far more freedom for people to indulge in habits which twenty or thirty or forty years ago would have been regarded as socially unacceptable. The degree of tolerance which has entered our society is too high. There is a great struggle among the liberals in Hampstead as to the misuse of part of the Health by homosexuals, and the liberal camp is divided. One set say they have every entitlement to do what they wish to do, another set of liberals say that they are interfering with the freedom of families who want to walk round with their children. I find that a very interesting conflict. But I do believe there is

115

a lack of restraint in public behaviour today, and I'm not absolutely certain that this is an advance in a civilized nation.

Most people hate to grow old, yet old age brings maturity and often peace of mind . . . what are your own feelings on this?

I count myself jolly lucky at my age to be kept actively working five days a week, because I've come to the conclusion that as you get older, you have to look at your mind, very much as when you're young you attend to the fitness of your body. The great risk of old age, unless you exercise your mind, is that you become a tremendous bore to other people. There is a great tendency for your mind to close in on itself, and then all you really do is go on about the past. The great virtue of journalism is that it keeps your mind concentrated. People ask why I don't write my memoirs. The practical reason, apart from the fact that I rather object to the idea anyway, is that I cannot possibly devote my mind to thinking of what's going to happen tomorrow which is, for journalistic purposes, essential, while half my mind is occupied with digging out what happened yesterday. And tomorrow on the whole keeps me fitter.

What weaknesses, if any, would you attribute to yourself?

I really admire people who have a bit more dash about them. I'm cautious, over cautious. I do too much thinking before I leap. If I'm pushed into it I will take initiatives, but I suffer from a certain passivity. It sounds a rather odd thing to say, but every now and again I get mildly alarmed at the extent to which someone of my rather limited intellectual capacities has succeeded in doing certain things. I've done a certain amount of self-education but not nearly enough, and therefore my capacities are more limited than you might suppose and occasionally it looks to me as if I'm like one of these children who are accused of getting very easy A levels and that is how I've slipped through my life.

PROFESSOR H. J. EYSENCK

Hans Jürgen Eysenck was born in 1916 in Berlin and is the best-known name in post-war British psychology. Educated in France and at London University (BA 1938, PhD 1940, DSc 1964), he began his career in the field of clinical psychology which led to psychometric researches into the variations of human personality and intelligence. Throughout his career he has been an outspoken critic of loose thinking, in particular claims made without adequate empirical evidence. He has published over seventy-five books and has been fiercely critical of psychoanalysis in its various forms. He has often held controversial views, notably in his study of racial differences in intelligence in *Race, Intelligence and Education* (1971). From 1955 to 1983 he was professor of psychology at the Institute of Psychiatry at London University. In 1988 he received the American Psychological Association's Distinguished Scientific Award.

When you look back on your childhood, do you remember facts and events or do you remember feelings and impressions?

Mostly facts. I don't go much by feelings and impressions. My childhood was reasonably happy and there was nothing in it that would cause me to worry. My main memories are of two things. One is of being talent spotted as a good tennis player and winning an open tournament. Unfortunately any future in the sport was cut short when Hitler came to power and I had to leave Germany. The other memory is of the struggle against Hitler and his ideas. I was about the only non-Jewish boy in the class who was anti-Hitler; the rest, and this was true practically all over Germany, were very nationalistic. I would have had a very tough time of it if I hadn't been big and strong and also good at sports, since it's difficult to beat up somebody who plays for your school. I was lucky in a way, but a year after Hitler had come to power it became hopeless. I had applied to go to university in Berlin but I was told that entry was conditional on my joining the SS, which of course was out of the question. I decided to leave and went to France with my mother and her second husband, a Jewish film producer, who naturally couldn't stay in Germany. I studied in Dijon for a while, but I preferred England where I had spent some time at school.

Why were you anti-Hitler at such an early stage? Most people saw him as a saviour to begin with.

When I heard Hitler speak, I thought it was evil incarnate. I simply can't understand how anybody could have failed to see that. When I read his book I became firmly convinced of it; it was so obvious, and I still don't know how people managed to avoid seeing it. The other reason was that I was very left wing, as many young people are, without knowing very much about it. I read a lot of Marx, but I wasn't convinced of the communists' notions, although they were the main opponents of Hitler of course. I was friendly with a number of communists but I think what really put me off was the tram drivers' strike in 1930 when they joined with the Nazis to oppose the Weimar Republic. I told my friends that the Weimar Republic was their greatest protection against the Nazis, but they wouldn't listen and preferred to carry out Stalin's instructions, even though – as I pointed out – Stalin was in Moscow and didn't know a damned thing about what was going on in Germany. Of course they all ended up in a concentration camp; they were brave bright people, but they were blinded by this curious notion that Stalin was infallible.

Professor H. J. Eysenck

You were abandoned by both parents and brought up mainly by your grandmother. Would you say that the absence of parental love and attention had a measurable effect on your adult life?

I don't think it had any effect at all. It certainly didn't worry me at the time. I occasionally met my parents, at Christmas for example, but I can't say I missed them very much. I was always very self-sufficient and had a busy life, playing tennis, football, rowing, and I was also reading a lot, both literature and science. My life was full.

Did you have a special feeling for your grandmother?

Yes, I loved her very much. She was an exceptionally good woman, in the best sense of the word, but she had a terrible life. Her husband died when she was young, she was a very promising actress and singer and then she broke her leg which was badly set and she became a cripple. Finally she ended up in a concentration camp. I don't really like to think about it. We tried to bring her over to England but just as we were about to succeed, the war broke out and of course everything fell to pieces.

You are quoted as saying: 'The fact that my mother did not love me is not important, because such a thing cannot be measured. It is very difficult to see how a mother affects her child. If it cannot be tested, it does not exist.' Some would see that as a defence mechanism against the absence of love in your early years. Do you deny there is an element of that in it?

I'd be very surprised if there was. There has been a lot of study recently along genetic lines of personality development, and what has been found is not only that genetic factors are by far the most important but also that environmental factors exclude the family. There is no evidence that the family has any effect environmentally on the personality development. I don't believe in all this defence mechanism kind of thing. As you know, I'm not very fond of Freudian theory.

Yes, we'll come to that. You left Germany to escape the rise of Nationalist Socialism. Was that a difficult decision to make – did you feel you had any real choice?

120

I had no real choice but to leave Germany, because I am incapable of lying or pretending. I simply had to say what I felt about Nazism and it was touch and go even as I left whether I would be allowed to leave or whether I would be sent to a concentration camp.

It can't have been very easy living in England after the war broke out. How did you manage to avoid internment, for example?

They came for me twice, but I managed to talk them out of it each time. It was obviously a stupid policy and the police realized this and were quite ashamed. So they were quite happy when I asked to be allowed to finish my PhD before internment. They departed in a very civilized fashion.

Were you ever made aware personally of much anti-German feeling at that time?

I never encountered any kind of hostility whatsoever. I think most people realized that Germans over here were refugees, and therefore they were welcome.

Do you still have feelings of being an outsider in any sense, or are you totally assimilated?

I don't think you ever become totally assimilated, particularly in a country like England . . . in America perhaps, but in England you are always a bloody foreigner. Again it doesn't worry me since I don't really go much for nationalism. I feel a good European.

I read somewhere that you were not in favour of the reunification of Germany.

I wouldn't put it quite like that. I think reunification was inevitable, but it does pose very great problems for West Germans, and I don't think they have even begun to realize how big these problems are and will be, and that for the next twenty years they will suffer financially and in every other way. There's also always a fear that Germany will become predominant in

Europe and will revert to its old bad ways. People reject that notion but I don't see how you can. They were beaten in the First World War after which there was the Weimar Republic – at first a very democratic regime – but then twenty years later we had another war. I feel we should not simply take it for granted that because Germany at the moment is democratic, it will always remain so. There is a very nasty rise of neo-Nazism in Germany already; it is very powerful, much more so than most people realize, and it is a worry.

In The Psychology of Politics, *published in 1954, you predicted that left-wing fascism would rise in Britain and parallel the right-wing fascism of Hitler's Germany. This has not really happened in any great measure. Why not, do you think – or is it still waiting to happen?*

It did happen to a considerable extent with the militant tendencies which assumed power in the Labour Party. That was an index of how very strong left-wing fascism became in this country. I never predicted that it would succeed; all I was pointing out at the time on the basis of my research was that there are very marked resemblances between the left-wing militants, communists and so on, and the right-wing militants. It wasn't at all appreciated at the time, particularly since Uncle Joe was still our friend, and it caused a lot of argument and hostility, notably at the London School of Economics and other left-wing institutions. But I think it was a reasonable prediction, and it was justified.

For you psychology is a science based on experiment and deduction, and science works on the assumption that every event has a determining cause. Do you really think that the nature of man can be properly determined by excluding all unscientific *methods of investigation?*

There are no methods of investigation other than scientific ones; if you rely on intuition and analogy and other mental activities you cannot arrive at any relatively certain conclusion. The only way to do that is by scientific methods, so what we cannot prove by science we cannot prove at all. That is not to say that other things may not exist. You cannot prove the existence of God, I cannot disprove it, so if you want to believe in God, that's fine, but it is outside the field of science completely.

Do you believe in God?

No, I don't. We have shown by studies of twins that there is a strong genetic element in religious belief; you are predisposed to believe or not to believe. I happen to be predisposed not to believe. In a sense I'm quite sorry. My grandmother, for instance, was a very devout Catholic and it helped her a great deal in her troubles. So obviously religious belief can be very helpful, but it's rather like beer. I was born hating beer, even the smell of it. I know I'm missing something because lots of other people have fun drinking beer, but I can't help it. And so it is with religion. In addition of course there are rational arguments against the existence of God to be taken into account. The arguments are perhaps too well known to go into here, but to have a baby born with Aids is not in my view the act of a merciful omnipotent God.

If I follow you correctly you would say that to understand people we must look at the world of statistics and experiment, not at the world of philosophers, poets and novelists, nor even into our own hearts. Does it not worry you that your approach would seem to exclude vast numbers of thinking people?

No, it doesn't worry me. There are two ways of gaining knowledge. For example, when we look at a table we tend to see a solid object with a colour and so on, but in physics the table is largely emptiness, with just a few atoms and electrons and protons. Of course common knowledge is also knowledge of a kind. Newton taught us the law of gravity, but when I'm playing tennis and I hit a ball straight at the opponent's backhand and he replies with a lob, I don't even have to look at it to know that this is going out by a foot. I don't have to pay attention to Newton's law to make this very accurate prediction, so we have a great deal of knowledge which is factual, and the same applies in psychology, otherwise we couldn't live alongside one another. We know who's hostile, who's friendly, which people will react to certain things – and so on, all this is common knowledge, not scientific knowledge, and in many cases it is still superior to anything we can do scientifically. But it has two disadvantages: first, it cannot be communicated, that is to say a person is good or bad at judging other people and he can't teach others; secondly, it may be wrong and often is wrong. This is illustrated by the contradictions embodied in sayings such as 'absence make the heart grow fonder' and 'out of sight, out of mind'

– both are true in a sense. In my field, however, we already do very much better than commonsense psychology. For instance, in the treatment of neurotic disorders, we do a lot better than Shakespeare or Proust if they had been faced with these problems. Poets, dramatists, artists and so on articulate common psychology; they mostly do it extremely well, and we can learn a lot from it, but it is not scientific knowledge. It is therefore not of particular interest to me as a scientist. As a man of course, it is – I love Shakespeare, I love reading good poetry, but professionally I have to put these things on a scientific footing. I'm not for a moment pretending that we've gone very far in this, but most of our problems as human beings are psychological. We know quite enough about botany, agriculture and physics to make sure of a very good living for everybody who is on the earth at the moment, but what stands in our way is our lack of knowledge of psychology. Why are there warring factions in Yugoslavia? Why is the Russian communist experiment failing? Why do we have strikes? These are all very real problems which we are incapable of solving because we lack scientific knowledge of them. I hope in 200 years time perhaps psychology will be an adequate science to deal with these difficulties. It will take a long time but it is necessary because commonsense is not helping us very much.

But there are certain people who for some reason or other seem to be able to do the right thing without there being any scientific basis for it.

Yes, I won't deny it for a moment. In fact that is one of the things one can investigate – why some people are better than others, what kinds of personalities they have, and so on. These are all scientific questions.

Your own autobiography is studded with quotations from philsophers and literature. Is there not a contradiction there?

No, because what they say can often be perfectly correct even though it isn't arrived at by a scientific process. We may now know that they were right. The real necessity for science, since philosophers are always contradicting each other, is to quote the ones who were right and not the ones who were wrong.

The most common worry which your critics express about your theories is that they are somewhat cold and dehumanizing. This seems to be given some weight by your own insistence that you are a very unemotional man. Is there not a substantial element of subjectivity in your science?

I don't see any subjectivity at all. In any case, if you want to find out the facts you have to be unemotional about it. Supposing you are faced with a very young child who keeps banging his head against a wall – it is a very serious problem which may eventually kill him. The question is, why does he do it, what can I do about it? It is just as cold and unemotional a problem as what happens in a black hole. The answer itself is a very simple one: you can cure practically every young head-banger by a method of what is called 'time out'. Whenever he starts banging his head the mother is told to pick him up, put him in another room, shut the door, and leave him there for ten minutes. In that way he learns that when he bangs his head something slightly annoying happens to him, and he therefore stops banging his head. But people who feel emotional about the problem say that the mother should rush to him because he is missing her companionship or love, pick him up, kiss him and so on. What that does in effect is to reward him for banging his head, so he goes on doing it even more. I naturally feel very sympathetic towards the child, but that doesn't help him in the slightest. What does help him is a scientific approach to the problem he presents.

But do you believe that any great virtue attaches to being unemotional?

I don't think it's either a virtue or a weakness. Artists tend to be very emotional and it is part of their nature. If they weren't emotional they wouldn't be artists, so it is a virtue for them, but not for scientists.

If I can press you a little further on the matter of being unemotional – you describe how your responses were once tested by electrodes, heartrate, breathing pattern, etc., and your reaction was so muted that it was at first thought that the equipment was faulty. Doesn't this in itself set you apart from most other people, and doesn't that in turn have serious consequences for your theories?

I don't see why it should, because a theory is tested by its consequences. In other words, if my theory about the head-banger is wrong, then it shouldn't work. The fact that it does work proves that it is the right theory, and the same goes for any of the other theories. They are tested quite independently of the personality or the prejudice or anything else pertaining to the scientist who puts forward the theory. It is an objective thing: either it works or it doesn't. When I put forward a theory for the treatment of neurosis, the question is a very simple one: does it work, or doesn't it work? In fact it does work, it works better than any other theory, so up to that point it is correct. Of course, like all scientific theories, it won't be a hundred per cent correct, it will be improved and changed as time goes on, but it is independent of the personality or anything else that the scientist presents. I don't deny that I'm unemotional; on a continuum from very emotional to unemotional, I'm at one extreme.

You belong very much to the behaviourist school of psychology, that is to say that people behave as they do largely because of genetics and conditioning. You have even claimed that feelings of happiness are genetically determined. It is difficult for the layman to see how this can be so since events which promote or remove happiness are not generally known in advance.

The point is that we very much overestimate the importance of factors which supposedly bring happiness. There are some people who have everything, millionaires like Getty, and yet they are perfectly unhappy; the converse is also true. Events are very much less important than a person's individual reactions to them. I know people with very little who are profoundly happy; it is an innate gift. Similarly some people react with emotion to events which fail to move others. Nobody is saying that genetics is a hundred per cent responsible for our actions; what we are saying is that the genetic factor contributes about sixty per cent to personality differences, and seventy per cent to intellectual differences. This obviously leaves a wide margin for environmental factors to determine character.

Since you have always been an experimental psychologist and to my knowledge have never actually treated patients, isn't there a danger that your theories are too academic, too ivory-towered, too removed from the ordinariness of real life?

If they were, they wouldn't work. The point is that they do work, they're pretty universally used now over the whole world in the treatment of neurotic disorders and they're very much more successful than any others. Before I retired, I had a very large department, about fifty clinical psychologists using these methods. I never had to do the treatment myself – it would have been far too time-consuming a business, it's impossible to combine the two. But if I take the very simple example of compulsive hand washing, a very serious problem which can destroy a person's life – he spends all his time washing his hands, he can't have a sex life, he can't work, he has no family life, he has nothing. Psychoanalysis had been tried, leucotomy, electric-shock treatment, everything, but nothing worked. We put forward a very simple theory of how it works and how it could be cured. It has been tried out independently by three different large organizations, and we now have a success rate of about ninety to ninety-five per cent. So, I don't have to do it myself, other people can do it much better. I'm not very gifted as a therapist, but the crucial point of the theory is that it works.

But since most of us don't go through life being rigorously scientific, most of us behave quite irrationally, at least some of the time; how do you take that into account in your study of people's behaviour?

I don't see the problem. We do find that most people behave irrationally much of the time, but so what? The theory doesn't say that they should behave rationally, the theory says that emotions are very powerful, it studies the way emotions are conditioned to external stimuli and so on. It is exactly what we would predict.

You have often argued that those who commit crimes, for example, do so not because they are deprived or frustrated or socially disadvantaged but largely because of genetics and conditioning. Some of your critics would say that you have never really confronted the hopelessness of some people's lives, the sheer scale of suffering or deprivation, which is why you can dismiss it as perhaps irrelevant. What do you say to that?

I wouldn't dismiss it for a moment. It is obviously a very sad feature in the lives of many people. The question, however, is quite a different one: does it cause criminal behaviour? I grew up in Germany when we had an unemployment rate of thirty per cent, in some places much more. There was no welfare state and some people were actually starving; but there was very little crime. There is far more crime nowadays, and most of the criminals are not undernourished or deprived. If the theory were right, then there should be a perfect correlation between crime and income, but there is no correlation at all, if anything there is a negative correlation. People who make that kind of assumption simply don't know the facts.

But surely somebody who is starving and who sees a loaf of bread is more likely to steal it, than somebody who is not hungry?

That is not the nature of crime as we know it. My wife is a magistrate and she has never had a case before her of anybody walking into a shop and stealing bread. This is not an illustration of actual crime as it happens. The usual kind of crime is of a youngster, often middle class, stealing a car and driving off; stealing bread just doesn't occur any more. Much of the crime is committed by middle-class youngsters, as well as by working-class youngsters, in which deprivation may be a factor, but certainly not a major factor. The most deprived seldom commit any crimes at all.

As a scientist, how would you go about reducing crime and delinquency figures?

There are two ways. The first one is proper punishment. As you probably know, between a third and a half of all crimes against property are committed by people on bail. It's absolutely beyond comprehension how a justice system ensures that people will continue to commit crime by putting them on bail. The second one, probably much the most important one, is that is has been shown that you can reduce the criminality recidivism by over fifty per cent by suitable psychological treatment, in the form of behaviour therapy. Typically all the studies have been done in America, since the Home Office doesn't care about this and doesn't encourage research in this area. What we need is a more psychological approach to the problem. There's also the question of the original punishment. Essentially what we do at the moment is exactly the wrong thing. When a youngster commits a crime, what happens? He gets a caution, which tells him in effect that if he does it again he will really be punished, sent to prison perhaps. When he commits another crime, he gets another caution, and again he is told that the next time he really will be punished. So by the time he gets any kind of real punishment he's already firmly convinced rationally, as well as through conditioning, that crime pays, that nothing really serious happens. What we should do is exactly the opposite. The first time somebody commits a crime he should be clobbered, so that he really learns that the consequences of criminal activity are very serious. That would be the correct psychological approach; but instead what we do is to persuade people that the consequences of crime are very benign.

On the other hand, many psychologists argue that punishment has never been a deterrent to crime.

It just isn't true. You won't find anybody who has made a serious study of the literature saying that. A lot of psychologists say that because they haven't looked at the evidence. After all, many people, even in psychology, tend to talk in terms of their prejudices, and only a small minority have actually studied the literature, and among those you will not find anybody saying that punishment doesn't pay.

If environmental factors count for so little, doesn't this have serious consequences for the way in which we behave towards each other, our whole moral structure indeed? I mean, what is the point in behaving well towards our children, for example, when this is going to have no effect – since everything is genetically set in advance.

I never said everything is genetically determined, only sixty per cent which still leaves a very wide margin. Obviously anything that happens to us determines in some way how we shall react later on. Genetics points you in one direction, but events in life can point you in another. What I've always said is, man is a bio-social animal, determined by logical factors and also by social factors, and we've got to take both into account in what we are doing. I can take somebody who is predisposed to react anti-socially and by a suitable system of punishments alter his behaviour.

You said of your son by your first marriage that you didn't think that he suffered unduly through growing up without a father. Isn't that another

Professor H. J. Eysenck

defence against something which might otherwise be difficult for you to face up to?

I don't see why I should need a defence. He has grown up very successfully, he is a very good scientist, he has a happy personal life, married with several children. I don't see any evidence of any kind of deprivation, or any kind of bad effect this may have had on him.

Although you hold Freud in very low esteem, and indeed very few people nowadays accord his work the status of scientific theory, we are left with a huge legacy from Freud, in the sense that it is still the natural idiom in which most people discuss their psyche and their relationships. Do you think this does any great harm? And will it eventually change?

Freud has always been particularly successful with what I might call the litterati, writers and the media, and not as successful with scientists who can actually test his theories. In previous centuries literary allusions were based on Greek and Roman mythology, and everybody knew this and understood it. Now Freudian terms have taken their place, and we talk of defence mechanisms, libido and the Oedipus complex. Writers joyfully make use of all this directly or indirectly, and they like it very much. Maybe it will change when we have some other mythology to take its place, but what is important to recognize is that Freud is mythology, not science.

Freudian theories have permeated not only our way of thinking but our institutions, such as schools and prisons. Psychotherapy has had an immense impact on Western culture. If it is so completely without basis, why do you think it has so far survived?

For the same reason as Marx. It is a theory which is superficially attractive because it is intelligible to most people without any scientific knowledge. It is presented in language which is quite attractive, and although it is propaganda rather than fact, most people don't realize that, and they become convinced. We're all interested and concerned with other people, our own motivation, their motivation and so on, and Freud enables us to talk about this in a way that appears to be scientific. It's easy to pick up because Freud is no more difficult to read than Proust or Stendhal or any other novelist. If you compare it with the theories of Pavlov, for example, which I think are scientifically correct, you actually have to learn a new vocabulary, you have to know about physiology, you have to read a thousand articles and a hundred books if you want ever even to come near to understanding what it is all about. Naturally the man in the street can't do that, so instead he reads Freud, or more usually a book describing Freud in elementary terms, and then he thinks he knows about psychology. Just as most of the communists I knew in Germany had never even read *Das Kapital*; they had read only a second-hand account of Marxist theory and thought they knew it all.

However much Freud is discredited it seems likely that people will continue to discuss their libido or their unconscious. Since these are theoretical notions whose manifestations are not really observable, does that lead you to discount them completely?

What I think about Freud essentially is that what is new in Freud isn't true, and what is true isn't new. There are a number of things in Freudian writings which obviously are perfectly correct, but these don't come to us via Freud. For instance we talk about Freudian symbolism, that some shapes remind you of the penis, and others of the vagina. But of course this was really quite explicit in Roman literature two thousand years ago. The trouble is, when people don't know that the ancient Romans already had the same ideas they say, oh how wonderful, this is obviously correct. Similarly with the unconscious. The unconscious has been postulated and talked about and discussed by at least two hundred philosophers and medical people over the last two thousand years. So I think many of what we call Freudian notions are not original at all. People call them Freudian, that's all.

Do you accord any importance to the Freudian account of psycho-sexual development – I mean, would you allow that our subsequent sexual development has its origins in the young girl's affection for her father, and the boy's for his mother?

I don't think for a minute there's anything in this. The Freudian notion of sexual development has been studied extensively by well-trained psychologists who have followed the actual behaviour and development of very young children, both their own and other people's, and although they started out with a belief that Freud was probably right, they discovered nothing of the kind that Freud describes in all this. Children simply don't develop in this fashion; it just isn't true.

Is homosexuality decided genetically in your view?

In many cases, as is demonstrated by studies of twins, there is a genetic component, but there can also be an environmental component. Sailors in Nelson's navy, for instance, had no outlet for their sexuality other than with other men, so for most of them it would have been an environmental factor. Similarly, if you are a prisoner for twenty years, then obviously the circumstances are such that you are almost forced into homosexuality regardless of your genetic predisposition.

Do you think sexual problems can be treated, and if so how?

There's no doubt they can be treated, but *how* is a different question. It depends on what kind of problem it is. Impotence, for example, has proved very resistant to most forms of treatment, and the rate of improvement is not very high. Premature ejaculation has proved to be fairly easy to treat and cure, so it does depend very much on the kind of disorder, the reasons for it, the type of person and so on. But certainly in due course I believe we'll even learn to deal with impotence.

How important do you rate sex in our lives?

Obviously sex is extremely important; it is linked with our personality and everything else, and it is certainly a very interesting topic of study. I have written several books on it because it is such a fascinating area. I was particularly interested in the genetic contributions which are very strong, and also the relationship to personality. For instance, we postulated and found that extroverted people have sex earlier than introverts, have sex more frequently, and with more different people, in more different positions and so on. This was predictable and found to be actually so. We also found that a happy sex life is almost impossible if you have a strong degree of neuroticism. Neurotic people seldom have happy sex lives and their marriages often break up. It is a very serious business.

You have sometimes said that you have no empathy with irrational fears. Why not?

Empathy means that you have some experience of the problem. Feelings of depression, anxiety and so on are just alien to me, so I find it difficult to empathize. I can objectively know that people do have anxieties and phobias, and I can account for them in terms of their developmental history and conditioning, and I can treat them with behaviour therapy, but I have no empathetic feeling for them. Just as I have no empathetic feeling for homosexuality or for many of the more esoteric sexual practices that people indulge in. I can't imagine getting any sexual satisfaction from being beaten, for instance, but many people do. Many people get sexual satisfaction from having a woman urinating over them; this is so absolutely alien to me I can't understand it, though I have to acknowledge that it exists.

Your most controversial book is probably Race, Intelligence and Education *published over twenty years ago. Do you still stand by everything you wrote then?*

The book has been much maligned, usually by people who have never read it. Essentially what happened was that Jensen in the United States wrote an article in which he suggested that the difference in IQ between blacks and whites in the States was about fifteen points and had been so ever since the First World War. He went to say that this might not be due to deprivation and environmental factors, but might in part be due to genetic factors. That produced a great controversy, and I thought that as the topic was an important one and most people seemed to take sides without knowing anything about it, it would be useful to present the facts in book form. I think I did this successfully, because the book has never been criticized by experts in the field as being factually incorrect. What people didn't like was even to acknowledge the possibility that genetic factors might be involved. If you look at recent publications you find that the majority of experts agree a hundred per cent with everything I said. It was not a maverick voicing an opinion, it was a distillation of what are agreed among experts to be the facts and an attempt to explicate these for the

133

general public. This I take to be a very important task, because there obviously is an enormous problem as we can see from the riots in Los Angeles now and those we have had here from time to time. We are not likely to solve such problems on the basis of ignorance.

You have said that your book and others you have written were designed to prevent the truth being concealed by the prejudices of the liberal intelligentsia. Are you wholly against what might nowadays be called 'politically correct' ideas?

I think the politically correct ideas have gone well beyond what is admissible in a democratic society. For instance I have always opposed any kind of racial or sexual discrimination, I think it is a crime against the Holy Ghost, but what you get now in the guise of political correctness is discrimination against majority groups in favour of minority groups. But discrimination is discrimination always, and affirmative action, so-called, is to my way of thinking a racist policy. Political correctness disregards facts and imposes certain attitudes on people which are essentially anti-democratic.

Where do you stand politically?

That's very difficult to say because I have always kept away from party politics. It seemed to me quite obvious that different parties were right on different issues. If you belong to one party you are forced to put all these things together in a kind of average, whereas I prefer to judge each issue on its own merits, so I have voted in due course for all three parties. I have voted for Attlee's Labour Party, I voted for Mrs Thatcher's Conservatives, and in between for the Liberals as they were then. I don't think any of the parties has the universal truth at its disposal. This is mixed up with a general feeling I have always had of favouring the underdog. In the sixties, for example, the trade unions were far too powerful and consequently I began to lean in the direction of control which meant going over to the Conservative Party. In the nineteenth century capitalism was much too powerful and the working classes were suppressed in ways that were completely unacceptable, so naturally I would then have been in favour of building up the trade unions. In other words, what you need in society is a balance between opposing forces, both of which have something positive to say for themselves. In a capitalist society you must have a certain degree of freedom for the capitalist to run his particular organization; on the other hand, he must not be so powerful that he can suppress the people who are working for him.

In 1973 you were physically attacked at the LSE and prevented from lecturing. Was that in some way do you think symbolic of the times? Do you think the same thing would happen today if you had just published your book on race and intelligence?

The answer to the first question is yes. In fact, as I was being attacked the first thought that came to my mind was that I had predicted the uprising of the fascist left and that was what I was experiencing. It was just the first occcasion where a speaker was attacked at a university for political reasons, and of course it spread and even now you have people being spattered with eggs and tomatoes, which is a tragedy for the cause of free speech. It's exactly what happened in Germany to Jewish or Marxist lecturers who dared to speak their minds and were attacked by Nazi yobs and suffered exactly the same kind of fate. It is very difficult to say if the same would happen now. I think people are getting a bit more realistic, so perhaps not.

What effect did the physical attack have on you at a personal level? Did it change the way you thought about anything?

No, it didn't really make any difference to my thinking. I took it as proof that I was right about the fascist left. It had much more serious consequences for my family. Even my children were attacked by their teachers at school on the basis of what they thought I might have said, which is of course completely unacceptable in a democratic society. In fact, we changed our name by deed poll for a while in order to protect the children, but then it blew over and we reverted to the old name.

In your research into the importance of personality in determining our susceptibility to various diseases, you say that personality can to a large extent be changed by therapy. Why can't delinquents be changed by therapy in a similar way?

Professor H. J. Eysenck

They can. The evidence is that you get a fifty-three per cent improvement in the recidivism rate by a suitable type of behaviour therapy. The reason why it isn't done in this country, God only knows. It's a kind of conservatism, I suppose; the Home Office is no hive of innovation.

You are the most widely read psychologist in the country, in Europe perhaps. Do you ever see that as an awesome responsibility?

Yes and no. My attitude has always been that a scientist owes society just one duty and that is to tell the truth as he sees it, that he shouldn't pretend for any reason whatsoever that he has nothing to say, or keep quiet on sensitive issues. When I wrote this book on race, I had a lot of letters from geneticists and social psychologists who said they agreed with everything but asked not to be quoted. I think that is the wrong kind of attitude. People accused Germans when Hitler came to power of lacking civil courage; well, that is also a lack of civil courage which I think is very serious. If there are problems, it is important that we should investigate them experimentally and that we should publish the results; the debate should then take place on the basis of these results. Affirmative action has not improved the position of the blacks; if anything it has made matters worse in the United States where there is a much larger proportion of them in what they call the underclass. As a policy it has failed, therefore the theory on which it was based is probably the wrong theory. But there was no serious discussion at all, it was simply imposed without empirical evidence. To take a very simple example, we have found recently that even in well-nourished white American children living in the countryside rather than in the inner cities, about half of them have a deficit of micro nutrients, vitamins and minerals. We found that we could increase their IQ by eleven points by giving them vitamin and mineral supplements. Can you imagine how much you might improve the IQ of inner-city children who are really deprived? But nobody pays any attention to this – they are so homed in on other notions of environmental influences. We could easily raise the IQ level of most inner-city children by an enormous amount, thereby making them more successful scholastically, in their life experience, careers, and so on. But we don't do it, we don't even discuss it, we prefer to ignore the facts.

You have always claimed that you are seeking the truth, however unpalatable, but in that pursuit you have been accused of indifference to people's feelings and sensibilities. Is that something that worries you at all?

It doesn't, because I don't believe it's true. You might also say that Galileo and Darwin were indifferent to the sensibilities of religious people. If the truth is unpalatable, that's too bad, but you can't neglect it for that reason. You have to know what the facts are; you can't solve problems on the basis of imagination.

Some people think that you enjoy conflict, that you deliberately invite controversy. Is there any truth in that?

Nobody would seek the kind of confrontation I had at the London School of Economics and on other occasions. Obviously it would be much nicer if everybody accepted my ideas immediately, gave me the Order of Merit and made me Lord Eysenck of Brixton. In the scientific field it's true that I quite enjoy criticism, because you learn a lot from critics who pick out the weak points in your position. You can then either change your position, or strengthen it. That is the life blood of science. But the pointless, political sort of controversy – no I hate it, and I'd rather be without it.

You once said, 'Perhaps my constant rebellion and my desire for recognition have something to do with the past, but I do not wish to explore it further. There is no sound method for doing so.' Are you at all afraid of what you might find if you were 'to explore further'?

It isn't that, it's really something quite complicated. If a psychologist writes an autobiography, he is expected to be an expert on motivation, and therefore he is expected to know about his own. But the study of motivation is a disaster area as far as psychology is concerned because we simply have no methods for investigating it. How would I find out why I did a certain thing? There is no way scientifically to find it out. Of course I could give a sort of intuitive answer, but it would be a pretence; it would simply reveal what kind of person I am, whether I preferred to pretend always to have good motivations for what I do, or whether I'm honest enough to admit bad interpretations, or a mixture of the two. But it wouldn't reveal the real truth about why I did something. It's not that I'm

137

afraid of finding out, it's that I don't know any way of finding out. That is the simple and honest truth.

You have said that you have a very thick skin, and that your wife and family have suffered much more than you from criticism and hostility. Is susceptibility to that also genetically determined, do you think?

I'm almost certain of it. Right from the beginning, when I was a schoolboy, criticism just flowed off my back. When I thought Hitler was wrong, I said so, and whatever anybody else said simply didn't matter to me. I couldn't pretend otherwise simply because other people disapproved of me. Similarly, when I first brought out my article in which I showed that there was no evidence that Freudian psychotherapy was any good, there was a lot of criticism, but I just had to grin and bear it. Nowadays it is widely recognized as being correct.

In your book on marriage, you say that sixty-four per cent of factors which make for marital happiness can be measured. Even if that is so, it still leaves thirty-six per cent. Do you really believe that marriage is a proper area for scientific enquiry?

Why not? Every human activity can be looked at scientifically, and marriage is no exception. We find for instance that in happy marriages, there is a good deal of agreement on things like political attitudes, social attitudes, and when people marry others of roughly the same intelligence, that makes for a good prognosis. These are facts. It may not help us in choosing a good marriage partner, but the facts are interesting to know, and to my mind at least they may be important.

Do you think ultimately science will be able to prove everything, or that we will be able to understand everything through scientific research?

It's a good question, but one that doesn't have an answer. I'm not a prophet. I would like to think the answer is yes, but I'm very doubtful. There is an obvious limit to what science will find out in physics; maybe it did all start with the Big Bang, but how can we ever know what happened before the Big Bang? I don't think we'll ever know all the answers, but we know a lot of the answers, and that's the important thing.

Life, like marriage, can never be an exact science. By claiming that if things cannot be tested and measured they do not really exist, aren't you approaching life as it were a purely scientific enquiry?

I'm not saying they don't exist. What I believe is that everything that exists, exists in some quantity and can therefore be measured. There are a lot of things we can't measure at the moment, but that doesn't mean we will never be able to measure them. Certainly at the moment there's a great deal of life that we can't say anything sensible about, but it is important for society to study those areas where it can.

Would you allow that science, philosophy and religion are different paths towards the truth, and that they all have their contribution to make?

No, I wouldn't say so. If you talk about truth you can only deal with science, in the sense that truth must be recognizable. 'I know that my Redeemer liveth' – this may be a valid statement, but I cannot accept it as truth because there is no way of proving it. If somebody else says there is no God, no Redeemer, he may also be right. How can I ever tell which of them is correct in his assumptions? How can I discern who is speaking the truth? The only truth that is acceptable is one that is transmitted by science because it depends on fact and proof. I'm not saying that religion isn't important, that art isn't important . . . that's quite a different matter . . . but truth is entirely related to science.

But would you accept that philosophy and religion all have a contribution to make?

I wouldn't dream of denying it. Science is only one part of life and other aspects like religion and art may be more valuable than science for many people; but they are not a search for truth in this sense. We have to remember there are great individual differences between people. For me truth and facts are absolutely vital. I would always prefer to know the truth, however painful.

Professor H. J. Eysenck

What do you think is the greatest harm that can be done by your profession?

I don't think my profession as such can do any harm. Scientific knowledge of atomic fission and fusion can be made to create energy or create bombs: it's up to the politicians. The scientist does not do harm because he has no power whatsoever; the harm is done by people misusing science, which of course is always possible.

What would you consider your greatest achievement?

Probably that I helped to steer people away from a purely environ-mentalistic notion to recognition that man is a bio-social animal, that biology does play a very important part, that heredity is crucial. When I started in psychology this was fairly universally rejected; now it is recognized and absolutely established.

If you were to live your life again, would you do anything differently?

The trouble with a question like that is that you can't normally do what you want to do in life; what you do is determined by circumstances. I wanted to be a physicist or astronomer, but the facts of life made it impossible for me, and I was sidetracked into psychology. If I had had a choice I would have preferred to be in the hard sciences. In psychology I wanted to work in the field of learning and conditioning, but the only job I could get was in the clinical field, so I was sidetracked again. Of course, the competition in physics and astronomy is much greater than in psychology; you are dealing with a grade of intelligence that is very much higher, whereas in psychology I found it quite easy to get to the top. In the hard sciences I might easily have been second rate.

REUBEN FALBER

Reuben Falber was born of Polish parents in London in 1914. His childhood was marked by poverty and he left school at the age of fourteen. The rise of fascism, Hitler, Mosley and the growing threat of war led to a serious and lasting interest in politics, specifically in communism which he saw as offering an alternative in a society 'which had no solution to poverty and war'. He joined the Communist Party shortly after the outbreak of the Spanish Civil War in 1936, and played an active role in a variety of ways, including writing articles for the *Daily Worker*, *Morning Star* and *Marxism Today*. In 1968 he rose to the position of assistant general secretary and, in recent revelations, admitted responsibility for 'laundering' large sums of money from the Communist Party of the Soviet Union.

Mr Falber, your wife has accompanied you to this interview. Do you involve her in all areas of public life?

My wife involves herself in political life and activity of her own volition. If she wants to take part in any form of political activity she does so. It's entirely her decision.

Would you say she is complementary to you in public life?

Not complementary, no. Although we broadly agree with each other in our political opinions and in what kind of activities we should undertake, we are independent people who according to our inclinations and abilities make our contribution to the causes to which we have devoted our lives.

May I ask the most brutally frank question before we proceed further? Do you not feel that your life has been wasted? The idol you served turned out to have feet made of something rather worse than clay.

No, I don't think my life has been wasted. Subjectively, I've enjoyed it. If I had my life all over again I would like to do the same, to devote my life to something which I believed was good for humanity of which I'm part. Whatever may be the present circumstances, I believe that people like me over the last fifty or sixty years have helped create a body of opinion in this country and internationally which is bound at some stage to bear fruit. We have held up not only the banner of socialism, but we have never submitted to Thatcherism. From the moment Thatcher was elected it was the communists in Britain who argued that Thatcherism was a phenomenon which differed in many important respects from traditional conservatism, and that it was necessary for the left to understand this, and to adjust their policies, their propaganda and argument accordingly. I therefore think that the change which has taken place in public opinion in this country in the last few years is in part attributable to the work which people like us have done.

How do you think Mrs Thatcher deviated from traditional conservatism?

She was able to strike a popular chord. She was able to associate herself with people who wanted to improve their life at a time when there was a serious economic recession, not as bad as the present one, but nevertheless a serious economic situation in Britain which was having its impact on people's living standards. It was affecting the delivery of the social services, the provisions of the welfare state, and Mrs Thatcher was able to use to advantage the dissatisfaction people felt. Her success resulted from her ability to recognize the changes in the outlook of the populace and the aspirations of a new and emerging generation of younger people.

Do you think that communism has failed? I know there will be people who say it has never been tried, but the Soviet Union had more than two generations to try it and they could not get it to work.

You ought to look at the works of one of the people whom you interviewed in *Singular Encounters*, John Kenneth Galbraith, who in an article in the *Observer* a year or two ago made the point very tellingly that in the earlier years of the Soviet Union it did work. They transformed a very backward country into a highly industrialized one; about ninety per cent of the people had been illiterate and under communism they became literate and highly educated. The Soviet Union had, and probably still has, more qualified people than any other country. For whatever good it did the people, they won the race to get into space. And therefore it did succeed to a certain extent. Where it failed was in its ability to turn these things into what the people wanted, in the shops and on the table. The bureaucracy which it had to create in order to establish a developed modern industrial state was unable to deal with personal needs. In other words, it was a system which worked in terms of doing big things, but for ordinary people life is not full of big things.

What do you think was the real cause of the failure? Was it intractable human nature – greed and self-concern?

I don't think you can attribute it entirely to that. There was an attitude created among the population that if you wanted to improve life it had to be by collective effort; the kind of attitude which I think is developed to some extent in this country, where people are willing to pay higher taxes in order to get a better health service, a better education, clean up the environment, and so on. That feeling was very strong in the Soviet Union and when I read the press reports from Moscow over the past few weeks I have a feeling that Yeltsin is going to run up against that in his efforts to privatize everything.

In theory the working classes in different European nations were to rise up in a sort of rolling wave of revolution. Why did it never happen?

The working class didn't want it. Obviously. At the end of the First World War, with the exception of a few idealists or adventurers, the over-whelming majority of the working people did not regard revolution, in the sense of an armed struggle, as a way forward, and Frederick Engels, as far back as 1891 or '92, in an introduction to a new edition of one of Marx's works, argued very strongly that the armed insurrections he and Marx had written about in the mid nineteenth century were no longer on, and for two reasons. Firstly, because in Europe working people were beginning to see the use of the ballot box and the right to organize as the way forward. Secondly, Engels pointed out that the revolutions of 1848 had taken place in cities built very different from the cities which existed in 1890. He spoke of Hausmann, who had re-built Paris, Budapest and the other European cities with broad avenues along which big guns could be deployed, and he argued that after 1848 revolution had not a cat's chance in hell. The concept of revolution therefore died in the nineteenth century. It did revive at the end of the First World War when you had unique circumstances – Russian and other European societies were collapsing – but apart from that brief period, armed insurrection has never been on.

Do you think it is still an option for the future?

No.

What is so puzzling is why the ideal should have failed. The first generation of revolutionaries were really, even heroically, self-sacrificing and committed. How did it all go wrong after that?

If I had the answer to that question I'd be one of the heroes of the left. It's a question on which the left has been arguing for many years, and there is no simple answer to it. It's easy to say it went wrong because of what Stalin did. But you then have to ask, was it inevitable that Stalin should have acted in the way that he did? I don't think it was. One of the answers is of course that the first successful working-class revolution took place in the most backward country in Europe, the working class being a small, even a minute, percentage of a population overwhelmingly peasant, illiterate, unorganized in every respect, as you can gather if you read any of the classic Russian novels. It was Lloyd George who said round about 1920 that capitalists were lucky that the revolution had taken place in Russia and not in Germany. The Germans would have made a much better job of it, and I think there is something in that. Lenin anticipated that revolution in the West would come to the aid of the Russian revolutionaries; he never really thought that the Russians could hang on to what they had gained in the revolution unless there were revolutions in the West to back them up. Well, these revolutions either didn't take place or when, as in Germany and Hungary, they did take place, they failed.

When did you begin to suspect that all was not well? For example, did you believe the reports about Khatyn Wood where the Soviets slaughtered 5,000 Poles?

No. I didn't believe the reports.

You still don't believe them?

Probably I have to believe, but you must remember at the time when the reports were first published we were at war. The Soviets had their backs to the wall; they were the ones who were fighting Hitler, more than we were, and we saw them in a certain light because of what they were and what they were doing. We regarded these reports as coming from enemy sources hostile to the Soviet Union. The objective was to undermine sympathy in this country for the Soviet Union and particularly to undermine the military cooperation between Britain and the Soviet Union in the opening of the Second Front. That was how we looked on things at that particular time, and in the light of subsequent events, I think we were wrong. I ought, with other communists, to have believed the report. A lot of things I didn't believe at the time I later found – I have to say, unfortunately – to be true.

Given the theory of communism and the brotherhood of man why was anti-Semitism so common? After all, the usual explanation offered for anti-Semitism is that Christians regard Jews as collectively responsible for the death of Christ, but the Soviet Union was atheistic?

I think that anti-Semitism, like any form of racial prejudice, is very deep seated, and it can't be legislated away. Anti-Semitism, in countries like Russia, is part of religion and one of the big mistakes the communists made in the Soviet Union and in other countries was in believing that by education itself they could eliminate religious belief. We also failed to understand this.

We . . . you mean, the British Communist Party?

I mean people like me also failed to understand the strength of the hold that religion has on people. Also you can ban religious education in the school, but nevertheless, religion, taught in the home, is carried on from generation to generation, and in Russia, Poland, Hungary and Rumania, anti-Semitism is very deep seated. It's existed for two, three hundred years or more, and you can't eliminate it by legislation or simply by improving education. For years the Soviet authorities fought against it, maybe with some measure of success, I don't really know . . . but when popular support became a little more difficult for the Soviet leadership, some of them at any rate succumbed to the temptation of not resisting anti-Semitism, of letting it go on; that's a slippery road.

Can one be a dedicated communist, and still be a believer in God at the same time?

I don't see why not. Communism is a concept of the kind of society that we want to live in. There are many people who avow that Jesus Christ was a communist; there have certainly been many Christians who were communists. A classic example of course was the Dean of Canterbury in this country. I also remember people coming back from Italy in the years immediately after the war saying they had been to villages where the leader of the local Communist Party was the local priest who would gather the semi-literate population together and read to them out of the party paper. So I don't think there is any conflict between being a Christian – or a Moslem or a Jew for that matter – and being a communist.

Reuben Falber

Would you consider yourself anti-religious?

No, I think being anti-religious is rather childish. When I was young, and first became converted to communist ideas, atheism went with it, but I soon realized it was rather foolish and footling and irrelevant to the main question.

Are you a believer now?

No.

As you get older, doesn't it worry you not to believe in anything, in an afterlife?

No.

You believe that your life will end when it ends on this earth?

I do.

And that's the end of the story?

Yes.

Did it ever occur to the British Communist Party that the huge, sprawling, and virtually ungovernable Soviet Union might not be the appropriate model for a nation with a quite different history and tradition?

Oh yes, it occurred to us. I can't speak for the communists of the 1920s and the early 1930s, but certainly from the time I joined the Communist Party in 1936 the talk of the kind of society we wanted to establish was something very different from the Soviet model. I recall a book called *Britain without Capitalists*, and the outline there of the way in which the industries would be run didn't correspond with the way things were being done in the Soviet Union, for the simple reason that the Soviets had started with virtually nothing in the way of industry, and we were starting with a highly developed technological society. Also, the social conditions were different. In 1951 we produced a programme, *The British Road to Socialism*, which quite clearly stated that it was possible to establish a socialist society in Britain by the democratic process of securing a parliamentary majority. It would be based on socialist principles and would begin to introduce legislation which would socialize society, and that was entirely different from anything that existed in the Soviet Union or Eastern Europe or China.

Just how ignorant were British communists of what was really happening in the Soviet Union? Germans often explain that they did not know about the Nazi death camps, but it is quite hard to believe. In the same way there is always the suspicion that the communists were quite content to take Lenin's view that you can't make an omelette without breaking eggs.

German people lived in the country where these things were taking place. There were German people – I don't know how many – employed in or around the concentration camps and certainly hundreds of thousands living in the neighbourhoods of the camps. The British communists did not visit or live in the *gulag*. I've been to the Soviet Union half a dozen times; I've been to all the other countries in Eastern Europe which were under Marxist leadership, and what I saw was what they showed me. I never had the opportunity of seeing anything else. Understandably they didn't show me the bad sides of society.

But can you honestly say that you didn't have any suspicion of what was going on, even if you didn't see it.

We didn't believe it was going on to that extent. I'll tell you a little story which was told by a man who had been the *Daily Worker* correspondent in Moscow in the period just after Stalin died. There was a British communist who had gone to work in the Soviet Union in some technical capacity, and he had been jailed and sent to the camp. After Stalin died he was released and all the British communists who were working in Moscow, as journalists, translators, and so on, organized a party for him; and all of them, including the communist who had been jailed, regarded his jailing as just a mistake, that somehow there had been a miscarriage of justice. And the man who was explaining this, a man called Dennis Ogden, an academic, an extremely intelligent and able man, told us that what they didn't realize was that the injustices, the jailings, the camps, the executions, weren't just a collection of mistakes, but had become almost a system of government.

Do you believe the end justifies the means?

The way the question would have been posed in my younger days would have been: Do you believe that the killing of a few hundred people in Russia in November 1917 was justified by the victory of the revolution, and I would have said yes. But if you ask me, do I believe that all we now know can be justified, the answer is categorically no, because that is completely in conflict with what we wanted. The means became an end.

What was the British Communist Party's attitude towards the show trials of the 1930s? They could not have been ignorant of just how many of those who had actually led the revolution were now disgraced and dead. Did no one wonder why or enquire?

I was not then in the leadership of the British Communist Party, but I, along with other members of the Communist Party, accepted the Soviets' version of events, that they were spies and traitors. In that, of course, we were terribly wrong.

Do you ever think in retrospect that you were really naïve?

We were naïve in some respects. You see, we saw the Soviet Union as the first country where the revolution succeeded. It was a country where a workers' state was established, where the capitalists were no longer in power, and it was ours. I think we were right to look at it in that way, but that of course clouded our judgement. Because we had this attitude, everything the Soviet Union did was right, and every criticism that was made of the Soviet Union was regarded as coming from people who had no love for the country, who wanted to undermine support for it in Britain. And therefore we rejected what was true; we wouldn't believe it.

Do you think now with hindsight that various British governments were right to distrust and resist the Soviet Union? You presumably would not have wanted imposed on us what the Communist Party imposed on the Russian people.

The Soviet Union could never have imposed anything on Britain. Our society is the outcome of the relationship between political groupings, opinions, and so on. I don't think that British governments in resisting the Soviet Union were resisting an attempt to impose upon Britain the society which existed in the Soviet Union. It was the spread of left-wing ideas of any description that they wanted to prevent. You must remember that Nye Bevan was branded as if he were a communist; he was hated by the capitalist class, by the right-wing press in this country, and by the Tory Party, as much as they hated Willie Gallagher who was a communist MP.

When at the end of the war the government sent back thousands of Cossacks who were promptly murdered by the Soviet authorities, did the Communist Party of Great Britain know about it?

No.

And when you did know?

Well, a lot of nasty things happened at the end of the war, and this was one of them. When we began to know what was happening, we expressed our opinions. After the Khrushchev speech at the 20th Congress in 1956, when it was quite clear what had been happening, we began to speak out; initially in private discussions with leading people in the Soviet Communist Party, and then later in public.

When you look back would you have done things differently?

Of course. You must understand the context in which these events took place. If there hadn't been a cold war after 1945, if Churchill hadn't made his famous Fulton speech, then international relations would have been very different. We would not have felt the same urgency about defending the Soviet Union as a part of the fight to prevent a third world war. In a different context we would have been able to take a very different attitude towards international relations and also towards events in the Soviet Union. We would not have seen reports of Cossacks being sent back as part and parcel of a campaign of hostility to the Soviet Union; we would have been more objective.

Where do you feel that the real allegiance of communists lay? I mean, in practice. There was (and I suppose still is) the suspicion that communists are not to be trusted because they may betray their fellow citizens in the interests of some larger international ideal.

I think the allegiance of British communists is to the British people. I've always thought that. I don't think there is a larger international ideal which could lead to the betrayal of Britain.

Some of course did just that: Philby, Burgess, Maclean, Blunt. They must have been responsible for the deaths of many of our agents. Did you feel that anyone who resisted the Soviet Union deserved what they got?

Spying is a dirty business. I also think it's a rather useless business. From the little I've read about what spies do, it seems to me that they spend their time collecting information which is either freely available or else useless once they've got it. It's an activity which I think no communist in this country should ever have had anything to do with. Maclean and Philby were never members of the British Communist Party. The one person involved in espionage who was a prominent member of the Communist Party was the late David Springhall and he was expelled from the Communist Party because he had broken what was really a cardinal principle.

Would you in the fervour of youth ever have contemplated spying for the Soviet Union?

It's a very hypothetical question. I don't think anybody would have approached me – I could never have been any use to them – therefore it's very easy for me to say that I wouldn't have done it. My way of working for solidarity with the Soviet Union was to try to persuade people that the kind of society which existed there represented the future. That was the way I looked at things in my youth; the idea of spying never entered my head.

Do you think it is ever possible to coerce people into doing what is good for them? It seems it is only really possible to coerce people into doing things that are good for someone else . . . all oligarchies do that.

I don't think people can or should be coerced into doing anything. People have to be convinced that they need to do certain things to their own advantage. It's only on the basis of conviction and people understanding the path that has to be taken in order to improve their lives that we'll ever get any change.

Did you ever think that 'truth is what serves the party'?

No. What I thought was that the party represented truth.

You still believe that?

Well, there isn't a party now. I think that the kind of ideals which I still hold are the best ideals. Things are true or not true – that's obvious in real life, but in the language we're using truth is a bit of an abstraction, and saying that truth is what served the party, which I now know is wrong, is as good as saying that it's all right to lie, which I've always believed was wrong. I've said things which were untrue; I argued that the people who were executed were traitors, but I believed it at the time. I never deliberately said anything which was untrue because I thought it would help to convince people.

Did you ever wrestle with your ideals or doubt that you were on the right path?

Oh yes, notably in 1956, after the publication of Khrushchev's secret speech to the 20th Congress. Any communist who didn't wrestle in his mind was a peculiar person. After all we had for years and years been saying that all these things that the capitalist press had published about the Soviet Union were a pack of lies: the labour camps didn't exist, people were guilty, they were spies, enemies and wreckers. And then Khrushchev came along and said, not so. The whole basis of our belief was called into question. The conclusion we arrived at after a great deal of heart searching was that whatever had happened, capitalism was still an evil, and there should be a fight to end the capitalist system and establish a socialist society. We did not see the Labour Party as the force to do this, because its leadership accepted capitalism, and simply wanted to make some cosmetic improvements. A communist party was therefore necessary and our ideals were necessary.

Communist parties all over the old Soviet Union and Eastern Europe have transformed themselves into various sorts of nationalist and socialist groups, but can leopards really change their spots?

We'll have to wait and see. Judging from some reports of events in Eastern Europe where it seems that people have overnight become transformed from communists to enthusiastic privatizationists, one might easily say they have changed their spots. The bad spots are certainly there.

How do you think the West can be most helpful at present in trying to get some sort of stability into the Commonwealth of Independent States?

I honestly can't answer that question. It's easy to say we should give aid and trade, but they have to solve the problem themselves. They have to find a way of organizing their society to accord with the history and traditions of their country, with the resources available to them, and I think that they are best left alone.

It begins to look as if the problem of ethnic minorities is quite intractable – as much in the West as in the East, I'm thinking of the Slovenes and the Serbs, and the Turks and the Kurds. Do you think the communist ideal of internationalism might be transformed into some sort of federalist ideal to combat that?

Federalism is not in conflict with internationalism, but whether federalism will work in the CIS remains to be seen. Federalism in Yugoslavia worked while Tito was alive; he was able to win wide respect and impose his authority. But whether it can now work where there are such longstanding historical antagonisms as in Yugoslavia, or in parts of the Soviet Union, especially the Asian parts, is another matter.

Are you hopeful?

Hopeful but sceptical. It can only work if a basis of common interests is secured. It ought to be possible, but it is very difficult to achieve, as Yugoslavia shows. Even in Tito's time the more advanced parts of Yugoslavia, Slovenia and Croatia had to give up more than they wanted to in order to help the more backward parts of Yugoslavia – Montenegro, Macedonia, Serbia – and this created dissatisfaction and conflict which broke down the federal idea. It's very difficult to create genuine federation between societies at very different levels. If you take the concept of a federal Britain, that is a Britain with a Scottish parliament, an English parliament, a Welsh parliament and so on, that would bring problems, but the problems would be nothing compared with what we've seen in Europe. That is because the economic, social and cultural levels and differences in Britain, though important, are not all that great, whereas in Eastern Europe and the old Soviet Union they are very extensive.

China is still a bastion of communism, but do you think it will be able to prosper in the long run without transforming itself into a capitalist economy? So far it does not seem to have been possible anywhere else.

I think they're trying to convert their economy, or rather to develop the private side of their economy, and have been trying to do this over a number of years, but again they are meeting with a lot of resistance from Chinese people. Anyone who forecasts what's going to happen in China is really going out on a limb.

It is sometimes argued that 'market economies' are natural in the sense that taking what you have to sell to market and asking who wants to buy it is what always has happened. Do you think that's true?

There always has to be a market economy because it's only through the market that you can discover what people want and whether people are satisfied with what they're being offered. But there is a difference between having an economy which provides for that, and a market economy in the Thatcherite sense. The market economy has to be regulated and there are a number of services and goods which should not be supplied through the free market . . . the telephone, energy, postal services, transport, health service, all these things should be basically collective services.

I can understand this applying to health care, but when you talk about transport, telecommunications, energy, you would surely be using public funds to subsidize something which is basically inefficient.

Your statement is basically incorrect, based on a completely false assumption. I don't believe that telephones, gas, electricity or water are better for being privatized. Look at the pollution in the water supply. What's being done about it by the privatized companies? Virtually nothing at all, because if they spend any money it's at the expense of profits. I would extend my argument by saying that the great problem faced, not only in this country but on a universal scale, is that of the pollution of the environment in the interests of profit. I know it was polluted in the Soviet Union and other East European countries in the interests of the profit of particular enterprises; but we also know that in this country industry pays very little heed to the long-term effects. We will never be able to solve the environmental problem while the economies of the advanced world are based on private enterprise with private profit and not the common good as the objective. If ever Marxist ideas were needed, it's today. The three great problems we face are the environment, the north-south divide, and the appalling poverty in the Third World which is worsened if not caused by capitalism. The great social problems in our own country, the homelessness, the appalling mess in our cities, the growth of crime, all of these things are a consequence of the drive for profit.

I remember Khrushchev saying that when communism had triumphed they would have to preserve Switzerland because a free market would be the only way of knowing what anything was really worth. How else would one decide?

I don't remember Khrushchev saying that. I'll take your word for it. When it comes to consumer goods, a market is the way in which things are measured against each other. You decide whether you want to spend your money on buying a new cassette recorder or going out for dinner. But I don't really see that has any relevance to the way in which society is organized. There's no free market in electricity, in gas, in water – it's all nonsense. One of the consequences of deregulation of the buses is that free bus passes for pensioners are going to be a thing of the past. Bus passes are vital to pensioners – my wife and I know this and would be virtually housebound without them.

Is corruption not one of the great problems of any all-embracing totalitarian regime? If there's only one source for everything, even necessities, don't those who control the source become intolerably powerful?

Corruption is a problem of every regime. In this country we don't have control of sources, and yet we have extraordinary corruption. Look at the corruption in our police force and in local government. I don't speak of corruption in central government only because it doesn't come out so much, but I would be surprised if it doesn't exist to a very considerable extent. I don't think that the corruption in East European countries and in the Soviet Union was greater than in this country; it just took different forms.

If reports are true, then before the latest putsch *in Russia, billions of Communist Party funds were smuggled to Switzerland. That couldn't happen here surely?*

Well, Maxwell was able to pinch three hundred million pounds' worth out of the *Daily Mirror* pension funds.

Yes, but he was one individual.

But it happened. If you are talking about corruption, look at the extent of it at the BCCI, Maxwell enterprises, the Guinness scandal.

I suspect that one of the things non-communists now dislike so much about communism is its thirst for ideological correctness, because it seems to mean that no matter what a situation is in reality it must be made to appear appropriate, or it has been in the past. Did you never feel that having to pretend was counterproductive – literally millions of people starved but it was pretended that they did not.

Before 1917 people did starve in Russia, and after the Revolution, in the circumstances of war, there was a famine and millions starved. It was very brutal, but then they did succeed in establishing a society in which people are reasonably fed. I am very cautious in what I say about conditions in the Soviet Union, because I know I've always been shown what people wanted me to see. But I would say that over recent years people had enough food; it was difficult to get at times, and the quality was often poor. It's much more difficult now to get food in what used to be the Soviet Union – you've only got to read the press reports to see the extent to which people are suffering.

In your letter to me you were rather dismissive about the lives of some of the contributors to Singular Encounters. *Don't you feel that they might see the cause which you have pursued as an even less attractive idea?*

Lord White would have done, wouldn't he? The man who praised Hitler, as reported on the front page of the *Guardian* recently. He is all that I think is hateful in capitalist society, a man who is ruthless, concerned with nothing but his own wealth, his own power, and contemptuous – not just of people who disagree with him but contemptuous of working people, those who have made his millions.

You suggested that some of the interviewees had led rather useless lives. What constitutes a rather useless life in your view?

A life that's devoted to hedonism, to self-indulgence, having no concern for society as a whole, with a readiness to enjoy the fruits of life and one's own well-being at the expense of other people. A kind of selfishness I think it is, which stands out in one or two of the people you interviewed; White is a particular example. There are other people with whom I disagree, such as Lord Alexander who is a Thatcherite, but I wouldn't say he's led a useless life. He's a highly intelligent man who has devoted his career to the law and now to banking. But he's in a different category from somebody like White.

Left-wing progaganda has always made a great deal of the iniquity of imperialism, and rightly so, but what was Eastern Europe until recently if not part of a Soviet empire?

Relations between the Soviet Union and the Eastern European countries were very different from those between Britain and its colonies (which isn't to say that I think those relations were right). The relations between Britain and its colonies were based upon their conquest by armed force – and this applied not only to Britain but to France, Belgium and Spain. The relations between the Soviet Union and the East European countries emerged from a war in which the Soviet Union liberated those countries from fascism. It should then of course have left and let them get on with their own business, running their own countries. The reason why they didn't do that was their fear that these countries would be the base for a future attack on the Soviet Union. It was the cold war which was responsible for this; indeed many of the questions you pose really arise from the consequences of the cold war.

Do you have any sympathy at all with the Zionists?

None. It's never attracted me. I am Jewish but I have never felt any emotional attraction to Israel. This is my country. I was born here, I was educated here, I want to go on living here.

How do you view the problems in what used to be Palestine?

The Palestinians have the right to a state of their own, and the two-state proposition, that the Palestinians stay on the West Bank and Gaza, is realistically the only thing that can be argued for in the present circumstances. If that objective were realized, there would be a problem of how to deal with the Jewish communities which have been established on the West Bank. That has to be faced by both sides essentially, but it should not be posed as an argument against justice for the Palestinians.

You say apropos of the payments which were made by the CPSU to the Communist Party in Britain, that you have 'no regrets'. Do you ever have any doubts about the morality of receiving those payments?

No. You see, we regarded ourselves as part of a world communist movement in which we helped each other. Parties like the Soviet party had resources which were not available to others, so they helped other communist parties and we were in the position of being the beneficiaries. We were helped by the Soviet Union just as we did things to help people in Spain, struggling against Franco. When we were hard up ourselves, desperate for money, we went round collecting money, food, all sorts of things, to send to Spain to help the Spanish people. This was part of our international solidarity.

Were you accountable for this money? Did you have to fulfil certain conditions in order to receive payments?

No. For example, in 1978 I was in Moscow on business for the Communist Party, and the head of the international department of the Communist Party, Boris Ponamarev, sent a message saying he wanted a discussion with me. I went to the headquarters of the Communist Party, and Ponamarev launched an attack on the *Morning Star*. He was unhappy about some articles which were critical of a number of things in the Soviet Union . . . I can't recall the particular incidents but they were probably the arrest and imprisonment of dissidents. Ponamarev blew his top about this. I told him that we didn't censor the paper, that the editor of the paper wrote what he thought, and it so happened that what had been written did correspond with the views of the British Communist Party. That would have been about February 1978, and shortly after that I received a payment. There was therefore no connection between payment or non-payment and what we said. They didn't like what we said, but they didn't think that they could buy us.

What did you use this money for?

All sorts of things. The amount we received was rather small, and a lot of it was used to help some people who had worked for us as full-time officials in the early days of the Communist Party and had very little in the way of pension rights, for example. We also used it to maintain our headquarters, finance some of our propaganda materials . . . the sort of day-to-day activities of the party. The largest sum of money I ever received was £100,000, a lot of which was used for the maintenance of the *Morning Star*, the *Daily Worker* as it was originally. I never kept a count of the total received over the years, but I doubt if it was more than a million pounds, and don't forget, we're talking of twenty-odd years. A million pounds is not a large sum of money when you think of the money that's being used for propaganda today.

You were, you said, much disturbed by the way people deserted the party in droves after the invasion of Hungary and revelations about the persecution of Jews. Were you not just as disturbed about the invasion and persecution? How was it you were able to keep the faith?

Well, this was the time when we did our intellectual wrestling.

If I may take this matter a little further? After the invasion of Czechoslovakia in 1968 you said that you asked for the Russian subsidies to be reduced. This was because the invasion of Czechoslovakia was so unpopular here and partly membership fell off. One could understand why you might have felt you had to refuse any further money, but just reducing the amounts seems an odd response. Why did you not refuse it altogether?

We were receiving what was quite a substantial sum of money. To go from that to nothing at all would have created a financial crisis; therefore we thought we'd take things in stages.

You say that what you received was 'peanuts' compared to what the Tories had from John Latsis, whom you describe as 'a friend of the Greek Colonels'. I would have thought you would want to dissociate yourself from this sort of activity altogether rather than to fall back on the idea: 'Well they did it, so why shouldn't we?'

Well, why not? I see nothing particularly wrong in them helping each other; no more wrong for them to help each other than for us to help each other. But in the unlikely event of somebody like Maxwell ever coming along and offering us a large sum of money, we would have turned it down.

Would you really?

Yes, because we would not have regarded somebody like that as being a friend of ours, and not just because of what we know now. In my book, Maxwell's always been a villain. You know what the Board of Trade wrote about him in the Pergamon report.

The party was involved in many of the industrial disputes of the 1960s and 1970s. What was the object, was it just disruption? You surely could not have hoped to foment a revolution?

We were involved in these disputes because one of the jobs of the Communist Party was to help the working class defend its interests. We therefore backed the miners in their struggle against the Heath government; we backed the shipyard workers in the Upper Clyde in the defence of their jobs; we backed the motor workers, defending their jobs and conditions against the predecessors of British Leyland and Rover. That's been the major part of the work of the Communist Party throughout its existence – the defence of the conditions of the working class.

Recent access to secret-police files in East Germany (according to a report in the Independent *of 10 February) has revealed determined attempts to destroy marriages, to undermine careers, and to turn children against their parents. How can that sort of activity promote socialism?*

It doesn't. I think that society should provide the wherewithal for people to enjoy life and to live their lives as they want to, to live peacefully, to get married if they want to, to enter into other gender relationships if they want to – people should have all these rights, and none of that is in conflict with our idea of society.

What do you think happens next? Is there a way forward for the party?

Politics are dominated by the two big parties with the liberals hanging on, and all of them maintaining basically the present form of society. I think that the people who want something different have got to find a way of organizing themselves and creating a programme and policy which has credibility as the genuine alternative way of running our affairs.

When you look back on your life, do you have any regrets at all?

No. If I had my life again, I would like to do what I've done.

Did you ever feel that you have hurt anybody in trying to achieve your aims?

I'm sure I have unwittingly hurt people. And if I have hurt people, I would not argue that it was necessary, or that it furthered my cause.

LADY DIANA MOSLEY

Born in 1910, Diana Mosley was one of the celebrated Mitford girls, daughter of the eccentric Lord Redesdale who was to feature prominently in Nancy Mitford's novels. At the age of eighteen Diana married Bryan Guinness, later Lord Moyne, by whom she had two sons. In 1932 she met Oswald Mosley, leader of the British Union of Fascists, and fell instantly under his spell. Four years later they were married secretly in Dr Goebbels' house in Berlin. She bore two more sons before she and her husband were detained during the war under the defence regulations. Her publications include a book on the Duchess of Windsor and, in 1977, her autobiography *A Life of Contrasts*. For the past forty years she has lived in Le Temple de la Gloire, a country house south of Paris.

Diana, when we spoke about this interview you rather suggested that there was nothing new to say. My own impression from doing the research is that you have given a very uneven picture of yourself. It seems to me that you are perhaps misjudged, certainly misunderstood. You say in your book, A Life of Contrasts: *'Indifference to public opinion is an essential aristocratic virtue. It is rarer than one might imagine.' Looking in from the outside, it is a quality, however rare, that you seem to have in abundance. Is it really so? Are you not tempted to open up?*

I don't quite know what you mean by 'open up'. I don't think I've ever consciously dodged answers to questions. By saying that indifference to public opinion is an aristocratic virtue, I did not mean to imply that I consider myself aristocratic; I certainly do not. Of course I mind very much about the opinion of people I love or esteem, but not of journalists or acquaintances who – quite rightly – look upon me as not 'politically correct' or whatever the fashionable phrase may be.

You have been known to say that you don't understand all the fuss about the Mitford girls. By any standards family life was strange and eccentric and it has been well documented in Nancy and Jessica's books. Was it the case that the oddness seemed perfectly normal to you, or were you conscious that yours was a very singular milieu, unlike that of others, even in your social circle?

I think there's a misunderstanding here. Our life as children was exactly like that of hundreds of other children in the same walk of life. If you lived in the country in those days you probably didn't go to school if you were a gel, you probably had a governess, you had animals, you went out hunting, you went to neighbours' parties. I honestly don't believe there was anything in our childhood which was unlike that of a great many other people. There was really nothing odd about it. Some fathers were stricter or more violent than others. Although our father was sometimes rather violent, we loved him and were amused by him. He's been a bit exaggerated by Nancy, though not very much, since he is really more or less Uncle Matthew, but I think even in her novels she says we loved him. There was never a dull moment.

I realize that the memory of your brother Tom must still be painful for you, but can you tell me what was it about him that formed so strong a bond between you?

I suppose it was that we were very close in age, not even eighteen months between us. We were very fond of one another. He was a musical boy, and I loved music, so that was a bond. It's hard to say really, but until he was killed, we just were very close. I miss him even now, for many things. I can't imagine him as an old man.

When one studies the Mitford girls it's difficult not to be astonished by the sheer brilliance and individuality of all of them. It is not usual in large families for these qualities to be dealt in such large measure across the board. Would you say that such things are decided, as it were, genetically, i.e. in advance of upbringing, or would you attribute it more to family life and parental influence?

I think it's completely genetic. I don't think that upbringing has a great deal to do with what one becomes later on. We're products of our grandparents and great-grandparents much more. That's been proved scientifically, I think. For example, if you take identical twins who are brought up in different ways, they turn out the same in the end. It's just a curious fact.

In your early life at least, your father seems to figure much more prominently than your mother. Was he the decisive influence on you, do you think?

No, I really do not think so. We just took him for granted. In a way the person who meant most to me when I was a child was my nanny. I loved her far more than I did my parents and I very often felt guilty about that. One should love one's mother more than one's nurse, but in fact I loved nanny best. My mother was a great character; she had wonderful courage and was so honest that you couldn't even imagine a dishonest thought or act coming from her. But again, she was somebody we took completely for granted; she was just our mother, always there.

If you had a problem, would you have confided in her?

I wouldn't have dreamed of confiding anything in either of my parents. Possibly one of my sisters or my brother, but nobody else. It simply wouldn't have occurred to any of us to confide in them, I'm sure.

You and your sisters seem in retrospect all to have been quite fixated on a particular man. In your own case it was Mosley, in Unity's it was Hitler, in Debo's it was her duke, and so on. In your own ways you all seemed to have been besotted by powerful men. This is not something you touch on in your autobiography. Is it not something that has occurred to you?

Yes, it has occurred to me. Strangely enough, even Nancy who was devoted to her colonel, went over the top of the colonel so to speak in her tremendous feeling for de Gaulle. You see, she loved France, and she thought he was the ideal dictator. It was far more than the usual rather cool approval that one might feel about a president or a prime minister; it went much more deeply with her. You might say we all had that characteristic which must have come through our genes.

Your father does seem to have been a very eccentric man – he chased the children with a bloodhound, for example.

I don't think he was nearly as eccentric as people imagine. You see, he had a bloodhound, and it was rather fun to hunt with him, and we children were there, available. Most men love hunting after all. He didn't hunt us very often with his bloodhound, and in any case the bloodhound died. He didn't have what you might call a kennelful of bloodhounds; there was just one dear old one and he thought, well, let's give him a run.

But did there come a time when you realized that he was not like other men?

Well, he was actually very much like my uncles. It's true he had great hates which were rather unusual. There were people he disliked intensely for no particular reason, even children. Most people usually dismiss children and say to themselves, 'What a tiresome little gel or boy', but he managed to work up quite a passion of hatred for some child he didn't like. It didn't evidence itself in any way; one just realized he could hardly bear the child.

169

The same applied to grown ups, of course. He wasn't what you might call a very sociable man. He preferred walking with his dogs and chatting to the keeper.

I have heard it said that he was something of a philistine. Is this something you were aware of?

I suppose he was a philistine. He never went to an art gallery, he never cared in the least about sightseeing, and he liked only a very simple kind of music – Puccini's arias, for example; apart from that I cannot say that he had any sort of artistic interest.

In a sense you seem to have had quite a spartan childhood, plenty of space, but not much warmth, no fires in the bedrooms, and really rather strict 'rules'. I'm thinking of your Paris diary and its aftermath. Was that the usual pattern among the families you knew?

A good many gels of my age, who were friends of mine, had exactly the same experience, perhaps not quite so strict, but they were not allowed out except with a governess or a maid. That was by no means unique to us. When I got to Paris at the age of sixteen it seemed such a wonderful chance for freedom that I'm afraid I did one or two things which were strictly forbidden, like going to the cinema with a young man in the afternoon when I pretended to the old governesses that I was going to a violin lesson. I put it all in my diary and then of course there was the most fearful row when it was discovered. It's rather sad that my diary went west. Mother and father put it in the boiler.

You married Brian Guinness when you were eighteen. And he was also very young, twenty-three, I think. Do you think in retrospect that to marry at such a tender age may have been a mistake?

Not really. I don't think age makes much difference. I was nineteen when my eldest son was born and when I was twenty I had another son. About a year after that my husband and I parted. It was not because I married too young, but because I fell in love with Oswald Mosley and decided that I should prefer living on my own and being able to see him occasionally, to being married to Brian Guinness. He wanted a wife who would always be there, and that's what he got afterwards. He married a wonderful person and they were terribly happy, so I was absolutely right.

You paint a very different picture of the nightclubs of Berlin from that usually portrayed in novels and memoirs. Were they really as dull as all that? You called them 'grim places'.

Yes, you imagined you were going to find Marlene Dietrich, and then you didn't. Nightclubs are for people who are searching for something. My husband and I weren't, and we just did think them very dull – awful noise, second-rate jazz, hideous people, and lights going on and off. One's idea really was to get away to bed.

How did people you knew react to your divorce and your attachment to Mosley? I imagine not everyone was sympathetic.

Everyone was unsympathetic, without exception I should say. It seemed very unusual for somebody as young as I was to leave her husband, to live alone, particularly after having had such an amusing, entertaining and interesting life as I had had. To want to cut oneself off seemed very curious to most people. First they thought I was too young to be married, then they thought I was too young not to be married.

Were you looked upon as rebellious?

I didn't *feel* the least bit rebellious. I just followed my instinct. It's very difficult to look back sixty years, but I never regretted it for one instant, and by degrees everyone came round to my point of view. It seemed the normal thing for me and Mosley to be together.

The relationship between the three of you after your divorce is rather baffling. For example, you speak of the death of Mosley's wife, Cimmie, as a 'devastating blow' for him. It was also, however, the turn of events that allowed you to be together and to marry. Did you have a strong sense of fate intervening? Did you know Mosley's first wife?

I knew her, not very well, but she was charming and people were very fond of her. It was a devastating blow for me as well as for him. She was a young woman and the last thing either of us had ever expected was what happened. It might easily have meant a complete break with Mosley because it was terribly tragic for him. It might easily have worked the opposite way, and in fact it was only three years later that we did get married.

But what were your expectations when you fell in love with Mosley?

That I would live on my own with my children and that I would see him from time to time. I was interested in his politics, and I hoped to be able to play some part perhaps. Otherwise it was to be a life alone.

When you met Mosley he seems to have had the support of a great many men who were later prominent in public affairs – John Strachey, Aneurin Bevan, Arthur Cooke, and much later Richard Crossman spoke of the way in which he was a generation ahead of labour thinking. What went wrong? Was he unwilling to serve if he could not lead?

No. As you know he was first elected as a conservative, and when he crossed the floor he became an independent and then went the whole way and joined labour. But he never felt that labour would be an instrument of action; he always thought the Labour Party would break in your hand if you tried to do anything with it. It was dominated then (and I suppose up to a point it still is) by two such disparate elements – the trade unions and the intellectuals; and they did not want the same thing. I don't belong to the school of thought which makes out that one party is perfect and the other is devilish. By and large all politicians want the best for their country, but they go about it in different ways. England was at that time in a very poor way with enormous and growing unemployment, terrific suffering and hunger. That must never be forgotten, because to be unemployed then was far worse than it is now, awful though it must always be. Mosley therefore thought that the only thing to do was to make a grass-roots movement of his own. Some of the men you mentioned came with him, but there was a tremendous crisis in England after the Wall Street Crash in 1929. In 1931 there was an election and rather predictably the Tories won a sweeping victory and the New Party, as his party was called, was wiped out at the polls; even he was not elected. It was then that he thought he had better call things by their name and so he called his new movement the British Union of Fascists, later modified to the British Union, as you know.

Why do you think he went to such an extreme?

It wasn't considered an extreme then. In those days, for instance, a great many Tories were admirers of Mussolini. Hitler had not yet come to power. It was a different picture. The reason he called it fascism was because it was in a sense a world movement and he thought it was more honest. With the benefit of hindsight, I think perhaps it may have been a mistake, but on the other hand he didn't in the least want people to imagine it was anything it was not.

Historically speaking, it was not difficult to have some understanding of Hitler's charisma and the spell which he cast. Even your own brother, who was later killed fighting on the other side, seems to have found his politics attractive initially. How did it strike you at the time?

It struck me as perfectly normal and natural. Tom used to say that it would be either the Nazis or the communists, and that if he were a German he would be a Nazi. It wasn't only when he was a student in Berlin; he went on thinking that he would have been a Nazi – in fact, practically every decent German was. We must remember that nothing succeeds like success. Hitler not only had what people now call charisma, he was also – unheard of in the thirties – completely successful. He made promises at the polls and he kept them. In England both labour and Tories said they could cure unemployment, put the economy straight, make an earthly paradise; they each had a chance and neither of them was able to do it. Under Hitler, unemployment dwindled to nothing, and within two or three years a despairing country had been transformed into an extraordinarily prosperous one where people were happy and worked hard. Hitler always said he would give the people *Arbeit und Brot*, Work and Bread, but the interesting thing is that he put work before bread, whereas in England, they put bread first and then work a long way afterwards. Everyone was interested in Hitler. Churchill himself wrote at the time that Hitler was the person everybody would like to get to know, because he seemed to have a political secret which was hidden from others.

Lady Diana Mosley

You speak in your book of your conviction that fascism in Britain would have been a different sort of thing from that which overtook the Continent. It is difficult for many people now, after the horrors of the camps and so on, to understand how it was to be different. What was your own vision?

That is such an impossibly large question; to answer it properly one would have to go into every facet of life. Briefly, the British parliament would have had a great deal of power which of course the Reichstag did not have. Another point which is very important is that my husband was always against imprisonment without trial. He said concentration camps were a horror which should never have been allowed anywhere. And as to cruelty, it just wasn't in his nature.

What impression do you retain of that first Nuremberg rally? It must have been very different from the huge stage-managed affairs of later years.

Even so they managed to gather a million people for the first rally. The Germans are of course quite extraordinary when it comes to organization, and perhaps no other country could have done it, or done it so smoothly. It was an amazing achievement, and of course very interesting for a foreigner to see.

Were you mesmerized by it?

I wouldn't say one was mesmerized, but it was very striking and even very moving. You saw a country which had been reduced to despair pulling itself up by its own bootstraps.

With hindsight virtually everyone thinks of Hitler as a monster, but that is a public rather than a private judgement. He clearly commanded the allegiance of his fellow countrymen. You have never denounced him, and have continued to reiterate your admiration for him . . . were you ever able to see things from a different perspective?

No. I saw a man whom I got to know through a very strange chance because he was a friend of my sister Unity. Unity loved and adored him, thought him utter perfection. I never felt like that about him, but I did admire him very much for what he had done. I thought it quite amazing that of all the politicians in charge of big industrial nations at that time, whether France, the United States, England, he stood alone in having been able to solve the appalling problems of poverty and unemployment. That is never admitted now because it is said that no monster could possibly have done anything as clever as that. But in fact he did, and one day history will be written in a truthful way. That was the man I knew, the public man. As for the private person, I didn't know him all that well, but I was determined after the war that I would at least say what I'd seen, because by then he had become a monster, as you say. Of course the crimes in the war were utterly terrible and unforgivable, but I believe that THE great crime was the war itself, which engendered all the horrors, and not only all on one side, I may say. I have felt it not only a duty but almost a pleasure to describe the man I knew, because it's so monstrously unfair when people deny something which they felt very strongly at the time.

Have you regretted anything?

No, absolutely not. Why should I? A woman writer published something the other day about my being impenitent. I've never really understood what I have to be penitent about. I just speak the truth as I remember it, as I know it, as I believe it.

But obviously you didn't know then some of the things that had happened. Since the war there have been horrific revelations about Hitler . . .

Yes, horrific. But I can't change my mind about the man I knew long before all that happened. Like everyone else, I deplore the crimes and the horrors and the miseries, but I still think the basic reason that made them possible was the fact that we had a war, and for the war I blame Hitler and I also blame Churchill.

In your autobiography you suggest that the Jewish question was one which Jews rather brought on themselves and that it could have been solved by emigration. This is surely a somewhat naïve view, if only because there must have been millions of Jews, then as now, who thought of themselves as Germans. They were people who had fought as Germans in the First World War. Why should they have felt the need to leave?

I do see that very much, but at the same time, I'm quite sure that Jews who had fought for Germany in the First World War need never have left. Unfortunately there was this tremendous feeling of anti-Semitism not only in Germany, but all over Central Europe. I've always felt that it would have been far wiser, and also far more humane, to have had a round-table conference with, say, the League of Nations, and discuss how best to separate people who were not living happily together. I still feel that. That's what was attempted in Ireland, but because there were many Republicans who remained in Ulster, the fighting just goes on and on. If you force people who dislike each other to live together, it doesn't make for a very happy life for anyone.

But what was the cause of the anti-Semitism?

After the First War there was an enormous influx of Jews from Eastern Europe. As we know, one of their great strengths is that they always hang together, and, rightly or wrongly, they became more and more unpopular because people coming back from the front found their businesses had been taken over. This engendered an enormous amount of anti-Jewish feeling in Germany as a whole, not just in Hitler. I've always felt it could have been solved simply by separating them. Most of them would have loved to go to America, just as they do now. After all, most Jews coming out of Russia, go to New York, not Israel.

In your book you recount that Professor Lindemann, a regular visitor to Chartwell, said to you of your friend Brian Howard, 'Oh you can't like him, he's a Jew.' Were you aware of much casual anti-Semitism in those days?

No, I wasn't. He gave me quite a surprise by saying that. But there are double standards here. My father, for example, was very anti-German and was quite capable of saying the only good German is a dead German, but of course if anybody said that about Jews they'd be for the high jump, although it's supposed to be quite all right to say it about other people. English people often say they hate the Scotch, but of course when they meet the Scotch they don't hate them at all. It's rather the same thing with the Jews. Collectively, so to speak, they may be deprecated by certain people but individually they're considered brilliant, charming, clever.

How do you feel about the Jews yourself?

I feel they behaved very badly towards my husband who was not anti-Semitic. They attacked him not only in newspaper articles and newsreels at the cinema, but physically at his meetings, until in the end they practically made him into an anti-Semite. He never was one, it just wasn't in his nature, but he did think they were a perfect pest. They used to disrupt his meetings, jump up and down and shout, very often without knowing English, and therefore not even able to understand what he was saying. We now know they behaved in this way because they were having a really bad time in Germany, but having said that, it doesn't alter the fact that they were anti-Mosley long before he was anti-them.

You were very friendly with Goebbels' wife. In Leni Riefensthal's autobiography she claimed that Magda only married Goebbels to be closer to Hitler with whom she was actually in love. Was there any evidence for that in your view?

No. She did adore Hitler, but I'm certain that she was in love with the Doctor, at least when I first knew her. I think she got very fed up with him later. As minister of propaganda he had so many starlets around, and that probably annoyed her quite a lot. Nevertheless she was very fond of him, and devoted to her children.

Leni Riefensthal also describes a conversation she had with Hitler on the subject of Unity. According to Riefensthal, Hitler said: 'Unity is a very attractive girl, but I could never have an intimate relationship with a foreigner, no matter how beautiful she might be.' Does this accord with your own impression?

I don't think Unity ever thought of him in that way. She adored him, of course, and the great attraction for him was that she made him laugh so much. She was so unlike German women; she just always said what she thought, did as she wished. I remember him telling me that one day he had been driving in Munich when he saw somebody coming straight at him the wrong way down a one-way street. His driver had to brake and Hitler saw it was Unity. She merely laughed and said she had been trying to catch up with him. She had no idea of keeping any rules, and that in itself is very unGerman. She was lawless, completely.

You have said many times that Hitler adored Unity and was devoted to her. I'm sure you are tired to death of being asked if Unity was in love with Hitler, but if she was not, why did she try to kill herself when war broke out? Was there a chance that they could have been lovers?

No. There was a much nobler reason behind her suicide attempt. She had always told me she would kill herself if England and Germany went to war. She was always an extremely patriotic Englishwoman as well as being so in love with Germany.

But she was in love with Hitler, wasn't she?

Well, there are so many different ways of being in love. I don't think she was sexually in love with Hitler, at least not in my opinion. She was devoted to him, admired him, but he represented for her something quite different from a lover or a husband. That's my own view. She was appalled by the global tragedy of her two beloved countries going to war. When she heard Chamberlain say that war had been declared on Germany, she didn't really wish to live and see any more happen.

Unity was the one who chose consciously to adopt a national socialist creed. Did she ever change her mind when the consequences became apparent in the revelations after the war?

She wasn't really with us after the war; her mind had gone away. The bullet went through her brain and Professor Cairns, the brain specialist, told my father that it was not possible to remove it safely. It was therefore a kind of freak that she lived at all. The Germans had been afraid that she might do something and were therefore watching her. They knew she had a gun and on 3 September 1939 she went to Gauleiter Wagner in a great state and gave him a letter to send to my father, and also one for Hitler. She then went to the English Garden in Munich and shot herself. Wagner had had her followed because he had a feeling that she was going to do herself a mischief. No sooner had she fallen off the bench than two men ran up and took her to hospital straightaway. She was unconscious for several weeks and was looked after with extraordinary devotion by nuns. Hitler had been informed, of course, and he was constantly telephoning to find out how she was. On 9 November he came to Munich for the anniversary of the 1923 *putsch* and it was on that day she emerged from the coma. Naturally her brain had suffered terribly. Hitler offered her the choice between having a house in Germany where no one would pester her, or, if she preferred, safe passage to her family in England. She chose the latter. Hitler arranged the whole thing with a Hungarian friend of my brother Tom who was, in fact, a lover of Unity. He was perfect. He took her in a special train with nurses and doctors to the Swiss frontier and there handed her over to Swiss doctors. She was taken to a clinic in Zurich, and my mother travelled across France with my sister Debo and together they brought her back to England. This was in January 1940, long before France fell. Before that, my father had seen Oliver Stanley at the War Office and made him promise that Unity would not be arrested. Stanley gave his word and he kept it. To begin with Unity was paralysed, but by degrees she got the use of her limbs again. But her mind was simply different; it was never again normal. To what extent she realized what had happened at the end of the war I don't know, and I'm sure my mother kept newspapers away from her. She knew Hitler was dead, but whether she knew anything about the horrors of the camps, I doubt it. She never spoke of them to me and of course it was the sort of subject one never would have dreamed of raising with her. She was pathetic really.

In 1944 Adam von Trott was executed for his part in the failed attempt on Hitler's life. Instead of being shot he was hanged from a butcher's hook as Hitler looked on. His death was filmed for all to see, so there was no question of this being anti-Hitler propaganda. Was there anything about Hitler and the others that suggested this sort of potential ruthlessness?

First of all, I completely disbelieve that Hitler would have wished to see any person hanged in any way; that's just a figment of some foul person's imagination. You see, he was accused of these terrible atrocities and cruelties because he was in charge, but that's a very different thing from

179

doing it himself. I'm quite sure your story is untrue; nothing would ever make me believe it. As for Adam von Trott, he was a traitor to his country. He tried to kill the person who was fighting the war and losing it – I don't suppose there would have been very much sympathy in England for somebody who had tried to assassinate Churchill. His friend von Stauffenberg was one of the dirtiest fighters imaginable. He did what is always so much denounced when the IRA does it; he left a bomb so that it would go off and kill any number of people around, but not himself. If he had wished to rid the world of Hitler, all he had to do as a serving officer was to take his revolver, shoot him and take the consequences; that would have been the act of a man. What he did was the act of a perfect common or garden terrorist. There would have been no pity for such a man in England either . . .

Yes, but they wouldn't have hanged him on a hook.

Well, I don't suppose they did. But if it was done in a cruel way, Hitler would never have demeaned himself by going to watch, never. I simply don't believe it.

Why are you so sure that Hitler wouldn't have done it?

Because I knew Hitler well enough to be sure. I knew his character; he may have been cruel, but he wasn't mean.

You speak of Churchill as someone who was really in love with war. In your book you write: 'The difference between M. and Churchill was that M. wanted Britain to be strong in order to keep the peace unless any part of our possessions was threatened, while Churchill genuinely hoped for war.' And you quote in support of this statement Lloyd George who said: 'Winston likes war; I don't.' But if that really was the case, why did Churchill disarm after the First War and render the country quite unprepared for war?

He disarmed after the First War because quite rightly nobody thought there would be a war for ten years; this is what they call the ten-year rule. England became more and more poor (partly owing to Churchill's muddling as chancellor of the exchequer) so the ten-year rule was forever being extended, or reimposed. But in the early thirties he did begin to want to rearm, and he never stopped speaking in parliament. Mosley thought it fatal to have the very tiny air force which we had, and he always maintained that a strong air force and navy together could have kept any invader out. That's why he said that as long as England was not attacked we could make peace, a negotiated peace. By the time France fell and Mosley was arrested, I don't think it would have been possible to make peace, or at least it would have had to be such a pathetic peace that it would hardly have counted. All the same, several cabinet members were for it, but Churchill was against. I don't myself go along with the idea of the finest hour; it seems to me that if you declare war on a very strong country and have as your ally a rather weak country and the weak country is overrun and your army has to escape through Dunkirk as best it can, throwing away all its armaments such as they were, there's nothing very much you can do except have a finest hour. What was so utterly foolish was to declare war in the beginning, pretending it was going to help Poland; as Mosley said at the time, it was simply writing Poland a blank cheque which then bounced.

It must have puzzled you enormously, as it does me, why you were arrested and imprisoned. I suppose it's arguable that your husband might have been thought potentially disruptive, but what were the authorities afraid you would do? What could you have done?

Nothing. I've absolutely no idea why they imprisoned me. I was told recently by a professor that the Japanese who were arrested and put in camps in the west of America brought a successful action against the government and won their case. I thought that was wonderful, and wondered about bringing one myself until he told me that they hadn't got their compensation, so then the idea rather died on me. To return to your question, I think it was an extraordinary thing to have done, to my husband too, especially since our people were extremely patriotic. They all joined the army when they could, and long before he was arrested. Fortunately it's in black and white in his little paper which came out nearly a fortnight before he was arrested. He said there would be no question of where members of the British Union would stand; they would die to the last man in order to drive the invader from our shores. You can't say more than that. All he had argued beforehand was that until something happened, we should try to have a negotiated peace over Poland. But France fell so quickly, and then there was the terrible tragic farce of Norway, which was entirely Churchill's idea. And after he had made such an absolute fool of himself there, the next thing they did was make him prime minister.

What did you feel about Churchill's complicity in your imprisonment? After all, you knew him quite well, and he was your father's cousin, yet he had separated you from your husband and your children and imprisoned you for years without charge. Do you feel any bitterness towards him?

No, none at all for that. I feel bitterness towards him for the war itself. He was one of the people responsible for it, determined to have it. Sadly, I think the same of Hitler. I think that was their great crime, because it very nearly ruined Europe, and England was ruined completely. Not only have we lost our empire, which was supposed to be so strong but turned out to be so very weak, but also England itself changed very much as a result of the war, not all for the good.

Rumour has it that Churchill was prepared to allow you a bath and running water, but you refused it. Is there any truth in that?

Yes, it's completely true. I was sent for by the governor and he said: 'There's a message from the cabinet. Lady Mosley's to have a bath every day.' Of course it wasn't possible, so I just laughed and so did he. All we had was a horrible foul little bathroom with a very old-fashioned geyser which did only three baths twice a day. There were about sixty of us, so we had a rota, and I could no more have gone in front of the others than . . . well, they were all my dear friends.

What did prison life teach you?

Nothing, except to hate discomfort, which I always have hated.

Did it leave you feeling bitter?

No, I just despised the government so much really. If you don't respect people, it doesn't engender bitterness.

Were you ever offered any sort of explanation afterwards? Large numbers of those arrested with you were eventually freed, but you had to wait many years. Even after the war ended the authorities tried to prevent you travelling. Why do you think that was?

I just do wonder really. It is very extraordinary. One reason is that the Foreign Office, as Enoch Powell so truly said, was a nest of spies and traitors; it really was, right up to 1951 when Burgess and Maclean very sensibly went off to Russia, which was where they belonged. And if you have a Foreign Office which is a nest of spies and traitors they don't want decent people travelling.

You say in your book: 'The paramount crime was the war itself. None of the atrocities could have happened in time of peace.' But we know now of course that both Dachau and Buchenwald were in operation by the end of 1933 . . .

Not in the sense that you mean. There were several concentration camps which my husband greatly deplored, but they had floating populations, so to speak. People would be told they were going to Dachau for three months, and out they'd come again. I remember an edition of an illustrated Berlin weekly just before the war which had pictures of people in concentration camps; there were very few, a couple of dozen perhaps, and they were all mentally deficient, or people who might have annoyed the government. They were neither criminal nor were they our beloved liberals or anything of the sort; they were just ordinary common or garden misfits.

Did you ever meet Eva Braun?

Yes. She was very pretty. She was also extremely loyal and brave, as we know by what she did when she flew into Berlin. She was flying to her death and she knew it.

You once said: 'Men who wage war give cruel orders which are executed with violence and provoke tragedy. This applies to them all, Hitler, Stalin, Roosevelt and even Churchill, in so far as he had the power.' Many people regard it as breathtaking cynicism that you make no distinction between the first two, Hitler and Stalin, and the last two, not even a distinction of scale.

But I said 'in so far as it was in their power'; I call that a distinction. If Churchill had had absolute power, which thank God he did not, then who knows what he might have done? When you think of the lies that have been told about Hitler since the war I should think Roosevelt and Churchill would have been *capables de tout.*

I realize how dreadful it must have been to be imprisoned for years without even the shadow of a charge, but in view of the fact that there were crowds protesting at your release even as late as 1943, do you think that perhaps you would not have been safe had you been released earlier?

That was the most terrific canard there has ever been. I know Clementine Churchill said to my mother that she thought we were probably much safer in prison, but my mother replied that she thought it was for us to judge. There was never a breath of any trouble after we got out. The *Daily Worker* even went round Shipton asking all the villagers to demonstrate against the Mosleys and not one of them would. We also discovered from an old man who lived in a villa about half a mile away that he had been approached by the *Daily Mirror* who told him that the Mosleys were going to be his new neighbours, and he said, 'Oh, how interesting,' which wasn't at all the reaction they'd hoped for. You see, English people are not like that really. You might get communists demonstrating outside the underground if they think enough people are watching, but they are not going to do the slightest harm. No, that aspect never bothered us. What we minded was not having passports. We had to buy a little yacht to get away from England.

Presumably you were not a political animal until you met Mosley. Did you actually share his vision intellectually or was it something you took on board as part of your profound love for him?

It's not quite true to say that I wasn't interested in politics; I was. The first time I had a vote was in the 1931 election and if in our constituency there had been a Lloyd George liberal standing, I would have voted for him because Lloyd George had very clever ideas about unemployment and all sorts of things. I often thought afterwards that was why he and Hitler got on so very well. They liked each other enormously when they met, and Lloyd George wrote wonderful articles in the English papers praising him. There's a beautiful story about when he was on the *Berg* with Hitler. He was in bed one morning and he rang for his secretary Sylvester and told him he wanted to lay a wreath on the war memorial. Sylvester brought him a wreath, and gave him a card to inscribe. Lloyd George wrote on the card: 'To the brave men who died for the Fatherland'. Sylvester asked, 'Don't you think it might be better to put *their* Fatherland?', and Lloyd George thought perhaps it would, so he added the two little letters. It's terribly nice isn't it?

It is often said that you were the driving force behind Mosley. Would you agree with that?

No. He had the driving force within himself. He didn't need me for that. I suppose I must have influenced him a little bit, but not very much. He was much more of an influence on me. He was so clever, so brilliant.

It is also alleged that Mosley was something of a philanderer. Was this a problem which loomed large in your marriage or were you so devoted to him that you accepted and forgave his transgressions?

Well, I suppose one never completely accepts. Jealousy is a very real emotion which nearly everybody who has been in love must feel and know about, but he was an exceptional person, and therefore very attractive to women. He himself adored women, and that's just a fact. I never blamed him for that.

But did you suffer?

Only marginally really, because it was so taken for granted. It's very hard to say looking back; I'm sure there were moments when I was jealous, but not unduly, not enough to matter.

185

Lady Diana Mosley

You were upset and angered by the publication of your stepson Nicholas Mosley's book, Beyond the Pale. *I was told that you were shown the book in draft form and decided to make no changes and that it was only afterwards that you had second thoughts about what he had written being made public.*

It's completely untrue to say that I was shown it in draft. He sent it when it was already too late to make any alterations, which is an old trick, as we know. I didn't mind him saying that Mosley was a philanderer, because it was just the truth. What I minded was that he tried to make him such a trivial person, whereas in fact he had been a tremendous worker all his life and had had brilliant ideas. None of that is dealt with at all in the book.

You mean the balance was not right?

Not only was it not right, it was simply ridiculous. The other point is that as he was his son, he'd been told he could have the papers, and I didn't bother to look through anything. There were very intimate things, such as letters between him and his first wife, which I didn't think it was right for Nicholas to publish. I implored him to take them out and the answer was always that it was too late. He has a complete obsession about his father, which may not be entirely his fault, because the truth is that the most interesting thing about him is that he's the son of an extraordinary man. Journalists know that too, so they always get off the subject of his probably not very interesting novels, and ask him instead about his father. The book about Mosley is fundamentally such a dishonest book, because nowhere is it suggested that he was a brilliant thinker or that he could have made a difference to the world had his ideas been accepted. Instead he is portrayed as some kind of playboy, which is too absurd when you think of what the man was. That's why I object to it.

How did he get on with his father?

Very well. My husband was very fond of him and very good to him always. But of course it turns out that Nicholas must have been fearfully jealous; it can't be explained in any other way. The dishonesty and the obsession must be the fruits of tremendous jealousy.

Is there any truth in his suggestion that during your marriage to Mosley you suffered from appalling migraines which disappeared after his death?

It's quite true that I did suffer from appalling migraines, but what I had was a brain tumour. It was operated on and removed, and I'm alive to tell the tale. Mercifully, it turned out to be benign, but it had been pressing on the nerve for years. However wicked Mosley may be considered by his rather dreadful son, I don't think he could have made me have a brain tumour.

With the imminent arrival of a united Europe, and apprehension about immigration and its troubles, you must feel that both your husband's goal of an integrated Europe and his fears about widespread immigration have become part of mainstream politics. Do you feel that many of his views have been shown to be right?

I think his views are quite extraordinarily right. When you look back at what he wrote, you realize that he had amazing powers of seeing what might happen. It's been the most wonderful joy for me to see what's happened in the last two years, to see the utter and complete failure of socialism and the reuniting of Germany, which is something I'd always known would happen but imagined might be long after my death. As to immigration, what happened in the 1950s was a great tragedy, and it still is. The proof is in the number of laws which had to be made to force it down the throats of the unfortunate English who really should have been asked, either in an election or in a referendum, whether they wished to be the hosts of an enormous population with a completely different culture from their own. They might have said yes, but I doubt it. Luckily there was a referendum for Europe and there was a large majority in favour. And every time the English try and put a spoke in the wheel of Europe, as Mrs Thatcher tried to do, I mind less and less, because as time goes on, if you have twelve countries and one of them is always the one that is bloody minded, it doesn't really matter very much; the other eleven have their way and the twelfth comes hobbling along afterwards. Of course I should love to see Europe with England at the very heart of it, as Mr Major promised, but if we're not to have that, we still have Europe. I'm a complete European. I love England, but I could be as happy living in Spain or Germany or Portugal or Italy as I am in France. The reason I live in France is that the house I've been in for so many years has so many memories, I don't want to leave it.

187

Lady Diana Mosley

*You yourself have always had a very bad press. You said in an interview in
The Times five years ago: 'People think I'm a sort of gorgon.' Do you think
there has been a deliberate campaign of vilification or is it just the usual
tabloid thirst for copy?*

It's fashionable to attack me and people follow the fashion. I can't say I've
minded very much or that I've done anything to stop it. I don't get hurt in
the least. I'm very thick skinned. I also feel very fortunate in that I have
children and grandchildren and great-grandchildren, not to mention a
great many friends. The people I write to and receive letters from don't
attack me, so I don't very much mind whether the papers do or not.

*Have you ever had the same sort of hostile reaction in France that you have
suffered for so long in England?*

No. They're not a bit interested in attacking private people. In fact they
have a very good law which forbids interference in people's lives, which is
an absolute boon. Nobody has ever bothered me in the forty years I've been
here.

Even an apparently innocuous activity such as appearing on Desert Island
Discs *can provoke an outcry after nearly fifty years. Can you in any way
understand the strength of the public feeling against you?*

I don't think it's public feeling; it's really rather a small number of people.
Apparently what happened was the BBC decided to broadcast the
programme when it was Yom Kippur. I'm not sure what Yom Kippur is,
but it's something very important for Jewish people who immediately
made a tremendous fuss and said they couldn't listen to Mozart and
Beethoven and Wagner at Yom Kippur. The poor old BBC had to think of
another date, but the next one turned out to be the Jewish New Year or
something quite important. Again there was a tremendous outcry so they
had to put it off again. In the end I wrote to them and said that if it was an
embarrassment, then they should cancel. But of course they didn't want to.

*Your beauty is legendary in its own time. Your looks astonish still and yet
you are said to feel indifferent on the matter. Can this really be true?*

I suppose I was quite glad not to be a monster, but people exaggerated quite a lot by pretending one was so beautiful.

But didn't men fall for you all the time?

I don't think they did. Men don't ever fall for someone who doesn't fall for them; that's my opinion. Women usually make the first move if there's going to be anything. In any case, there's something much more important than beauty, and that is charm, which is something you can't describe adequately. But there's no doubt it's far more powerful than just having big eyes.

You were friends of the Windsors in Paris and you even wrote a biography of the duchess. It is a very sympathetic account of a royal love story which is at odds with the widespread opinion that she behaved appallingly towards the duke who was in turn masochistic, and so on. Why did you want to paint such a romantic picture to the world? Were you really not aware of the negative side?

I was well aware of it in the sense that it is always being written about. But I tried to write what I knew about, what I'd actually seen. I just don't go along with the idea that he was masochistic or that she was beastly to him, or any of those things at all. Perhaps I did bring out the nice side, but one thing is for sure, he absolutely loved her. The reason I wrote the book was not at all because writing about royals is an amusing way of spending one's life, but the Americans had gone really beyond everything in their unfairness. It seemed to me that somebody might perhaps try and put the record straight.

You have said that the one thing you regret is not having been able to do more to help Mosley to achieve his aims.

I regret most being unable to do anything towards his campaign for peace. From the beginning of the war until I was arrested I was either pregnant or nursing a tiny baby, so there was nothing I could do.

But, looking back now, do you regret anything else, or wish that things had been different?

Does it sound very smug to say no? When I have regrets in the stilly watches of the night, it's always about having been unkind to somebody or not fair, but I suppose everyone has those sort of regrets. Otherwise in the big lines of my life I wouldn't have changed anything. I would choose the same life again, and in fact it's wonderful to be able to say that. It's like Nietzsche's idea of *die ewige Wiederkehr*.

Is there anything in life you'd still like to achieve?

Not for myself, but for the people I love. I long for everything to go right for them. Of course, everyone has to live life in his own way, and nobody knows that better than I do.

Born in 1909, John Murray was educated at Eton and at Magdalen College, Oxford, where he took a BA in history. In 1930 he joined the publishing firm of John Murray, and during the war he served with the Royal Artillery. His publications include *Byron: A Self-Portrait* (1950) and *Complete Letters and Journals of Lord Byron* (12 vols 1973–81). Since 1968 he has been senior director of John Murray and in 1975 he was awarded the CBE.

When I was doing the research for this interview, there was very little in the press cuttings which was revealing about John Murray the man as opposed to John Murray the publisher. Have you deliberately tried to keep out of the public eye?

Yes, for two reasons. First because any importance that I have is because of the authors I have published. Secondly, my personal life is so traditional as to be hardly believable. My main claim to fame is that I am the only publisher who has typeset in the nude, something I did when I was with Robert Gibbings who ran the Golden Cockerel Press. As a young man I would go and help him and unfortunately I hit the short period when he was in his nudest phase and as I was only about fifteen or sixteen years old I found this very embarrassing. It was all right for him because his nudity seemed like a fur coat. But my own life is essentially dull, except perhaps in two regards: it is a good example of family nepotism – that's the first; and the second is that during my schooldays I had a bad spell of stammering which impeded my education. But I did get over it and this is encouraging to anyone who has a stammer. It was a most terrible handicap but I went to see a man called Lionel Logue who subsequently helped King George VI with his speeches. He put me through a very interesting training and taught me something which I often now tell young stammerers; that is, with your hand in your pocket beat time with one finger in rhythm with what you are saying and this will help you get over the blockages. Other than that my life has been routine. I mean, it's boring to say that one's first memory is of sucking gooseberries; one can do without that.

How would you do a thumbnail sketch of your own character?

Ask me what I think about the characters of my authors, and I could tell you very easily, but until one gets older one doesn't really examine one's own character. Nevertheless, I have given this some thought and I would say that I have no greed, no wish to have yachts or a second home. I do have incorrigible curiosity, and I also have a terrible vice – envy, envy of other people's literary skill, for example. I try to pretend it's something else, such as admiration, but it is actually envy. On the positive side I have flexibility, which I consider a strength. Of course as a publisher one learns to be flexible within the yardstick of truth and to give way wherever one can. This is the sort of quality which would make me a good ADC. It stems from the fact that my great childhood friend here in Albemarle Street was the butler. I so admired his handing round at table, decanting the port, serving the drinks. Barnes in his waistcoat looked like the backside of a wasp. He had a little bit of paper which was the blacklist of authors for whom there was never any spare chair at luncheon. I admired his style so much, the way he helped gentlemen on with their coats, and so on, that I asked him to teach me everything in return for being allowed to play with my train in the nursery. To my amazement he agreed. He did show me everything, and I now feel equipped to be a very good ADC. Indeed, I am afraid I embarrass American publishers when I help them on with their overcoats since I always put my hand under the coat to pull the jacket down. They look round at me with the gravest suspicion.

You were at Oxford in the 1930s and contemporary with John Betjeman and Osbert Lancaster. To an outsider it always seems as if they must have been exciting days. Is that how you remember them?

Oh yes. And they remained my greatest, most exciting friends until their deaths. That was why I published Betjeman – a fascinating occupation. You would be amused to see the typescript of *Summoned by Bells* with comments by Tom Driberg, John Sparrow (warden of All Souls) and me. Betjeman was certainly one of the most inspiring people in my life. No journey with John was ever dull . . . There's a charming episode I remember. He was rather extravagant and he used to take people to his club and have oysters and champagne. I remember one day his accountant, called Masterson, came in and asked if we had any more royalties for John Betjeman – 'He is terribly in the red, and I find myself going down on my knees and saying, "Oh Lord, please prevent John Betjeman from going into the Garrick Club."' I also met Osbert at Oxford, and he too was a life enhancer. He used to come in, either before or after doing the cartoons in the *Express*, for what he called a snifter, usually a gin and vermouth, and of course the amount of gossip one got from him was absolutely fascinating. Both John and Osbert were much more knowledgeable and scholarly than I was, Osbert on arts, John on poetry and architecture, and I learned a lot from them. But we had a sense of humour in common, and I can think of no people with whom I've shared more laughter.

When you were at Oxford, did you sow your wild oats? Were you a womanizer at all?

Not at Oxford. I found no woman to womanize with at Oxford. Magdalen was still celibate. I did a little after Oxford, but I did it in moderation. Although I thought of women all the time, and was fascinated by them, I was frightened to get too deeply involved because I thought there might be no escape or that damage might be done. I usually found something I thought I couldn't live with permanently, so I was a very cautious lover, if that word is appropriate. I then met a girl, knew her on and off for about ten years, and married her. I'm still married to her fifty years on. We laugh sometimes to remember that we first met at a rat hunt in Buckinghamshire. We never caught a rat, but I caught a wife.

How did marriage and family responsibilities alter your life? Was that an area of great fulfilment for you?

Yes, and it increased the possibilities of my career. I'd been an active publisher for about ten years before I married, which of course confirms my view that the male should have settled what he wants to do before he gets married. My wife was very intelligent, read books, liked people, and that was a wonderful bit of luck because it enabled one to entertain authors rather more happily than it is possible to do by oneself.

As you get older, are you more sure or less sure about your ideas and opinions?

Less sure. Goethe writes somewhere: 'To be uncertain is uncomfortable, to be certain is ridiculous'; and that applies to me with one exception, which is the Net Book Agreement. I'm rather bigoted about that and I only wish that the greedy boys would look more carefully at the reasons for it being started in about 1900.

I don't know whether you're religious or not, but how do you feel about that area as you grow older?

I think if anything I've become a little less religious. I certainly go to church now less often than I did. Of course, the chains of habit are too weak to be felt until they're too strong to be broken, and though I read the lesson in the Anglican church up in Hampstead when I'm asked to do so, I feel a little ashamed that I attend church less often. I try to analyse this and I can't, but there may be something of old Voltaire on his deathbed when he was asked by a friend to confess his sins and denounce the devil, and Voltaire said: 'Oh my dear fellow, this is no time to make enemies.' But I firmly believe that churchgoing is important for unifying a community.

Was there tremendous family pressure on you to become John Murray the sixth?

There was pressure, but not tremendous pressure. I don't think that excessive pressure was needed because I'd been brought up with authors around me. I've certainly never regretted my time in publishing or wished I had broken away from family tradition.

Your own son is set to be John Murray the seventh. Did that come about easily or was it a source of family tension?

I put no pressure on him. As in my case it seemed a natural progression of events. Looking back on family history, the great oddity to my mind is that every Murray but one had one son, and none of them revolted. One of the Murrays had two sons, my grandfather and my great uncle. They didn't agree with each other because my great uncle was artistically inclined and he wanted books to be produced with lovely gilt bindings. He was far too extravagant, whereas John Murray was a very careful man. So my Uncle Hal retired and became a wonderful watercolour artist. To return to your question, one of the things I always did when I knew my children were getting home was to hide the typescripts and relax back in the chair, hoping to give the impression that a publisher's life was one of lovely laziness. Whether I succeeded or not I don't know.

How well do you get on with your son? Is there a generation gap in thinking?

Our views are different on some subjects, but he has sense at the back of him. I have not come across a subject in which, even though it uspet me, I didn't think he was right. I can say that perfectly truthfully, but then he's a remarkable fellow.

The publishing world which your son now inhabits is very different from the one you started out in. Are you confident about the future of publishing?

I'm not confident about the future of general publishing but this is a widely held view. Fortunately, in the last century we started educational publishing which now acounts for sixty to seventy per cent of our turnover. This is the future, a difficult future, because the government doesn't keep pace with new curriculums by providing money for teams of authors to produce new series of books. General publishing is difficult. I think I'm almost the longest serving publisher on the Publishers' Association Council, and many years ago I did a private survey. I cross-examined about fourteen of the larger publishers in order to discover how many of their books paid, and the figures were not uninteresting. More than half of all the books they published made a loss, another twenty-five per cent just covered the costs, and the number that made a profit was absolutely minimal – under ten per cent. Nowadays the reasons are of course perfectly clear: auction of rights, squeezing by powerful retailers, inadequate funds for public libraries and so on. But I needn't tell you all that, you must know it all.

One of the changes in publishing is that what used to be called flair has given way to market predictions, trends and committees. Do you regret the passing of the good old days, so to speak, or are you resigned to the changes?

Oh no, you can't be resigned to them. I believe that if the man who has flair has the persistence and energy to publish a book and has the stamina to follow his enthusiasm right the way down, he'll make a sucess of it. I don't want to be conceited myself but I remember well that my grandfather had not published any poetry for a long time, and since I knew Betjeman at Oxford I came back with a sheaf of his new poems. My grandfather said, 'My dear young fellow, we can't start publishing that sort of thing.' I told him I thought they were so good and would catch on and that some of my friends had been very excited by them. I felt so strongly that I offered to guarantee them with a hundred shares of Bovril that he had given me for my eighteenth birthday. He agreed, and I never had to sell the Bovril shares.

Have you ever discovered the secret of successfully predicting a book's sales?

That's a difficult one. This immediately raises in my mind the failures and successes for which I have been responsible. I have a perfect example of a book about which people were lukewarm turning out to be a great winner. There wasn't much hope in the office for a book called *The Story of San Michele*. We only printed about a thousand copies, so little did we think it would succeed. Then H.G. Wells reviewed it in the *Evening Standard* and said it was the most extraordinary book with plots that would keep a short-story writer happy for the rest of his writing life. From that moment it shot off, has been published in eighty-two translated foreign editions and has sold something like eight million copies.

Do you still get unsolicited books which turn out to be winners or are they mostly commissioned now?

It's increasingly rare that typescripts coming out of the blue are any good at all. If commissioned, they are mostly by authors we already know. I remember a long time ago, however, commissioning a fascinating book, thanks to Bernard Shaw. He had just met the Benedictine nuns at Stanbrook who were writing a book about the abbess, and he advised me to go down and see Dame Felicity. The Benedictines at that time had a double grille through which one had to speak. I arrived at the abbey, rang the bell, and the lay sister opened the door and asked me to follow her. She then turned to me and asked if I were accustomed to talking through a double grille. I told her I was not and that I was petrified. She said, 'Mr Murray, you needn't worry, it's not like them Carmelites what have spikes on their grilles.' For about two years we worked on the book. The manuscript had to be put in a drawer in the double grille which she pushed to me and I then made comments and pushed it back; I never saw her face. If it was autumn when I came there was always a little basket of plums in the double drawer for me to take home and if it was spring there was a little basket of eggs. It was a marvellous book and a good financial success. It told the story of the abbess, and the correspondence between Bernard Shaw and the abbess and Sidney Cockerell in which they communicate about death and religion. It became the play *The Best of Friends* with John Gielgud as Cockerell.

How well did you know Bernard Shaw?

I knew him very well. I cured his wife of lumbago. I prescribed hot cabbage water with salt and pepper to drink, twice a day. It never fails. I used to be a martyr before I was married. I lived upstairs in the flat and I sometimes couldn't get out of bed, and had to wait till the staff from the advertisement department rolled me off and put on my clothes. Then somebody told me about hot cabbage water which I still drink now.

But Shaw, what sort of a man was he?

I was fond of him, but ye gods, he was unpredictable. He could be more rude than anyone but Evelyn Waugh. He used to come to parties here and he was heartlessly rude. I remember we had an author called Mrs Campbell who told me her long-felt wish was to meet Bernard Shaw. So I took her up to introduce her. He pierced her with a steely, terrifying look and said, 'I only know one Mrs Campbell and you are not she,' and turned away. But if you were on the right side of him he could be very kind. Evelyn Waugh was rather similar. He had a terrible urge to shock people; he couldn't stop himself. I was never at ease with Evelyn. I was always afraid he would do something unpleasant to somebody I was with. He was never nasty to me, because I probably wasn't worth being nasty to, but funnily enough when he wasn't like that I was fond of him and of course I had infinite admiration for him. I know of no one except P.G. Wodehouse who had that marvellous literary skill of economy, who could describe a situation and a scene in the fewest words.

Which authors have you felt proudest to have published in your time?

Many come to mind. Apart from John Betjeman and Osbert Lancaster, Kenneth Clark played an important part in my life. As a result of my interest in architecture, I'd read *The Gothic Revival* which was a very early book he had written while still at university. I asked if we could reprint it and, because of that, we then published most of Kenneth Clarke's other books, including *Civilisation* with the BBC. I'm keen on that example because, going back to before my time, there is a precedent with Charles Darwin. John Murray Three had read his *Voyage of the Beagle* and was so impressed by it that when he heard that the publisher was remaindering copies, he wrote to Darwin to ask if he could buy up the rest of the edition. Darwin said he would be very pleased, though he thought it would be a harzardous undertaking since the book hadn't sold very well. Murray bought the sheets, rebound them and, treating it as though it were a new book, relaunched it. The whole lot was sold in a fortnight. He reprinted it, and from then on Darwin sent Murray all his books. There's a fascinating letter years later from Darwin saying: 'You very kindly said you'd publish my next book. It's not what I thought it was going to be, and I release you from your promise to publish.' Murray replied that he didn't want to be released – fortunately, as it happens, since the book was *The Origin of Species*. The curious fact about this story is that Darwin wrote to Murray exacting a promise that he would not print more than a thousand copies. Of course it went like a bomb. Now the question is, what were Darwin's motives in trying to restrict Murray? Did he honestly, kind man that he was, not want Murray to lose on it? Or was it that, although he wasn't a churchgoer, he was very reluctant to shake the religious views of other people? I think that's why he did it. Murray did finally persuade Darwin to let him reprint. And I wish I'd been there to hear the arguments that Murray gave.

I delighted in the Sherlock Holmes books, and in a way that was what first endeared me to authors. I was a schoolboy on my holidays and my grandfather was ill. He said, 'I think Sir Arthur Conan Doyle is calling today; will you be kind to him? I hope he may be bringing another typescript.' Conan Doyle brought the last volume of the Sherlock Holmes stories, and I was so staggered by this distinguished man's courtesy to a young whippersnapper like me that I thought: if this is an author, let me spend my life with authors.

People often remark that there is something very thirtiesish about you . . . the dress, tweeds and bow tie, the high brow, the longish hair and your debonair manner . . .

Who says that? By God I'll . . . I wish I could get hold of him . . . though it was probably a lady. I don't regard myself as being of any particular period because I am convinced that I'm not yet grown up. I don't relate to any age, in fact I forget my age. My physiotherapist used to quote the following:

> Man is not old when his teeth decay,
> Man is not old when his hair turns grey,

> But Man is approaching his last long sleep
> When his mind makes appointments his body cannot keep.

I sometimes still feel like a child and I'm sure there are many who feel the same. As a consequence one is appalled by one's ignorance of what's going on in the wide world and, indeed, of all the literature of the past and all the things of the past. One feels an ignorant child.

But do you feel with age a kind of serenity you probably didn't have twenty years ago?

No. I don't . . . perhaps after the fifth glass of claret I might possibly feel it.

Do you still find yourself excited at the sight of a very pretty woman?

Oh, yes. I dream about them. At one stage I thought it would help me to go to sleep, but I have discovered that it doesn't. One of the reasons I love going on the underground, the Northern Line to Hampstead, is because I'm fascinated by the different fashions. I'm particularly expert on the kind of bottoms that authors have. I'm amazed that Americans always have such big bottoms and I think bottoms can reveal almost more clearly the character of the person . . . well perhaps not more than the face, but the way people move their bottoms gives a strong indication. And of course the sexual impulse is still there. But, alas, no competence . . .

Do you have strong views about censorship?

I think censorship is right under certain circumstances, if you don't want to be unnecessarily cruel to people or their beliefs. My view is very unpopular, but I've held it all along.

Have you ever regretted being a publisher rather than an author?

No, largely because I know too well that I am not equipped to be a good author. I have tried to write, and I can't do it. I can rewrite other people, I can prune like anything, but I can't write.

Authors come with a great variety of personalities. Is there a sense in which you have to judge the man or the women as well as the work?

That's a splendid subject. In our editorial meetings, if somebody suggests a book, I always ask if the proposer has met the author. If not, I always say, 'Well, I would advise you not to put forward an agreement till you've seen him and you have talked with him, better still till you've eaten with him.' I think this is frightfully important.

Tell me about Byron.

When Byron died Hobhouse (his executor) said, 'Byron liked keeping his friends in hot water and it looks as though his remains will do much the same for his executors.' Of course this is true, but he had such a magnetic quality that John Murray Two bent over backwards to please him. His demands were excessive: when he was abroad he was always asking for Edinburgh powders, or racing dogs, indeed every kind of thing. In fact, if a new author came tomorrow and I had reason to believe that he would be as complicated as Byron, then unless his skill was very great, I think I'd turn him down. But Byron was Byron.

You have edited Byron's letters. What is it about him that attracts you above all?

His immediacy. Let me illustrate it with an anecdote. You will know that we burned Byron's memoirs in the fireplace where I used to warm myself as a child. Though I wasn't present there was embedded in me a seed of guilt. Many years later I thought the only way to make amends for burning Byron's memoirs was to publish, collect and edit his letters. So we started. We had a great many here because of course he wrote to Murray but also got a lot from Lady Dorchester. Peter Quennell and I would meet one night a fortnight here in this room to decide if they were autobiographical enough to qualify as being memoirs, and secondly whether they were unpublished. One night, Harold Nicholson was here, sitting in the armchair, and we were reading a long unpublished letter, a fascinating account of what Byron had been up to that day – a riveting letter – and at the end, it gave the date, a Friday in March 1813. Harold Nicholson sat up in his chair, slapped his knee, and said, 'So that's where he was on Friday night!' You see, that curious immediacy, the effect of our wanting to know every detail of Byron's life is very extraordinary. And it hits anybody who approaches him. We still have Byron's boots here. They came through Lady Dorchester who had a row with the Lovelace family and consequently left Byron's letters and many of his things to my grandfather. When the dust settles on his boots I clean them now and again and laugh at myself.

How would you most like to be remembered in the publishing world?

I suppose that I have been of some help in encouraging authors to create. I can't really think of anything else of lasting value.

If you were to live your life over again, what are the two things you would be unlikely to repeat?

I'm reasonably safe on that score. I've only done one thing that I feel any guilt about and I'm sorry I did it. From the point of view of my work, I can't think of anything that I would rather not have done; which is terribly dull. My main interest lies in the relationship between author and publisher. I was very pleased, for example, to discover a letter to Murray from an author who was a flop; he writes: 'Dear Murray. You are the only publisher at whose table an unsuccessful author can sit at ease.' Now isn't that a claim to fame?

Are you a gregarious character? I mean, is it possible for you to be seduced?

Oh I think so. Given the right circumstances, I'm eminently seducable.

Looking back, which period would you single out as being the happiest, most fulfilling, or the saddest of your life?

I suppose the happiest, most exciting in a way, was from about 1930 up to the war, because that was when I was meeting new people, new authors. The saddest was when my mother, of whom I was very fond, became utterly helpless. Then there was the recent sadness of going to see Freya

Stark; I published all her works and adored her, but when I went to see her last autumn in Italy, she hadn't the foggiest idea who I was. That I found almost unbearable.

People regard John Murray's almost as a dynasty. Indeed Albemarle Street is a kind of last outpost of ivory-tower imperialism. How has this affected your life? Do you feel yourself to be in charge of something sacred?

I like the word imperialism. For a firm that's been famous but never very big the word imperialism is very curious. It is sacred to the extent that it contains so much that is personal to so many authors who provided literature in this country. I regard myself as a custodian of all these things. We have all the early manuscripts and authors' letters dating from 1768. If American publishers are being really beastly to me I like mentioning to them that we were publishing books when they were still our colony.

Most people who count as oldies would claim to have learned some important lessons in life. What are the lessons you have learned?

I hardly dare give them to you, they're so awfully dull. Modesty, because it safeguards against disappointment. By modesty I mean keep your head down or it'll be chopped off. In so far as anyone can, try to develop a sense of humour, try and see the funny side of whatever it may be. And patience is vital, because then you don't waste whatever your endocrine glands provide. The one that infuriates my wife is thrift. She gets very upset and confuses it with meanness, which it is not. It's not wasting what you don't use, it's sending newspapers to be recycled. You can train yourself to be thrifty, yet never be mean. I turn out lights that are not being used, I try not to throw away food if it can be used. But on occasions, delicious occasions, a really good blow out is marvellous.

CONOR CRUISE O'BRIEN

Conor Cruise O'Brien was born in 1917 into a strongly nationalist Dublin family. He was an outstanding student at Trinity College, Dublin where he took a BA and PhD. His doctoral dissertation, later published as *Parnell and his Party* (1957), was a remarkable mingling of political analysis and literary insight. Between 1956 and 1960 he was a member of the Irish delegation to the UN. His book *To Katanga and Back* (1962), widely considered to be his finest work, is an autobiographical narrative of the Congo crisis of 1961 when he served in Katanga as representative to UN secretary general Dag Hammarskjöld. Following academic office in Ghana and New York, he was elected Irish Labour TD (MP) for Dublin in 1969, became minister for posts and telegraphs in 1973, and was defeated in 1977 because of his opposition to IRA violence in Northern Ireland. Between 1979 and 1981 he was editor-in-chief of the *Observer* and has been pro-chancellor of the University of Dublin since 1973.

You have said that in your youth you were more strongly drawn to the Protestant than to the Catholic ethos. Why was that?

The second school I attended was a Catholic convent school and I have unpleasant memories of the severities practised there, not actually by the nuns, but by some of the lay teachers. My recollections of Catholic teaching are of being told, this is how it is, repeat after me; it was all authoritarian. Then I went to my main school, and found that I was invited to discuss, to question, and I liked the atmosphere. What appealed to me was not Protestantism, but enlightenment, and I have related to it ever since.

This was a Protestant school?

It was a school attended in equal parts by Protestants, Jews and liberal Catholics, that is to say Catholic families who did not want their children to get a Catholic education for reasons which I later came to understand. I remember being confused on my first day there when the headmaster said that the Church of Ireland boys would stay for prayers. It never occurred to me that the Church of Ireland could be anything other than Catholicism and I knew our family were supposed to be Catholic so I stayed for prayers, and witnessed the horror of people kneeling on one knee only. But I got over that initial shock.

In 1916, the year before you were born, your uncle was killed by a British officer during the Easter Uprising. Your maternal grandfather had associations with the Irish Republican Brotherhood, forerunners of the IRA. To what extent has your family background helped shape your own attitudes?

One of my uncles who was married to my mother's elder sister, was shot on the orders, as you say, of a British officer in Easter week, 1916, but another uncle, just a little older than my mother, was killed in the autumn of that year in France, wearing the same uniform as that worn by the killer of the other uncle. Those two deaths are an integral part of my life. I spent a considerable part of my youth puzzling out what it all meant. I'm still not sure.

207

Do you have a strong sense of history in your present ideological position?

Yes, I'm an historian, partly by training but more and more by inclination. I find that almost everything I read now is history in some form or other.

Is not history largely a matter of interpretation?

Yes, but you wouldn't find any historians who would deny that a world war happened between 1914 and 1918. From then on they could start interpreting, but again it is a fact that one side lost and another won, and the consequences of that are there. The historian interprets, but there are great brute facts which he can't interpret away.

Your mother was a Catholic, your first wife was a Protestant, your daughter is married to the son of a Protestant archbishop. Your second wife is a practising Catholic, niece of a cardinal. Have these different threads confused your sense of your own identity, or have they clarified it?

That's a good question. All I know is that I am happy with the results, except that my first marriage broke up, and that's always a cause of sadness to all parties. But relations with my five children and with my second wife are excellent, and I have learned a lot from my wife about Catholicism. She has taught me to be more comfortable with it, but makes no effort to induce me to believe in it. Indeed, I think if I showed signs of believing in it she would deter me.

I understand that now you do not profess any religion. Is that simply a lack of faith or were you driven from the church in some way?

I was never really near enough to the church to be driven from it. My father was an agnostic, my mother indeed during my father's lifetime would have declared herself to be an agnostic, as would other members of the family. Though I don't think I ever believed any part of it, I had my first communion, I was confirmed. This, according to the teaching of the Roman Catholic Church makes you a Catholic, whether you say you are or not . . . I say I'm not, but if I were to meet a bishop, he would say, well you are. When I think back to my childhood I think of it as something dark and oppressive in the background, something that I was supposed to be part of but didn't ever wish to be any part of. I was a very priggish little boy, an only child who had spent most of his time with elders rather than contemporaries, and when a pious aunt presented me on my eighth birthday with a missal, I looked at this thing and said, 'Thank you Aunt Mary, it will relieve the tedium of the mass.' [Laughs.] That didn't go down terribly well.

Do you think you might mellow in years to come?

I have mellowed. Until 1977 . . . and that's sixty years . . . I was actively hostile to religion in general and most particularly to the Roman Catholic Church. After my father's death, my mother, acting at his request, sent me to the non-denominational school as it might now be called. I learned around that time that a contemporary of mine, who also belonged to a family of Catholic background, was taken away from the school because his mother had been warned by a priest that every day the boy stayed at that school lengthened her late husband's sufferings in purgatory. I believe my mother got similar advice, but the poor thing sweated it out, and kept me at that school though she was being mentally tortured by those people. So I didn't grow up with any feelings of kindness towards the Catholics. Then my wife in the late 1970s was involved in a very bad car accident; her right leg was broken in thirty-three places, she was in intensive care for quite a long time in a hospital in Ireland run by nuns, and their care for her and kindness to all of us was something really marvellous. When the recovery happened it was very much 'thank God', and something melted then. I ceased to have the hostility towards the religion that I had before. But that didn't incline me at all towards belief in any credo.

You have had academic appointments as well as political, administrative and diplomatic ones. What drew you to the universities?

A desire for knowledge, for instruction, for leisure in which to turn around and think, to meet other people interested in ideas; and I found all those. Most of my teaching has been done at various American universities, and I have enjoyed that. I found that American students start with absolutely nothing in the way of knowledge of the subject, but they learn prodigiously fast, and are very highly motivated and full of curiosity.

Most recently I was a research fellow at the Woodrow Wilson Centre in Washington DC, and I found it delightful actually to be paid for reading books which I would be doing anyway.

The universities are currently in turmoil. What do you think their function ought to be in the late twentieth century? Has Cardinal Newman's 'idea of a university' been superseded?

All kinds of things are going on in the universities. There is, as we all know, the multi-cultural agenda which in broad outline I dislike. The idea of the politically correct is obnoxious to me, but I did have a curious experience in that regard. When I went out to the Wilson Centre I said I would like to work on the phenomenon of the multi cultural, the politically correct, and of course race studies and gender studies are part of that. This was during the period of the Senate hearings over Clarence Thomas and Anita Hill's accusations against him. This was a strange happening, because within that agenda, race studies and gender studies people have been allies, but here the black rights people and the women's rights people were opposed. A poll showed that sixty-seven per cent of blacks were for Clarence Thomas, whereas all feminists of whatever colour were for Anita Hill. This prompted me to read black feminist writings. I had expected – and I'm not proud of myself for having expected – to find a great deal that would be propagandist and attitudinizing. To my surprise and delight I found a very considerable body of valid and splendid historical writing by black women thinking about the past of other black women, not to make some propaganda point, but to find out. I also found that the alliance in gender studies and race studies is essentially based on white feminists and black rights people, males mostly, zeroing in on the white male. It is manichean stuff and the white male is the arch enemy, but the black feminists are aware that white women can be racist and that black males can be sexist, and this gives it a richness and a maturity that the other lot don't have.

In view of the turmoil which appears to be typical of sub-Saharan Africa, do you have any sympathy at all with the South African whites and their dilemma? If they prevent majority rule they are anti-democratic . . . if they permit it they may be completely overwhelmed.

I certainly have a lot of sympathy with many white people there, especially the Afrikaaners. De Klerk is working on the right lines; he is not about to give in to the ANC, but is looking for a power-sharing formula in which the whites would still have considerable power. It now looks as if Mandela is prepared to go down that road, which means on his part a sizeable compromise. I think the ANC as we know it is about to split, and what you will have will be a coalition of all those, white or black, who have anything to lose. It is basically the people on the outside who are going to be unemployed. This is not an exhilarating prospect, but it's better than the apartheid state. I'm politically now fairly optimistic, but the demographic and social and economic realities are absolutely horrendous. Anyone you talk to in South Africa is more likely to be talking about crime than about poverty; if you're a young black and can't get a job, crime is your only career.

I believe you visited South Africa three years ago and in Capetown you were forced to leave the platform by anti-apartheid demonstrators. What exactly happened there?

I'll tell you exactly what happened. In 1986 the World Archaeological Congress was held in Southampton, and scholars from every country in the world were invited, including South Africa which has one of the richest schools of archaeology. Then, under pressure from the ANC and the academic left in Britain, the South African scholars were disinvited; they were told they were not wanted here, not because of any flaw in their scholarship but on account of their South African nationality, although these scholars were actually from universities like Cape Town which were desegregated. This struck me, as it struck a number of other academics, as a dreadful thing to do. So I protested against it. Then, having been invited to give a course of lectures at the University of Capetown, I publicly announced that I was accepting, thus breaking the academic boycott of South Africa. I was to give a course of fifteen lectures. In the beginning there was no serious trouble, then I was invited to a debate on the subject of the cultural boycott. Naïvely I accepted, thinking a debate was a debate. When I arrived in the hall there was nobody on the other side of the debate, and although I insisted on making an initial statement, the evening consisted mainly of hostile questioning. The first question was, 'Why did you come here to South Africa – was it to mock the sufferings of the oppressed people?' That was just a foretaste of what was to come the following night when I gave a public lecture about the Middle East and Israel. There was quite an audience, mainly Jews from off-campus, but the same crowd gathered outside in the corridors around the lecture hall and chanted slogans just when questions had started from the audience; I was most edified by my Jewish audience who went on as if nothing had happened. They thought, wrongly, that this was an anti-Semitic demonstration, but it was actually part of the cultural boycott. The audience remained attentive until the mob broke down the doors and surged in and drove us all out. When I met my regular class in the morning, a class of about a hundred people who were racially distributed as in the general population of the University of Capetown – about fifteen per cent black students, the rest white – again the mob broke down the door. The vice chancellor, Stuart Saunders, rang me later that day to say that if I tried to give the remaining lectures there was a danger of much more serious violence, so I had to call them off. The impression it left on my mind was that I wouldn't like to be in a South Africa that was run by the ANC. I wouldn't mind a government of which the ANC was part, but not in control.

So there was no hostility directed against you personally – it was simply as a result of the boycott?

Yes. Of course, they subsequently claimed that I had treated them in an intolerably patronizing manner, but in those circumstances you either bow down or you are accused of being insufferably patronizing. On the whole I'd rather be accused of being insufferably patronizing.

You were devoted to the whole concept of the United Nations. What was it that attracted you to the UN?

To enter the United Nations for the Republic of Ireland; we were admitted in 1955 and took our seats in the General Assembly in 1956. It was like returning to the world, because Ireland had been neutral in the Second World War and, understandably, rather cold-shouldered by the victors. We had been vetoed by the Soviet Union for membership of the United Nations for which we had applied as soon as it was set up, and it had been a pretty claustrophobic existence before that.

Katanga was described by Brian Urquhart as 'the most frustrating, nerve-racking and isolated of all the UN posts in the Congo'. Did you feel honoured to have been chosen by Hammarskjöld for the job or did you think you were being exiled?

Katanga was the great challenge to the United Nations at that time. I did feel honoured, and I knew it was a high-risk post and also that it was for that post I had been chosen. Formally the request to the Irish government was to second me for service in the political and security council affairs department in New York, but I always knew I would be sent to the Congo. And I had no sense of being isolated or banished or anything of the sort.

You had been selected by Hammarskjöld for your qualities of courage, independence of mind and spirit, as a radical young man who would be able to put Hammarskjöld's own ideas into practice. You for your part admired him equally. This mutual high regard must surely have made the break all the more painful when it came?

Yes, it was very painful indeed. Your summary is correct, but I'd like to add an element or two to it. This is the background to why I was appointed to go to Katanga: in January 1961, Mnongo, then minister of the interior of the so-called independent state of Katanga, announced the death of Patrice Lamumba, the prime minister of the Congo. Mnongo said that he had escaped from captivity in Elisabethville and had been killed by some villagers angered by his bad behaviour. But the whole world believed that Lamumba was actually murdered by the government of Katanga, specifically by Mnongo himself. There was outrage throughout the world, in the third world in particular, and also among American blacks. The United Nations and Hammarskjöld in particular were being blamed, with – though I didn't know it at the time – a good deal of substance, because Hammarskjöld's instructions to the UN forces who controlled all the airports at the time were not to intervene between Mr Lamumba and his official pursuers. This meant that with United Nations troops looking on he was handed over in Elisabethville to be murdered. The revulsion that followed this caused the United Nations, and Hammarskjöld in particular, to change course. My instructions were to try and bring the secession to an end. He picked me for that because the Irish delegation of which I was part had an anti-colonialist record. Also he wanted someone who was not part of the communist bloc, or African, or Asian, and not part of the Western alliance either; and I had those qualifications. But the break with him was a very grim thing. The first I knew of it, that I had lost contact with Hammarskjöld, occurred in this way. We had moved to arrest Tshombe and his ministers (Tshombe had been helped to escape by the British) but whether Hammarskjöld knew exactly what we were going to do or not, I don't know. He certainly knew what we had done because it was reported to him, and he issued a statement in Leopoldville in which he represented Tshombe's people as having been the aggressors, which they were not; we were. But he gave the impression of the United Nations being peacefully engaged until fired on by Tshombe's lot. Of course, the meaning of that was that Tshombe could have a ceasefire any time he wanted. The legs were cut from under us. I'll never forget the reading of that dispatch.

I know it's going back a long way, but how would you sum up what went wrong in the Congo? A lot of people say that you were going to be sacked by Hammarskjöld, had he not been killed. Is there any truth in that?

I think so. Once he nullified what I had done, he couldn't live with me. He would certainly have got rid of me.

How much did your personal affairs contribute to your resignation? There must have been enormous pressure on you from the press, given that you were living, not with your wife, but with the daughter of a cabinet minister.

That was raked up, but the decision had already been taken on political grounds because I had become identified with a policy that had not worked and had to be repudiated. It was, incidentally, a policy to which they reverted after I went, because they did use force to end the secession of Katanga, partly because they were embarrassed by what I had revealed. My wife's presence in the Congo then became a convenient way of notifying my government that I would have to be withdrawn.

What are the practical limitations of the United Nations as an organization?

I think one has to distinguish between the United Nations when there is consensus among the permanent members, and when there isn't. For most of the existence of the United Nations there was no consensus. For example, when I was in the Congo only one of the permanent members supported the secretary general in what he was doing. The Soviet Union openly opposed, Britain and France covertly opposed, so that's the context in which I and Hammarskjöld had to work at that time. No wonder it became a bit crazy. But then of course in the late 1980s, towards the end of the Iran-Iraq war, five-power consensus emerged. The secretary general in his mission to Baghdad and Teheran was backed by the embassies of all the five super powers, a blissful condition which I had never thought to live to see. That five-power consensus is still there, though there is of course uncertainty as to whether it can be preserved. Nobody knows what's going to happen in Russia.

But do you think it's a good thing for the super powers to dominate the United Nations?

There is only one super power, and it dominates; that is a fact of life. But there is a qualification to it; the United States likes to get the blessing of the security council on what it is about to do. It was the United States who determined that a war should be fought over Kuwait . . . nobody else. But the fact that they need to get the agreement of other powers is welcome as a limiting factor. If for example the United States at the time of the Vietnam War had needed to get consensus in the security council, I don't think it would have got it.

You were once interested in Yeats' relation to the ideas of Nietzsche. Was Yeats in any real sense a fascist?

No, he wasn't; he was a person who in certain moods was attracted to fascism. He was attracted in the 1930s when the Blueshirts – I won't say emerged – but limped out in Ireland, imitating the paraphernalia of Mussolini and Hitler. They were never really a very formidable lot – they never killed anybody for instance. In 1938, the last full year of his life, his poetry is more seriously fascist. He wrote, 'You that Mitchel's prayer have heard, Send war in our time, O Lord.' The poetry of that time is certainly attracted towards Nazi Germany; it never fully flowered, but that's where it was all tending in the last few years. Yeats felt the pull of violence, and violence attracts the imagination. He was a sort of heat-seeking missile.

A lot of politicians were also attracted to Nazi Germany at the beginning

There was something very powerful and attractive about success after success from 1935 onwards. Everyone's eyes were riveted on what was happening there and a lot of lesser politicians hitched their wagon to that, to their later regret.

You are known in some nationalist quarters as the fascist of the left. How do you react to that?

First of all, I laugh at the said nationalists using fascist as a term of abuse, because during the Second World War the IRA was pro-Hitler. Their chief of staff went to Berlin and they were trying to liberate Ireland with the aid of the Nazis, so when they call me a fascist I ask them, who do they think they're kidding?

But is there anything you might have done that could label you as a fascist of the left?

Yes. And not so much of the left either. I am in favour of the introduction of internment of the para-military godfathers on both sides of the border in Ireland, and the IRA in opposing that would of course have liberal allies.

For a long time you have been pro-Israel and anti-Arab, and have been especially vitriolic about the Palestinians. How did you come to adopt this position?

I would like you to quote – if you can – anything vitriolic I have ever said about the Palestinians, or indeed any Arabs. I have never attacked them. What I have said is that I don't think it is possible for Israel to obtain peace with the Arabs by handing over territory. There will always be, and for quite understandable reasons, a great many Arabs who don't want peace with Israel except on the basis of the destruction of Israel. That is not true of the people who are at present negotiating with them on behalf of the Palestinians, but there are other Arabs out there who will not give Israel peace on the grounds of anything that could be negotiated by the Palestinians.

Wouldn't you acknowledge that there are people on the Israeli side who are equally extreme, if not worse?

This is part of my case. This is why territory for peace is not possible either on the Arab side or on the Israeli side. If, for example, a government in Israel were to say that the Palestinians can have the West Bank and Gaza, that they can set up their state there, and the settlers will be withdrawn, that would mean civil war in Israel.

But one has to acknowledge that there will be no peace ever unless there is a compromise on both sides. Whereas in the old days one could have accused the Arabs of intransigence, today the intransigence seems to come more from the Israelis. The majority of Palestinians want peace, and your stand on the issue, if I may say so, does not help the cause of peace.

You're quite right in that the Palestinians in negotiating on the basis of autonomy have come a long way; they have come to it in the terms of Shamir's own offer. I regret that he now seems to be backing away from what he offered, and as you say that is an unreasonably instransigent position.

Let's talk some more about this. I have the impression from reading articles you have written that you are very pro-Israeli. Presumably you don't deny that Begin and the Irgun gang modelled themselves on the IRA of Michael Collins?

Indeed, Shamir's own clandestine name, Michael, is after Michael Collins.

Since you are opposed to the IRA, how do you reconcile the two positions in your own mind?

217

The IRA of 1919–21 were acting at least nominally under democratic authority; they were the armed forces of the First Dáil which was an elected body representing in free elections the majority of the Irish people. The modern IRA since 1922 has no democratic mandate at all from anyone; they are an unlicensed body of terrorists.

But Begin and the Irgun were themselves terrorists at the time. In one way you seem to oppose terrorism, in another way you don't condemn it.

Essentially the Zionist movement has its roots in Europe and is an outgrowth of the European history that produced Nazism. Chaim Weizmann said in 1921: 'We must have Palestine if we are not going to be exterminated.' That seemed a very extreme and bizarre thing to say in 1921 but by 1933 it was not. And the degree of sympathy I have for Israel is based on the realization that Israel is the result of horrendously extreme conditions. That is why I write as I do. It's an emotional issue with me.

But what about the poor Palestinians? They weren't responsible for the Nazi atrocities?

No, they were not, and they have suffered as a result of the Nazi atrocities. But they haven't suffered quite as much as the Jews. Of course, nothing that one can say or do will make amends to any of those who have suffered, either among the Jews or among the Palestinians. But one has to look at the here and now and see the best that is actually available. I have a high regard for the present negotiators on the Palestinian side, I think they are very brave people, but there are high risks, especially if they succeed. I wish that Shamir would meet them halfway. Palestinians are not at present demanding territory; what they are asking at the moment is autonomy, and I would hope that they get it.

Most Israelis recognize that the 1982 invasion of Lebanon was a terrible mistake, yet you defended it strongly at the time. Would you now agree you were wrong?

I didn't defend it strongly at the time. I merely went against some of the denunciations of Israel that were going on at the time. I defended it to this extent, and would still defend it; the PLO on the soil of Lebanon were claiming to be carrying on a war against Israel, and they had their vast heavily armed encampments there for the destruction of Israel; I put the point that if in the Republic of Ireland you had a similar situation with the IRA, legal and condoned by Dublin, carrying on bombings of Britain from the Republic, British intervention in the Republic would be the probable outcome and would be rather generally accepted. That is the parallel I drew. That was regarded as outrageous.

I regard it as outrageous. Shall I tell you why?

Am I interviewing you or are you interviewing me?

You are being interviewed, but I wanted to pick up on your reference to the destruction of Israel. Nobody can destroy Israel today; the world would not allow it.

Under certain conditions the destruction of Israel could indeed occur. For example, if as a result of an attempt at peacemaking the people of Israel should be divided to the point of civil war; that would be the end of Israel. There are great divisions in Israeli society, there's no doubt about that.

One more question about Israel before we drop the subject. You are known as a vocal champion of Israel, perhaps an uncritical one . . .

Not true. You wish to *portray* me as uncritical.

Not at all. It seems almost a case of 'My country right or wrong.' Whereas there might have been a case for supporting the state of Israel to begin with, what do you say about Israel's treatment of the Palestinians – well documented by Amnesty and Israel's own human rights organization?

The Israelis are in occupation of a territory whose inhabitants reject them and resist them. And these things happen under those conditions. I wish that Israel could withdraw from the territories it occupies. I find it difficult to see that it can, for reasons which I have set out analytically and

219

not emotionally. The treatment of the populations of the West Bank and Gaza is based on the laws, regulations and practices with which Britain governed all of Palestine, under the mandate. The military regulations are there; they are the British ones.

But you were always anti-colonial . . .

Yes . . . all right . . .

I'd like to ask a question in a different area now. There is a great deal of talk and a lot of effort to suppress the idea of freedom of information. You have been a member of government – did you feel the need to keep the public in the dark as far as possible?

I don't recall keeping the public in the dark about anything in particular. In this domain I am blamed for being the author of the legislation currently in force which prevents spokesmen for the IRA and other para-militaries from broadcasting; and there are those who hold that this is a limitation on freedom of information. I defend it on the grounds that all broadcasting codes prohibit incitement to crime, that terrorist violence is of its nature criminal, and that the spokesmen in question have no other purpose than to promote this criminal conspiracy.

During your time as minister for post and telegraphs, it has been suggested by some that you will be remembered chiefly for attempts to censor and control RTE. Is that an unfair assessment?

I would accept it to this extent: that if prohibition of broadcast interviews with spokesmen for terrorist organizations is censorship, then I am a censor. Beyond that not at all, never one step beyond it. While I was minister and responsible for broadcasting, the RTE regularly ran a series of satirical broadcasts about the government of which I was part, including pieces about myself. They ran it every week, for two years I believe; it was still running when my government fell. I don't think that's censorship exactly.

Mary Holland recalls that when she went to work for RTE in the mid-1970s people were 'quite simply frightened out of their minds'. Were you aware of that at the time?

Utterly ridiculous. Nobody was ever frightened out of his mind at RTE, nobody at all. They were frightened under Mr Haughey because he intervened regularly; whenever he objected to a programme, he was on the line. We never interfered with RTE at all.

Yet Mary Holland described the atmosphere as follows: 'Self-censorship had been raised to the level of an art and caution lay like a thick cloud over everything.' Do you accept that it was like that or at least appeared to others in that way?

I think it appeared to Mary Holland like that, but it's a ridiculous portrayal. I don't think you'd find anyone in Dublin to agree except Mary Holland and some Republican sympathizers.

In an interview with Bernard Nossiter of the New York Times *you attacked the* Irish Press *and said that you were collecting clippings printed in the paper with a view to having the editor, Tim Pat Coogan, arrested on the grounds that the letters supported Sinn Fein. The interview was duly published in the* Irish Press *and it was suggested that only the ensuing public outcry prevented you from putting your plan into practice. How do you defend your position on this issue?*

It's not true that I suggested that Tim Pat Coogan should be arrested; I didn't. I simply showed Bernard Nossiter certain letters that they had published which amounted to incitement to violence.

In 1978 you left politics and became editor-in-chief of the Observer. *Why did you do that?*

Because it was an attractive thing to be asked to do. I had been writing for the *Observer* on and off for a good many years. I was invited by Lord Goodman to meet with him and the new proprietors of the *Observer*, and then they offered me the post of editor-in-chief of the newspaper which I was happy to accept.

There is speculation among your opponents that you got the job at the Observer *because of a possible connection with the British Intelligence Service. Do you find this an absurd idea?*

Are my opponents the IRA? I imagine they are, since nobody except the IRA has its spokesmen talk like that. I have never had any connection whatsoever with British Intelligence or any other intelligence organization . . .

But have you ever heard it mentioned before?

I've seen it chalked on walls by the IRA, but I won't dignify it by further discussion.

During your time at the Observer *there were suggestions that you used your editorial powers to censor articles on Ireland, notably from Mary Holland. What do you say to that?*

An editor *is* a kind of censor. You decide what goes in and what goes out, and if you don't like things you want them to go out. Mary Holland wrote a piece during one of these IRA strikes, a tear-jerking thing about the dependents of the people who were on the dirty strike, and the whole article was an IRA sympathy kneejerk performance which appeared in the *Observer* magazine, not something that normally engaged my attention. When I saw it I naturally complained about it to the editor, but it was too late to stop it. I certainly did create when I saw it, and Mary would of course have seen it as censorship.

Do you think any sort of reconciliation is possible between Rome and Canterbury? I recall you speaking of the Pope's missionary attitude towards Protestantism. The two positions do seem to be hopelessly intransigent.

When the present Pope talks about the unity of the Christian churches, he means unity under him and according to his laws, and if I were an Anglican I wouldn't be too keen about being incorporated into all that; but that's their business. I'm neither an Anglican, nor a Roman. I wish the Pope well.

You were one of those who were instrumental in deleting from the constitution the reference to the special position of the Catholic Church in Ireland. How powerful does the church remain in Ireland?

The results of two referenda would suggest that the church still does have a lot of authority. They defeated the referendum which would have made divorce legislation possible in Ireland, and they succeeded, most ironically, in inserting the provision which appeared to make abortion illegal in all circumstances but is now found actually to have legalized abortion in certain circumstances; so they really shot themselves in the foot over that one. Their authority is now less than it used to be, even considerably less, despite the results of those referenda, for the real test of authority is on the matter of contraception. The teaching of the church is still implacably against artificial contraception, and yet it is quite clear that married Catholics are using contraceptives – the reproduction patterns are the same as those of other groups – so the teaching of the church in a centrally vital matter has gone. Also the public reaction to the original court decision in the rape-victim case was quite negative in relation to the church. You may have seen a piece of mine in *The Times*, an open letter to the Catholic bishops. That letter in a more extended form appeared in the *Irish Independent*, the largest circulating newspaper among Irish Catholics. The fact that such a letter could appear there is a sign of the times.

Yet last year in an interview you described abortion as 'a great evil' . . .

My point about abortion is that it is an evil always, but there are a number of cases in which it is a lesser evil.

How long do you think the Catholic Church will be able to hold out against letting their clergy marry, with all the ramifications of providing for widows and children and housing and pensions and divorce and remarriage and the whole secular round? Do you think it will come eventually?

I don't know. The convention of celibacy is so long established that the rule won't go unless there is such a shortage of clergy that they make the concession. I would certainly wish to see celibacy at an end. It is a bit sick to have celibate males deciding how other people should behave in bed. In fact it's disgusting.

In an article in the Observer *written twenty years ago you said that socially you belonged to the Irish Catholic community, that you were motivated by affection for it, identification with it, and a fear that it might destroy itself and you through infatuation with its own mythology. Twenty years on do you still believe that, and is it any closer to destroying you?*

I feel more relaxed about it than I would have then because the power and authority of the Catholic Church have been eroded. It doesn't inspire the same amount of fear and therefore revulsion that it used to when I was younger.

The trouble in Ireland is always put down to the differences between Catholics and Protestants, but how true do you think that is? Some of the IRA appear to be extreme left-wing revolutionaries who have only the most tenuous connection with Catholicism.

I don't think that's true. Indeed if you look at the times when emotions have been greatly raised, for example during the hunger strikes when men died, you wouldn't have seen too many volumes of *Das Kapital* around, but you saw the missal, the rosary beads, the holy water, all the paraphernalia of Roman Catholicism. Catholic Ireland was there; the Marxist stuff was very much top dressing. There is a story that illustrates this in the foundation of the Provos. There was a time before the split in the IRA, when the leadership was Marxist, and in that period, the late thirties, they were trying to detach the IRA from anything that would identify them with Catholicism. They sent a circular saying a decade of the rosary at the funeral of any given IRA volunteer was to be discontinued, but eight battalion commanders sent it back with the word that they were not going to obey. Those eight battalion commanders were later the founders of the Provisional IRA, so the good Catholic boys are the core of the Provos. For that reason the Catholic clergy in Belfast encouraged the emergence of the Provisional IRA because they thought it meant saying goodbye to those bad communists who had been in charge. And of course by bringing about a purely Catholic and Nationalist IRA which fitted much more naturally into the scene than the old Marxist stuff did, they produced in fact a more dangerous strain of the virus. To do them justice they didn't foresee the lengths to which the Provisional IRA would go, and I think those of them who are still around now regret what they did in 1969.

Do you think the Anglo-Irish Agreement can ever do any good? It seems so obvious that whatever the political talk about guarding the rights of the majority, it does put Northern Ireland into a quite different category from the rest of the United Kingdom – because of deep-rooted historical differences.

As long as the majority of the population in Northern Ireland want to remain in the United Kingdom they should be allowed to do so, and we should leave them alone and stop trying to nudge them in the other direction. By nudging them we appear to be partners with the IRA. When I say 'we' I mean the government. The historical differences and the differences in political allegiance are there, but you can't argue the population of Northern Ireland out of existence, nor can you induce people who fundamentally disagree, to agree. It is therefore an inherently unpleasant and enduring situation.

But do you see there ever being a solution to it?

I think it could be ameliorated. One thing that would have a positive effect would be for the Republic of Ireland to amend articles 2 and 3 of its constitution, which lay claim to the territory of Northern Ireland. This claim is very offensive to a majority of the people there. I won't say that would change everything overnight; it would just reduce the temperature a little.

In 1972 you sketched two possible models for the Irish future, the 'benign' and the 'malignant'. What you said then has turned out to be largely true. Twenty years on, are there any new models?

I'm afraid not. As long as the British stay, you'll have the IRA and in turn the Protestant para-military response to the IRA. But if Britain goes you'll have full-scale civil war. That's my malignant model, and I still believe in it.

Do you enjoy popularity in Ireland?

When I walk down O'Connell Street, for example, I'm likely to be stopped four or five times by somebody who wants to talk to me, and those people are invariably friendly. That's not to say that there aren't other people who recognize me and cross to the other side of the street. Let's say I never feel uncomfortable in the parts of Ireland I do walk around in. I wouldn't go to South Armagh, or Anderson's Town, places which are the IRA turf, but I would regard myself as popular with everybody except people who are pro-IRA or very traditional Catholics.

I hope you don't find this offensive, but a lot of people say you're a British stooge, and I wonder how you react to that?

For 'a lot of people', read the IRA and *their* stooges, some of whom you have clearly been talking to. Give them my regards.

People have seen a parallel between you and Paul Johnson – both intelligent journalists, and initially socialists who have become increasingly right-wing.

I can understand that. We're also both pro-Israel. Paul would probably be to the right of me, but otherwise there's a parallel, certainly one that I would not resent.

You are known to be a very good family man. Has the experience of adopting two-half African children been a rewarding one?

Richly rewarding. This is one thing I'm extremely happy about, because there is a close and loving relationship, not merely between my wife and myself and those two children, but also between the three children by my first marriage, and the two young adopted ones. That is a great joy.

Why have you spent so much time out of Ireland? Do you prefer to live somewhere else?

Ireland is the place where I like to live, but I couldn't bear living in it if I couldn't get out of it often and for long periods. As it happens I have never spent an entire year in all my long life outside Ireland.

ENOCH POWELL

Enoch Powell was born in 1912 and educated at King Edwards, Birmingham, and at Trinity College, Cambridge. He was a fellow of Trinity from 1934–8, and was appointed professor of Greek at the University of Sydney. In 1939 he returned to England to enlist as a private in the Royal Warwickshire Regiment, was commissioned in 1940 and rose to the rank of brigadier in 1944. He joined the Conservative Party in 1946 and entered parliament in 1950 as MP for Wolverhampton. Because of his opposition to the Common Market he did not stand for election in 1974, but returned to parliament in October of that year as an Ulster Unionist until he was defeated in the 1987 general election. He married in 1952 and has two daughters.

You were a very precocious scholar, both at school and at university. Was there a price to pay for all that solitary dedication?

I think one has to examine the term 'precocious'. I was not precocious in the sense that I was enormously in advance of the year of birth to which I belonged. It is a handicap to be too far ahead of your contemporaries, and I doubt if I actually was. I was probably put in a form of an average age a year older than mine, but no more than that. Precocity is therefore an idea to be handled very gently in this context.

You said of your early days that what drove you was the urge to 'rise'. What was it to rise in your sense?

My father used to say to me that if I were not a teacher that would be contrary to the laws of biology because both he and my mother were teachers. My father always said that the great thing in life was to write and speak good English. The nature of attainment as it presented itself to me in the first two decades of my life was therefore academic.

But was it something you wanted or were you driven to it?

I was not driven. I have no sense of having been physically or mentally pushed, but the implication of the environment was that there was no point in education unless one was academically successful.

In retrospect, who do you think was more influential in your life? Your mother or your father?

I think it was my mother, whom I remember describing, in the preface to a book published in the 1940s, as my first teacher and certainly my first Greek teacher. But it was a household in which learning was respected and the prizes in life were prizes to be won mentally.

You have often been described as a puritan, which is a word sometimes used unkindly. Is it a label that offends, or do you think of it as a badge of honour?

231

I think of it as a severe inaccuracy. After all, I am a high churchman in the Church of England and how a high churchman can be a puritan I do not understand, because puritan and Anglican are incompatible terms. A puritan is distinct from and opposed to an Anglican. Which is why the attempt was made by William III in 1689 to find a *via media* between the Church of England and the puritans. All those characteristics which predispose a man to be comfortable and find his natural niche in the higher end of the Church of England are incompatible with puritanism.

You are using puritan in the intellectual sense. But it is a term also commonly used to mean someone who is offended by sex.

I think the word 'squeamish' is perhaps eluding us here. I'm certainly not that, and if puritan is used in the sense of squeamish I disavow the description. There is no subject to which the human mind cannot properly be applied.

People constantly use the word austere in reference to you. Would you accept their judgement as appropriate?

Here again the word is used in a narrowed sense. Presumably it's intended to describe a person who does not find life primarily and self-evidently enjoyable. Well, I enjoy life; life without enjoyment would be intolerable. Indeed, sometimes when I'm asked what I have been doing for thirty-eight years in the House of Commons, I am disposed to reply that I have been enjoying myself. I don't think that comes under the heading of austerity.

There seems to have been a marked reluctance on your part to take up the academic life. You said you felt a sense of enclosure when you passed in under Trinity Gate. Why did you persevere if that was the case?

I didn't persevere. I tried to escape from Cambridge and eventually succeeded. From the time that I became a fellow of Trinity I sought appointment as a professor of classics or of Greek at any university which had a vacancy and when one occurred at Sydney and I was appointed to it I accepted it. But all through those years I was quite certain that this was a very brief temporary phase, which would be terminated by the coming of a war. This notion was derived from my observation and knowledge of what was going on in Germany and Italy. I had close connections with contemporary scholars in both those countries, so that I was aware of the rising threat which I perceived as a threat to the independence and self-government of the United Kingdom, and which I believed would have terminated sooner in hostilities than it actually did. If you're interested in one of the reflections upon life from an older person's standpoint, one of the things which has surprised me most is that events take longer to happen than one would have supposed. One can be sure that there will be war, but one thinks it will come sooner. The causes are there but the causes are not necessarily effective at the earliest possible time. I've always under-estimated the speed with which things can happen and the promptitude with which the foreseeable can occur. I'll enlarge on that if you like.

Please do.

It has been one of the experiences of recent years that after eighteen years of trying to make people understand what was being done to this country by European unity, what they were losing and what they were being asked to sacrifice, I've observed that at last they have woken up to its importance. I wouldn't have thought it would have taken so long, but I was mistaken; my fellow countrymen had only one eye half open. They did know, and they show signs now of remembering that they were told. So I think if I were advising my younger self I would say: you must not suppose that because saltpetre, charcoal and sulphur cause an explosion, they will cause an explosion now. There has to be a set of special circumstances arising before that explosion occurs, so do not imagine because you can trace the causes of events, because events are predictable, that they are imminent. From this I would engage in another reflection; which is that one of the great laws of life is patience. Do not imagine that because such and such a thing is ripe to happen it's going to happen immediately. You may have to spend a long time waiting for it to happen, but if you are right the world will come to meet you. If you are wrong, then you don't matter. That might almost be written up as the favourite adage of my declining years.

Your inaugural lecture in 1938 showed you conscious even then of the difficulties which attended maintaining Greek as a central part of higher education. Do you think that the battle is still capable of being won, and does it matter all that much anyway?

All battles are capable of being won, even the most apparently hopeless battles. In the mid 1920s it was the received wisdom that classical education was on its way out, and I remember the revival of classical studies which took place in the late 1920s and in the 1930s. There is a natural predisposition amongst people who belong to Western culture to be inquisitive about the Greeks and when you show them what Plato said, or what Jesus said, they say, let me get at it. People will not be indefinitely content to be held at arm's length from that which is ultimately intelligible or appreciable only in Greek. So long as Greek thought is immortal, Greek studies will be immortal, because people will not submit to being estranged from the source of that thinking.

In your collected poems you recall, without being able fully to recover, what you called the 'compulsions' under which they were written. Did you ever think of yourself writing poetry in the consciously public classical manner or was it restricted to a more self-absorbed romanticism?

Self-absorbed romanticism is a rather cruel but not entirely inaccurate expression. I wrote poetry when I had to write it, in obedience to an emotional compulsion, as a form of self-expression. Of course I was aware that I was using form, that I was entering into a tradition. Nevertheless, the necessity to do so was internal; it was not an exercise, it was not a chosen activity. In fact I was liable to write a poem in the most adverse circumstances, on the back of an envelope in a train.

Were you at all sympathetic to the modernist tradition which was being established while you were growing up? Were you able to share Eliot and Pound's sense of a need to break from an older tradition?

I'm afraid I was absorbed in what you describe as the older tradition, and Tennyson and Milton were the principal fountains from which I drank.

Have you written poems which remain unpublished?

I suppose all poets have. 'Ev'n copious Dryden wanted, or forgot, /The last and greatest art, the art to blot' – that's somewhere in Pope, isn't it? The art to blot is part of the art of writing poetry, and the knowledge that you must scrap a poem is a sign that you may be trusted at any rate.

I have heard that you have written poems to your wife which remain unpublished. Is that correct?

I write one poem a year on our marriage anniversary and I have been guilty of jocularly saying that this is a part of my wife's pension. I give her a rose for each year we have been married and a poem, sometimes referring to the number of roses, sometimes not. And I can imagine a book being published one day with a reproduction of a print of a rose on one page and on the other side the serial poem for the year.

Philosophers and even historians, like Lola Martinez, now think of poetry as a valuable source of evidence. When you write poetry do you think of it as a way of exploring or as a way of persuading? Is it cognitive in some way, do you think?

It's communicative, that is certain. A painter wishes to exhibit the landscape which he has painted because he has seen something which he thinks his fellows may not have seen. Similarly a poet says, here, listen, that's what I felt. The perception brings with it an urge to communicate. We are after all a herd animal and communicating our perceptions is bred deeply into humanity. This has a political application. As a politician I sometimes used to be asked: How do you go about your business? And I used to say it was rather like Luther in his Reformation hymn: "I hear the nightingale in the dark hedge, the dawn is coming . . ." that is to say, I sing in the hedge to my fellowcountrymen in case the song I want to sing is a song which they also want to hear. But there is a compulsion to sing it and see if somebody else will react to it; it's part of the communication mechanism of homo sapiens. Homer knew that he would have an audience – perhaps he didn't know how large it would be – but if no audience had been conceivable, he would not have sung.

Why do you find it so hard to believe that Shakespeare wrote the plays and poems attributed to him? So far no one has been able to establish that he was not the author.

I find the whole chronology from the earliest quartos right through to the publication of the first folio in 1623 or 1624 highly suspicious. Here are works, some of the earliest of which are the most mature, which appear in unofficial editions in the 1590s, then suddenly in the 1600s this flow is interrupted, with one exception, which is *Troilus and Cressida* in 1609. Then in 1623 we have a volume which contains some of the greatest plays, which have not only never been published before but of which there is no trace of a performance. How do we reconcile this with the biography of an individual who undoubtedly existed (because we must believe the parish records in Stratford upon Avon)? I find the whole chronology challenging and I have seen no convincing or satisfactory explanation of the appearance of those plays before the world. In 1972, after the European Communities Bill had been forced through parliament, I thought I wouldn't remain in public life much longer. I saw no.point in seeking to return to a House of Commons, and when I thought of what I was to do, the answer seemed to lie in the authorship of the plays attributed to William Shakespeare, and the Greek New Testament. The Greek New Testament beat William Shakespeare by a long head, but it's a half-open door which always beckons me whenever I glance in that direction.

But do you think you will ever open it properly?

Probably not.

But if he didn't write them, who did?

A committee. You may laugh, but we underestimate the extent to which great art can be produced by two or more hands, and undoubtedly the furnace of court drama under Elizabeth and in the early stages of James I was fed by a group of people, and that group was a necessarily changing group, though there is a voice and a mode of apprehension detectable in that joint product. I have not been convinced of any specific proposal to put a name to that voice, but do not underestimate the possibility of a joint creation of great works of art.

But has it happened before?

Yes, it happened in the Old Testament, the content of which is largely a joint creation. We tend to associate works of art with individuals, but in so

236

doing we over-individualize. It's a natural human fault to exaggerate the importance of the individual – there's a Tory statement for you.

I wonder if your own poems form in the way you describe one of Shakespeare's coming to him: that is, as a germinal phrase carried in the head until a suitable framework is gathered round it?

That was certainly my experience, and incidentally it is also the sort of experience which is described by Housman in his lecture on the name and nature of poetry. I would think it quite common among those who write poetry, that it comes in pieces, that an emotionally charged blob arises in the mind, and a framework for this must grow around it.

At Cambridge you were a fervent admirer of A.E. Housman and in some ways he became a role model for you. How far do you think his homosexuality was an integral, even an inseparable, part of his creativity? And did this matter to you or detract from his greatness in any way?

I probably was not conscious of it in the years that I attended his lectures, and I doubt the practicability of detaching one element from all the rest in an individual's character, particularly an artist's.

But a lot of great artists are homosexual : . . do you think that homosexuality and art complement each other?

If homosexuality is a common human characteristic then that would account for what you've drawn attention to. To say that artists have two eyes doesn't prove that they are different from other men, because having two eyes is quite common, pretty well invariable. If this strain is common in humanity then we shall find it in all manifestations of humanity, amongst artists, amongst painters, amongst politicians. Only if we could produce a statistical survey of the incidence in mankind at large at a particular time and in a particular society, and then show that that incidence was greatly exceeded amongst artists, might we be justified in coming to any such conclusion.

Enoch Powell

How do you yourself look upon homosexuality? Are you tolerant of it?

Well, I voted for its decriminalization, for it seemed to me grotesque that male homosexuality continued to be criminal from the reign of Henry VIII when female homosexuality was not. Nor did I regard it as a proper area for the criminal law to operate.

But why do you think homosexuality appears to be on the increase?

Ah, I notice the word 'appears', and I agree with that. That which is more discussed appears to be more common. It's not a matter to which I've applied my mind. I daresay there are those who are in the position to form some rational answer to the question, but I do think we have to beware of the impression made upon our minds by publicity. Familiarity tends to multiply, so we must beware of amateur statistics.

You were keen to join up in 1939, even passing yourself off as an Australian to do so. What was the attraction of the army, was it a sense of achieved order, or a duty fulfilled, or some more basic urge to help defend Britain, the land itself, as Wilfred Owen wanted to do in the First War?

I can remember saying to my father that it was my intention to get into uniform on the first day if I could. It was a spontaneous resolve of mine, though I didn't achieve it. It was the 20 October 1939 before I succeeded in getting enlisted. I wanted to defend my country, which is quite a natural impulse.

I was told a story that a man who had been one of your fellow privates at the beginning of the war met you years later when he had become a major and you a brigadier. When he greeted you in a familiar way you had him disciplined for not saluting a superior officer . . . is there any truth in that story?

No truth. That's an easily invented type of story. Indeed, it's a very interesting specimen of myth making. I did put fellow privates on disciplinary charges on the first day that I was a lance corporal, but that was for urinating in the barrack room.

238

You spent part of the war in India which was then part of the Empire. Did you have any feelings for the imperial idea or did you think the time had come for withdrawal?

Like most Indians, I didn't think the time had come for that phase of India's immense history to come to an end. It was as surprising to the Indians as it was to the British. And I only came to terms with it when back in this country in the late 1940s I began to apply myself to the constitutional history of my own country, and to understand that there was an insoluble contradiction in the government of a population on the authority of an assembly to which they could not be elected. The Empire of India was a huge repudiation of the lesson of the American colonies, and one with which England is still struggling: that is, that you cannot govern responsibly to parliament those who cannot be, or who choose not to be, represented in parliament. That's the underlying axiom of what is meant in English by democracy, and it was curious that it was our earliest *conquistadores* in India who understood this better than it was understood at the end of the nineteenth century. In India that principle was apparently unavoidable, but persistently and tantalizingly breached. Now this is not the me of 1943 speaking to you, who came back to politics in this country with the vague idea at the back of his head that it might somehow lead to the viceroyalty of India, and then had to work out his understanding of what happened to the United Kingdom when it ceased to be the mother country of a worldwide empire. The me of 1943 has arrived at New Delhi station at two in the morning on a posting from the Middle East. He realizes that it is impracticable to report to General Headquarters India until a much later hour, so he undoes his valise and he goes to sleep on the platform, and when he wakes up, what he breathes he finds intoxicating. Eventually he becomes an interpreter in Urdu and one of his unrealized ambitions is to produce a critical and literary edition of the *Rise and Fall of Islam* by the Urdu poet Hali, which is really the story of the Moslems in India. I suppose in my eightieth year I am a real oldie, and one who has to be constantly aware that he carries a lot of previous beings around in himself and that they are liable to be still vocal. Just as one's dreaming self is also one's waking self, the past individuals are asleep there somehow, and occasionally their words are remembered and repeated.

What was it that attracted you so powerfully to India? As a country it can seem so hopeless, so overburdened with a huge population, so impossible

239

to organize, its democracy so fragile, its savagery scarcely suppressed . . .

You used the word 'organize'. I suppose one of the fascinations of India for the British was its organizability. Here are immense resources, human above all; if these are harnessed together, what a wonderful organization could one not create, and in many ways the British did. The creation of a railway system, the drainage system of the Punjab – these must have given immense delight and satisfaction to those who organized them. But what we couldn't organize was a solution to the inherent constitutional contradiction of the British Raj. Nor could Indians, for they were mainly using material which they had obtained from us, and British material is very dangerous when used by those who are not British.

In an article you wrote about E.M. Forster's Passage to India *you spoke very fairly about the difference between his India and yours. How far, or when, do you think it is right to ask for accuracy in novels? May a book not be a good novel even if it's a bad social history?*

The dramatization of the novel *The Jewel in the Crown* always seemed to me grotesque, because life in India was not spent as life was spent by the protagonists in that novel; but that's not to say it's not a good novel or drama. But if you present a drama to a person who has lived in a particular place and situation and say, what do you make of it? – he will react with the contrast between his own memories, his own sensations, and the drama. I'm not apologizing for my review, I'm explaining it. Although the political axiom is supposed to be, never apologize, never explain, I don't mind explaining.

And you don't mind apologizing when you're wrong?

As a politician I try to follow the rule I've just quoted. And I've probably explained too much in politics, more than I ought to have done.

You now adhere to the Church of England, though you were not religious as a young man, and religious faith is often thought, perhaps wrongly, to be unusual in modern intellectuals. Does your faith ever sit uneasily alongside your intellectual convictions?

No, because worship and intellectual activity are manifestations of different aspects of the person, and they serve different – God forgive me, I was going to say biological purposes – no, they correspond to different aspects of that extraordinary animal homo sapiens. Religion must have been very important for his survival, because he has it everywhere. One of the remarkable things which J.G. Fraser, the great anthropologist, found so alarming, was how frequently in places between which there could have been no interconnection or intercommunication, man hit upon the device of killing God and eating him. Now this is not a rational proceeding, but it may nevertheless be a proceeding which is beneficial or necessary to humanity. I hope I have not unduly alarmed you.

No. You have said that you are deeply aware of a dilemma and a contradiction between Christianity and human life. Some observers have suggested that despite your participation in holy communion and observance of religious practice it is as if you are somehow forcing yourself to believe, if you like; that you are really struggling with agnosticism.

Well, who is to look into the heart of man and declare what he sees there, and who is man to say what is in his heart? I can only observe that at no stage in the last forty years can a credible political motive be assigned to what I have done and said as a member of the Church of England. Self-interest is difficult to establish – a very modest disclaimer I realize – but then we're often led by motives of which we are unaware.

It is said that those who believe have the grace of belief, and that is something that comes from God. Do you feel that you have the grace of belief or do you have a constant struggle to believe?

I feel everything comes *from* grace; I have everything *by* grace. My wife and I, for example, are celebrating our fortieth wedding anniversary but our marriage was a grace; it was something I didn't deserve, something I've been given beyond my desert. I find the concept of grace, that is to say an input of indeterminate origin, unavoidable in a whole range of experiences. To arrive at a logical conclusion from premises is in a way an act of grace. Perhaps this is to acknowledge what a wonderful thing it was that man originated.

Enoch Powell

Have you any doubt in your own mind about an after-life?

If you had substituted immortality for an after-life, I would not have hesitated to reply in the affirmative. The expression 'after-life' is timebound; immortality is not. The individual, encapsulated by time, unable to think or understand or have his being except as bounded by time, ceases to belong to that framework on death, and it's therefore a misrepresentation to treat him as though he continued to exist on the same scale. Suppose time is a man-made illusion, which it probably is . . . in that case the meaning of immortality will be very different.

Presumably you have a view about the ordination of women, a matter which looks as if it might further fragment the Christian Church. Is it possible theologically in your view, and is it desirable politically?

We're going through a bad dose of feminism, aren't we? Certainly the chattering classes are. Under the influence of a worldwide cross-infection, we are calling in question specializations which have been necessary to the survival of humanity. It may well be that the preservative and the destructive impulses of mankind have been specialized in the sexes and that we are playing with fire when we introduce confusion into that specialization. The specialization can, of course, be defined and debated, but the anxiety is whether we can radically interfere without unforeseeable but damaging consequences. I would place the proposal for the ordination of women and the enthusiasm for it in the context of that movement which leads all political parties at present in the United Kingdom to say that they want to see more women sitting in the House of Commons, even though those who do the work necessary for putting the members there don't think so.

There is now and there has been for a long time a great deal of agitation about women's rights. I suspect that you are not especially sympathetic to the women's movement. Is it that you fear the consequences of a loss of natural complementarity, or what?

I am very happy to consider with an open mind proposals for a change in the law where the law differentiates between men and women, though I am not sure that to treat the female as an independent tax band will be something welcomed by all those whom it will affect. My wife was certainly alarmed when I told her that she will be making her own tax return in future and would surely not expect any help from me.

Since you are a member of the Church of England, I assume you believe in original sin. How is the outcome of that to be combatted in a society without any restraints on gain?

Covetousness, greed, are not matters which can be the subject of legislation. They belong in the category of sin rather than crime, and from sin we are saved by grace.

You acknowledged once that you are intellectually arrogant. Does that degree of self-confidence not isolate you in the political world of horse trading?

I'm also a corporate man, a person at ease in society, fulfilling the laws and obeying the conventions, just as – constitutionally – the shared responsibility for the advice tendered to the sovereign extends right through political life. I accept that the unity of that advice implies give and take between those who are responsible for it being tendered. In other words, I am a naturally compliant member of a cabinet. The intellectual arrogance leads me to perceive that the whole structure of cabinet government and of party government depends on bargaining and compromise. But I'm a good colleague, one who goes to meet his other colleagues halfway, more than halfway if necessary.

Can you tell me what is it to be a Tory?

To me a Tory is a person who believes that authority is vested in institutions – that's a carefully honed definition. We have made the law, not for extraneous reasons, not because it conforms with *a priori* specifications; it has been made by a particular institution in a particular way and can be changed by that institution in a particular way. A Tory therefore reposes the ultimate authority in institutions – he is an example of collective man.

Do you believe in the Thatcher philosophy which is sometimes character-ized as advocating greed and free enterprise as a way of life, irrespective of community benefit.

It is alleged that the speeches I made on the working of the competitive market in the early 1960s influenced Mrs Thatcher, but I wouldn't attribute to her the formulation which you've just provided. There is undoubtedly a role in the functioning of a human society for possessive-ness, for competition, for envy, and for many urges which live in a kind of balance and coexistence with the other urges within. For instance, if we take the question of denationalization: do we wish our railways to be run by politicians, or do we wish them to be run by those who will lose if they are ill run? The private enterprise corporation is founded upon the assumption that the resources which it puts to work are put to work most efficiently if it is managed by those who stand to lose if the customers' demand is not anticipated and met. That seems to me a very happy and ancient device which most nations have grown up with.

You have described yourself as a man naturally sympathetic to authority and its institutions. What is to be done when authority ceases to be impressive or even trustworthy, when for example a minister insists that the economy is recovering in the face of the facts, or when unemployment statistics are patently 'managed'?

No institution is immortal, any more than any other human thing is immortal, and there is no sovereign remedy against its deterioration. Institutions are not only created and strengthened, they also weaken and disappear. We cannot deny that.

You have been the subject of a great deal of abuse for stating your views about immigration. Have you modified them at all?

The aspects and consequences of immigration as perceived now in the 1990s are not the same as those which were perceived in the 1960s. In the 1960s the level of admissions was the critical subject; this resulted in a factor of almost equal importance being underestimated and largely overlooked – the age structure of the incoming population. Age structure is now asserting itself and will result in a progressive and on-going relative increase in what are called the ethnic minorities in proportion to the total population. What we don't know and what nobody can know, is how long institutions based upon the working of majorities can continue to operate. There is an on-going change in the population of this country, and one doesn't know how far that will be compatible with the continued operation of our parliamentary institutions. If you cannot change your mind between one election and another in reaction to what has been your experience in the meantime you cannot operate a parliamentary system. If an election is a census it cannot form a basis of parliamentary self-government. These are the questions which with the passage of time are now emerging, but I do find that, so far as I can judge it, public anxiety is as lively on this subject as it was thirty years ago.

Except our worst fears have not been justified?

My projections have been verified. What I said in 1968, I would say again if it were 1968.

In a discourse on Wagner's Ring *you say that Siegfried of course did not fully understand or intend the consequences of his actions. Did you fully understand or intend the consequences of your 'River of Blood' speech?*

Those words were never used. That phrase did not occur in the speech. I don't think one ever foresees the consequences of one's actions and certainly in politics one never knows which utterances are going to be heard and which are not.

The sting in Paul Foot's book about you was that you had exploited the race issue as an act of political opportunism and not, as you claimed, as a matter of principle. What is your comment on that?

That's what he thought when he started to write the book, but after he'd met me he thought better. In fact, I ruined his book for him. When I heard he was writing it, I sent him a letter inviting him to come and talk to me. This was fatal because one can see in the course of the book that he discovered his conception was not viable.

Enoch Powell

The story goes that when you went to Northern Ireland someone called you a Judas, to which you retorted: 'I am sacrificing my political career. Judas was paid.' Is there any truth in that story?

That interchange did in fact take place after I'd delivered the second of my Vote Labour speeches in the election campaign of February 1974, but it was nothing to do with Northern Ireland.

You once spoke of yourself as a 'Lansdowne man' in the sense that since by 1943 it was clear that the axis powers could not win, we ought to have had a negotiated peace. Does that view not place you in the strange company of Oswald Mosley who also advocated a negotiated peace?

It does not put me in the company of those who see war between civilized nations as ending with the destruction of one's opponent. The object of war is to prove to one's opponent that he cannot gain his aim by force. When that has been proved the justification for war is at an end, and that point should be sought. Unconditional surrender was the most barbaric and inhuman concept to bring into the Second World War. You do not have to destroy your opponent; you merely have to prove to him that he cannot win, and when he can be persuaded that he cannot win, then you must make peace. Otherwise you will have to rebuild him and there will be a lot of other fallout too.

Many people have drawn a comparison between you and Mosley: intellectually rigorous, patriotic, a natural leader, a powerful orator, uncompromising, destined for – but never quite achieving – high office. Is it a comparison which offends you?

It's a comparison which is quite strange to me. I've never come across it. I am of course a failed politician, if one assumes that the object of politics is to gain and keep high office. Mosley was a failed politician too, so I may be included in the same category, but there is a large category of failed politicians.

Yes, but failed politicians because they were incapable . . .

All right, I can be placed in the category of failed capable politicians; they're still a sufficiently large company to contain me and Oswald Mosley and dozens and dozens of others.

You once wrote that 'no time spent reading history is mis-spent for a politician'. But do not circumstances change beyond all recognition and invalidate the 'lessons' of history . . . may it not be an error to read the future out of the past?

It is an error in any case to read the future out of the past, because history is not repeatable. The lessons which we learn about the scientifically measurable and investigatable world are applicable because that world is a constant. But history is not a constant; it is an artistic presentation of change in progress, irreversible and unique change. I recently improved upon my dictum about time spent reading history, and I would now say time spent reading biography is not mis-spent, perhaps because the repeatable element in individual human life is more substantial than the repeatable element in social or national life.

Hailsham said of you: 'He has the best mind in politics, until it is made up.' Did you understand what he meant by this, and did you accept the implied criticism?

No to the first question, and therefore the second does not arise.

A lot of people have said in that context you're your own worst enemy.

Well, it depends what a man wants, what his standards are, what life means for him.

But if you were to live that period in your life again . . .

Don't frighten me with such a horrible idea. Imagine putting all my prejudices as an octogenarian into the body of a forty-year-old man – it's such a horrible notion that I decline to entertain it.

Maurice Cowling called you 'a closet socialist'. What do you think he meant by that?

He meant what I was saying earlier about a Tory being an aspect of collective man. Society is in the end normative, and politics is about the management and governance of a society. Society is prior (in a logical sense) to the individual; the individual in the last resort is an abstraction. Nobody has ever met an individual, we didn't start as individuals, we don't live as individuals, we only know ourselves as members of a collectivity. I think it was that aspect of my Toryism that Cowling may have had in mind.

It is said that an unofficial approach was made to you with a view to your becoming a life peer, but that you made certain conditions.

That's not a question I would ever answer.

Would you like to have been in the House of Lords? Conditions or no conditions?

You mean, would I have liked to have a different father? [Laughs.]

The House of Lords would have provided you with a forum in which to express your views . . .

I find no difficulty in getting my views on to paper, or getting what I put on to paper printed. Nor do I find any shortage of my fellow countrymen who are anxious to lend me their ears.

The House of Lords wouldn't interest you in the least?

You're putting words into my mouth.

Would it interest you?

I do not wish to say anything disrespectful about the upper chamber.

I am puzzled by your suggestion that the greatest act man is capable of is to choose death instead of life. I assume you are not writing in praise of suicide. Are you describing the capacity to sacrifice oneself for someone or something else?

Yes. It was the only way out for mankind that God could discover. It was the only way to save mankind, to allow someone to sacrifice his life for the remission of sins. It is an idea endorsed by the strongest authority.

Are there circumstances in which you would sacrifice your own life for that idea?

I suppose my decision to enlist is the only evidence that I have to offer. And I know now that I'm not the only person who put on uniform and took it off again who has a lurking feeling at the back of his mind that there must have been something wrong with him if he came back. When I was asked on a radio programme how I would like to be remembered, and I replied that I wished I'd been killed in the war, I received a large correspondence from people who wrote that they were glad I had said that, because until then they thought they were the only people to feel that way. A large number of people who voluntarily went into the forces in 1939 are dogged by the idea that they were left unscathed when others were taken. Those who survived concentration camps also have this feeling.

Now that you have reached a certain age, are you afraid of death?

The nearer Death comes actuarially, the more he tends to present himself in the guise of a potential friend, a hand laid upon the shoulder saying, never mind old chap, I'll come along in due course and carry you away. There's a wonderful line in Homer where the prophecy is made to Ulysses that Death will come to him from the sea, with the words (in Greek) 'gentle, ever so gentle'. And one does come to regard death as a gentle presence.

Many people have commented on your seemingly cold exterior, yet in private you are obviously a compassionate man. Are you aware of this tension between the public and the private personae?

The surprise that I sustain is how widespread and undifferentiated is the friendliness towards me, evidently entertained by large numbers of my fellow countrymen. It constantly comes as a happy but still remarkable thing to me. Perhaps that is an act of grace.

What in essence so attracted you to the music of Wagner?

Hearing it. There's a line in Carducci: 'When Wagner breathes into the sounding metals a thousand spirits, men's hearts tremble.'

What is your view on the current debate in Israel about Wagner's music? The Israeli Philharmonic wants to play Wagner but the public continues to reject him because of the association with Hitler and the Nazis.

That is their business, and I will thank them to mind their business in declining to express corresponding opinions about the affairs of the United Kingdom.

Siegfried proclaimed what you call the great moral discovery of humanity: that it is better to die than to live in fear. While it is an idea which greatly captures the imagination, is there not a case for saying that in practice it is all but worthless. Many people live in fear of life itself or in fear of God, but their life still has intrinsic value.

Well, that will turn upon the word 'intrinsic', won't it? We live because we cannot help it, and we die because we cannot help it. You remember in front of Bolingbroke Richard II says: 'Give Richard leave to live till Richard die.'

When you reflected on age you said that to your surprise it was 'a constant opening of doors'. Can you elaborate on that?

I'm surprised by how much new there still is to think and to see, and the apparent immunity of one's thinking mechanism from those ravages that are making their advance in other parts of the organism. That one continues to think and enjoy thinking, to observe and to enjoy observing, is a constant marvel.

LORD SHAWCROSS

Hartley William Shawcross was born in Giessen, Germany in 1902. Educated at Dulwich College, he was called to the bar at Gray's Inn in 1925 and was senior lecturer in law at Liverpool (1927–34). After service in World War II, he was attorney-general between 1945 and 1951 and president of the board of trade (1951) in the labour government. He was chief British prosecutor at the Nuremberg trials (1945–6), led the investigations of the Lynskey Tribunal (1948) and prosecuted in the Fuchs atom spy case (1950). He resigned his parliamentary seat in 1958 and was created a life peer in 1959.

Lord Shawcross, you have had a remarkable number of really quite different activities in your life. Which has given you most satisfaction?

A very difficult question. The one that I found most agreeable was being the father of a family.

Much more than being attorney-general or an illustrious QC?

My work as attorney-general was extremely interesting; looking back on it I feel I did it reasonably competently, and I remember it with a certain amount of self-satisfaction.

You have been in government, the head of various panels, and a businessman on a large scale with wide experience. Do those activities require the same qualities or very different ones?

They probably require different ones. The legal position, of course, demands an adequate knowledge of the law, and if you are an advocate, as I was, some power of exposition, but you're not generally concerned with problems of policy, except in so far as this involves a particular legal question. I would have thought that the most important quality is commonsense and a degree of honesty, integrity.

You began your political career as a socialist, but I suppose there would be few who think of you any longer in that light. Does that surprise you?

No. It depends of course what you mean by socialism. I was always a radical, still am. I come of a radical tradition, and in the 1940s, up to the 1950s, socialism was the creed of most radicals. Mr Kinnock is now saying very much what I said in 1951. He has abandoned socialism in the old sense, and socialists are really now social democrats in the Continental sense.

You sit on the cross benches in the House of Lords. What was it about socialism that began to make you uneasy, and when did that unease start?

It started about the middle of Mr Attlee's government when I found it really wasn't working. One of the first measures for which I had a major responsibility was the reform of the trade union law, including the restoration of the rights to engage in almost unlimited picketing. I was sure the trade union members would be loyal and would not abuse this right. But in fact, within a year or two, it was being gravely abused; we were having mass picketing and a lot of unofficial strikes. That I think was my first disillusionment. Then I was president of the Board of Trade which brought me into contact with industrialists and the working of industry. I was only there for nine months, but I learned a lot, and I then realized that state control of industry was not working efficiently, and that it was characterized by a great deal of bureaucracy which it was almost impossible to eradicate from the system. I also realized more and more how important the ideas of personal incentive and individual gain were to the individuals concerned. They wanted to do the best they could for their families, as I did myself, and that was what encouraged them most to hard work, rather than the idea of social service.

You knew Attlee well?

Very well, and I admired him. I think he will go down in history as a very able prime minister. He was of course deputy prime minister throughout the war, and responsible for a great deal of the more detailed work on day-to-day administration while Winston Churchill was the great leader. Attlee was a tower of strength to him, and although socially they didn't get on very well, Winston did rely on him as being an honest and responsible and helpful person during the war.

You turned your back on the Labour Party in 1958 . . .

To say I turned my back on them is a bit hard. I left them certainly and went to the cross benches. In the House of Lords when I spoke at all, which wasn't very often, I was often critical of the policies of Harold Wilson's government – who wasn't? – but on other occasions I supported them. I haven't completely turned my back on them, and I left my own constituency on very friendly terms.

Many people at the time and since said that it was in order to reap the rewards of the boardroom. How do you answer that?

There is some truth in it, but I could of course have remained at the bar. What happened after the fall of the labour government at the end of 1951 was that I went back to practise at the bar, and I built up probably the leading practice of the time, although fees were in real terms not so high as they are today; according to the newspapers, I was making the largest income at the bar, but I couldn't save anything. The taxation rate at that time left me with about sixpence in the pound. I had a wife who was much younger than myself and three children, and we had no private means. I was very much concerned with the obvious probability that I should die long before my wife did and probably before my family had grown up, and that I must make provision for them. That really forced me to go into industry where I could enter into some arrangement which insured a pension covering my wife. That was the basic reason for leaving the bar. I could of course have gone on the bench, but that didn't attract me for one reason and another.

There are repeated efforts made by the right to tar all socialists with the totalitarian brush. Is there any sense, do you think, in which socialists are bound to be anti-libertarian?

When I was a member of an undoubtedly socialist government, we were to some extent anti-libertarian because we believed in the efficacy of controls. A great many controls and restrictions on liberty were essential during the war, and we carried them on during the period of demobilization and reconstruction after the war, but it must be remembered that even after the Labour Party went out of office in 1951 and the conservatives came back, a good many controls had still to be continued, such as rationing of one kind and another and exchange controls. Some degree of restriction on complete liberty is probably necessary in any system of ordered government and is more likely to occur when that government is of the left rather than the right.

The larger-scale experiment with socialism – I mean communism – really does seem to have gone badly wrong. Why do you think that was? After all, it's not such a bad ideal.

There was a strong, largely underground movement of communism in this country in the period immediately following the war, naturally encouraged by the success of the Russians during the war. The communists made a very great effort, with some success, to secure control of the trade unions. I was very much involved in it in a way, because I was aware of the underground efforts the communists were making and I helped to support the more orthodox, right-wing trade union leaders who were fighting to maintain a degree of democracy in the trade unions. I was involved in the case which destroyed the communist leadership of the electrical trade union, for example. In the end communism failed because it took no account of the natural instincts of people both to improve their own condition and to enjoy a certain amount of freedom and liberty.

It looks increasingly likely that the immediate sources of trouble are going to be racial, ethnic and religious. How can troubles which stem from such sources be resisted? So much of the fervour and hatred is irrational, it surely can't respond to rational arguments.

I wish I had an answer to that. I don't think anybody has. The antagonism between the races is probably not so obvious as it was earlier, but I'm not sure about it. We are taught now to avoid offensive expressions that were quite common form in the old days. At that time to say that a man was a nigger was, I think, not nearly so offensive as it is to say it now. The religious conflict is much more difficult to deal with, and I'm afraid I don't have any answer to it. I'm a member of the Church of England, I go to church occasionally, but I'm not engaged in any religious crusade myself. I believe it's very important that people should believe in something, and I am very happy to include amongst my friends people of very different religions, but the antagonism which is appearing in some places now is very worrying.

As you get older, do you become more or less religious?

Possibly I have become a little more religious with age. It may be that as I get nearer the end I become more hopeful that the end will not be final, that there might be something beyond it, but it doesn't absorb much of my thinking even now. All I can say is that I have a little hope that I may meet round the corner those who have preceded me.

You said once: 'Things ended for me completely when my second wife died.' Has the passage of time eased the loss?

Not really. I have a family who are very caring of me, and I'm very fond of them. We are a closely knit family, and I have a very small group of friends and a particular companion, but I still think constantly of my second wife, and indeed of my first wife. I had two very happy marriages and I look back on them with great gratitude. My enthusiasm for life did rather come to an end with the death of my second wife, which came as a terrible shock to me. I had never anticipated living after her, and had fully intended not to do so, but circumstances made that course impossible.

Do you believe you will see her again?

I hope I may. I carry in my pocketbook, even today, something that one sees quoted much more often in memorial services. It's a prayer that was written by Henry Scott Holland: 'Death is nothing at all, I have only slipped away into the next room, I am I, and you are you; what we were to each other we are still; call me by my familiar name . . .' and so on.

You have argued powerfully against the resumption of trials of war criminals, and yet you were the chief prosecutor at Nuremberg. Are the two positions consistent? How do you defend the charge that this suggests if you can get away with it for long enough it does not count?

I am against these trials, wholly against them, because experience has shown that the evidence of identification on which these trials would depend is always one of the frailest forms of evidence. People's memories are very often misleading, and after even a few days, evidence of identification becomes unreliable. After forty-five years it's utterly unreliable and some of the recent trials have shown that. They seem to have made a mistake in the current trial taking place in Israel, and they've adopted the extraordinary course of having found the man guilty under one particular identity, and then, apparently accepting that the identification was quite wrong, they have charged him with a different set of crimes, which seems to me a monstrous injustice. There is no possibility that these trials could be fair; that's the only reason I am opposed to them.

Lord Shawcross

Did you feel any sympathy with any of the accused at Nuremberg?

No. I was opposed to capital punishment, I always have been, but I felt that if capital punishment was ever deserved it was deserved by these men. And I was very surprised that some of them got off altogether. Schacht, for instance, who in his earlier days had made a very important contribution to the Nazi movement. He was a natural genius who had built up the Nazi economy into the very efficient war machine that it became, and he was very fortunate to be released. Von Papen was another who had contributed significantly to the Nazi regime, and I thought that he should have been punished. I had no sympathy for any of them.

What about Hess?

I thought Hess was mad; the very idea that by flying to Scotland and meeting the Duke of Hamilton, he could bring about a peace, shows that he was a little mad. At the trial a team of doctors said that he was mentally affected, but that he could understand what was going on. They were perhaps influenced by the fact that they were representatives of the victorious powers, but his conduct during the trials was obviously that of a madman. I assumed at that time that the life sentence was meant to be commuted to a much shorter term, as it is in every country in the world except the former Soviet Union, who insisted that he be kept in prison.

Of all the criminals who were there, who impressed you the most?

No question about that, it was Goering, Goering was absolutely outstanding; a man of very great intellectual ability and with a very strong personality, who sat at the end of the dock, listening to the whole of the proceedings very intently. From time to time something would go a little wrong; you would ask a question to which the expected answer was Yes, and the witness would say No, and if then you caught Goering's eye, he would shake his head sadly, or smile, and you had to be very careful to avoid smiling with him. As Norman Birkett said, he could have dominated the whole court if he'd tried to. He was very remarkable, and at the end of it all when he had been sentenced to death, his last statement from the dock was that he had sworn allegiance to Hitler in death as in life, and he said:

'I swore that, I meant it, and I still do.' He had great courage, and he knew that he was going to defeat the gallows in the end anyway.

You were the chairman of the Take-over Panel at one point. Why is there such a thing? It seems at odds with the whole notion of a free market; if one company can gobble up another, why shouldn't it?

No reason at all, provided it does so by open and honest means. The panel was set up in order to ensure that it should be done fairly, not by insider dealing or intrigues of one kind or another which are unjust to the shareholders, or potential shareholders in either company. That was the whole purpose of it, not to stop take-overs, which have often been beneficial. Prior to the establishment of the Take-over Panel by the governor of the Bank of England there had been some bad cases of dishonest conduct. The open market is a very important thing provided it is open and honest.

How far do you think the government ought to interfere in business? There is a great deal of talk about the market place and the healthy effect of competition, but some of the most successful economies, like the German and the Japanese, are heavily interventionist.

That is a matter which is partly the result of our different history and upbringing. The Germans are much more used to intervention and discipline than we have ever been. I was born in Germany and I got to know a fair amount about Germany even before Nuremberg; *verboten* was a very familiar word in Germany and still is. I don't know so much about Japan but they are also much more accustomed to a dominant class than we are in this country. I believe we have a lot to learn both from the Japanese and the Germans, and it may well be that their system of supervisory boards is a good one which will require much more examination than we have hitherto been prepared to give it.

Twenty years ago you said that the British judicial system was at once the envy and the admiration of the world. Do you think you could find anyone to agree with that now? In fact do you still think it is true?

It is still true. Unfortunately there have been a number of cases recently involving apparent deliberate perjury on the part of the police. In my day, altering the verbals, as they call it, was virtually unknown. Recently there have been cases so bad that the judges at first couldn't believe what had occurred, and they were perhaps not sufficiently vigilant in scrutinizing the evidence given for the prosecution and the police; but I still think that our system of appointing judges with their independence and integrity is a good one. Of course, our system of justice is quite different from that of the French under the Code Napoleon, and theirs may have a lot to be said for it, but I certainly prefer our way of appointing the judiciary to the American system. I think our Bench on the whole is extremely good.

Don't you think that the time may have come for a radical overhaul of the legal processes and professions in this country? All sorts of things seem to be out of control – unsafe convictions, grotesque anomalies in sentencing, and so on.

The commission which is now enquiring into the administration of the criminal law will probably come up with some safeguards, but I would be surprised if any drastic revision were required. I think it very significant that in this recent case of the Guinness No.2 trial the forewoman of the jury found it appropriate to write a letter to the *Financial Times* criticizing very strongly by implication the action of the judge in stopping the trial and in suggesting that juries could not understand trials of this kind. And she made it pretty clear that the jury at least thought that they were following the trial very closely and wished it to go on. What is needed is very great care in ensuring honesty on the part of the police and very severe punishment for those policemen who are found guilty of offences such as have occurred. What has been happening is that police officers have convinced themselves that they have arrested the people who were guilty of the particular charge they've been investigating, but the admissible evidence has not been sufficiently strong to satisfy the very rigid requirements of our law, and they have therefore tried to improve on the evidence by concocting statements which they attribute to the defendants, but which were not in fact made. I think it very rare indeed, if ever, that the police concoct a deliberately false case against somebody whom they don't believe is guilty, but what they do do is to try and ice the cake, which is absolutely wrong and ought to be severely punished. On the other hand, I think we ought to do away with the rule that a person accused of an offence may refuse to answer questions. The rule we have now that no comment must be made by the prosecution on the silence of the defendant is one which seems to me to be absolutely contrary to the principles of justice. The innocent man demands the right to speak; it's his great sword; the guilty man shelters in silence.

Is it not time to prevent juries awarding absurd sums of money to people whose feelings have been hurt?

Yes, I think the awards by juries in these cases have been quite absurd, and are largely due to the juries' dislike of the activities of certain sections of the press in invading the privacy of individuals, or in casting doubt on the sexual probity of particular people. I think juries are averse to the sensationalization of sex in this way, and although they all read these papers, they don't like it when it comes to a particular case, and they feel that the press ought to be punished for it. It may be necessary in these cases, and possibly in all cases, to have damages fixed by the judge and possibly assessors with special experience.

What view do you take of the libel laws? Years ago Robert Maxwell was branded as someone not fit to hold an office of trust, but nothing whatever was done and the threat of libel actions kept everyone at bay until the pension funds had disappeared.

I was the first person to cross-examine Robert Maxwell, and it was in consequence of that, a very long time ago, that the board of trade, my old department, set up an enquiry and concluded, as the City panel had done, that he was unfit to be a director of a public company. It is quite extraordinary that responsible people, including the heads of many of the banks, disregarded that and accepted Maxwell as being an honest and reliable man. I knew Maxwell quite well, because I cross-examined him for about nine hours and I formed an opinion that he was absolutely unreliable; but I recognize that he had a great deal of personal charm which seems to have carried him forward in spite of the very adverse verdicts, first by the City panel, and following that by the board of trade. There's a lot of criticism to be made against some of the people who assisted him in his business activities, the banks who lent him money without sufficient safeguards, and the people in important places who consorted with him.

Were you affected by what you call his 'personal charm'?

During the case I came to realize that he had charm. At the end we had to settle the press statement at about 2 o'clock in the morning, and when we showed the draft to Maxwell, he was very upset by the terms of it, and he wept, literally wept. I was rather moved by that, and I made one or two modifications so that it was slightly less harsh. But the report we made was so damning none the less that I felt Maxwell must hate me, and as I didn't like him, I took care to avoid him in the years that followed. I don't think I ever spoke to him until about eighteen months ago when I went to a press luncheon at the Savoy given by Lord Stevens, then of the *Evening Standard*. When I saw Maxwell was on the list of guests, I resolved to avoid him, and I went to the end of the Lancaster Room, found some friends there, had a drink with them, and told them I was keeping out of Maxwell's way. But up he came, held out both his arms, and said, 'Hello Hartley, old boy, how good to see you!' He had never called me Hartley in his life, but what could one do but shake hands with him? He certainly had that sort of charm which I didn't succumb to myself, but many people did.

Regarding the right to privacy, you stated in 1970: 'The world is a much less private place than it used to be, and those who engage in public life are a legitimate subject of interest to the public at large.' Do you think this legitimate interest extends to sexual morality, bearing in mind that American political candidates are judged to be fit or unfit for office largely on personal matters which have little to do with politics?

If a man engages in public life, it is a matter of legitimate interest to the public to know what sort of man he is. Is he the sort of man we can trust? Amongst the considerations that many people would have regard to, would be his sexual fidelity. Within reason, therefore, there is a legitimate interest in the sexual behaviour of public men, that the newspapers are entitled to expose. I don't think they are justified in hounding men in public office, but if they find that a man is notoriously unfaithful to his wife, disregards the interests of his family, has one mistress after another, I think that is a matter for legitimate concern on the part of the public.

But does it make him politically a less able man because he's sexually active?

It's not a question of sexual activity; it's a question of sexual morality. Is he a man who is faithful to his word, is he true to his friends, is he true to his wife? If he's not married, and has no obligations of that kind, then his sexual activities are of much less concern, but if he is promiscuous, that is a matter which the public is entitled to have regard to in deciding whether he is fit to govern their lives.

After the recent revelations about Paddy Ashdown, his popularity increased significantly. What do you think this demonstrates? That we are unwilling to follow the American model; that we are adopting a more mature, less censorious attitude; or is it all orchestrated by the media?

I think it does show that we don't like the American attitude to these problems, and it may show a greater degree of sophistication. The Great British Public accepted that this particular incident had occurred a long time ago, that his wife knew all about it, that she had forgiven him, that their marriage was happily continuing and that it was quite unfair to rake up this shortlived incident of many years ago. I think it was a good reaction on the part of the British public, and a good reaction against the press publicity given to what after all is a fairly trivial incident.

Why should barristers have a monopoly of pleading in the High Court? This does not happen anywhere else in Europe and it looks remarkably like a lucrative closed-shop arrangement.

It's the result of the historical development of the legal system in this country. Here we have always had a division between those who are advocates in court and specialize in advocacy, and those who are attorneys, as Trollope called them, who do non-litigious work. The result has been that we have had a special class of person who has specialized in advocacy and court work. He has no direct association with his client at all. He has no incentive to put the evidence or take any measure which is not strictly honest, and he is supposed – these are the words of a famous judge – to act as a minister of justice. He is there to assist in the application of the law with complete independence. That is the theory. On the whole it's adhered to, although there have been notable departures from it, but I think our system has maintained a much higher standard of independence and

265

honesty in the administration of justice than would have been the case if the two professions had been one.

So you're in favour of maintaining the system as it stands now?

It's been very much modified by the reforms introduced by the present lord chancellor, and solicitors have been given certain rights of audience and more opportunity of going on the bench. I'm not dismayed by that. It means they can now be appointed to the bench if they have any obvious merit, and they can do advocacy if they think it worthwhile. But in America where the system doesn't exist, all the big firms have trial lawyers who specialize in the trial work and other lawyers who don't, and if you go with a case to a Wall Street lawyer, you probably end up by seeing all the partners in the firm, and paying a fee to each of them. Our system is probably much cheaper – although it's far too expensive now – and is very efficient in maintaining a degree of independence on the part of the bar.

When you were practising as a QC, which case gave you the most satisfaction to win?

I don't know that one really derives a tremendous amount of personal satisfaction from winning a case. I had some cases which I won but did not expect to, but I don't remember them with any particularity. I had a very bad memory for cases, and once a case was finished it was finished. In fact, I can claim to have forgotten all my cases; I don't know why that was, but they went completely out of my mind, and the only way I can remind myself is by looking at press cuttings. I'm astonished sometimes when I read the cuttings to know that I was in the case at all.

In 1970 you were warning of the consequences of 'a sickness in our society and politics which bodes ill for us all'. Do you think that prophecy has been fulfilled, or was it premature?

I was very disillusioned with the way that party politics were being conducted at that time; everything one party proposed was automatically opposed by the other. I thought we should try to seek a much greater consensus, and at one time when the country was in a bad state of recession

I almost suggested that we ought to have some sort of coalition government to improve matters. That was the sickness; we were all too suspicious of each other and not prepared to cooperate enough.

At one point you were chairman of Thames Television. Did you feel at that time any obligation say to ensure a high standard of production, or was it just a matter of maximizing your shareholders' profits?

I felt that we had a very great responsibility. I was in fact the first chairman of Thames Television. I remember I was in New York at the time I received a telephone message from the head of EMI telling me that they had joined up with another company to establish Thames Television. The television commission insisted on their having some sort of impartial chairman, and would I agree to take the job on? He also told me that I could quote any terms I liked. I was naïve about that, and I accepted a ridiculously small salary compared with what people get nowadays. My job as chairman was to help ensure that the company was very responsibly conducted, and we did some very good things. I was astonished when the franchise was not renewed; I think it's a great misfortune.

Are you in favour of the BBC charter changing, or should it retain total independence as it has now?

It ought to have independence, yes. On the whole it is the most responsible of the broadcasting organizations, and the present system has justified itself, so far as it concerns the BBC. I wish I could think that there was the same responsibility on the part of all the independent companies.

Every government in recent times has levelled criticism of bias against the BBC. Is this paranoia do you think, or is there some substance to it?

There's possibly some substance to it. The BBC think their task is to be critical rather than supportive and that is the reason why every government has criticized them for bias, but my impression is that on the whole people in television are more inclined to be left wing than right wing, and so there is always a certain degree of leftish slant. I believe the leaders of the BBC

Lord Shawcross

are on their guard against this, however, and as a rule succeed in avoiding anything that is at all scandalous.

In 1974 you made a statement on corruption in high places and how you were prevented by legal privilege of secrecy from disclosing your 'incontrovertible evidence' and thus having the offenders pursued. At the time you said: 'And so the evildoers continue to flourish.' Do they still continue to flourish, in your view?

I made that statement when I was still at the bar, and had a great deal of work concerning financial and industrial problems. Occasionally one came across cases of dishonesty, like the one that you're referring to, which were very serious. I think that cases of financial corruption in government or in the higher ranks of the civil service are very rare, but I've no doubt that such cases do occur and continue to occur. All that one can do is to be vigilant, and if they do occur to be severe in dealing with them. Recent developments in the City have been very disturbing indeed. When I first came into the City standards were undoubtedly very high and the old adage, my word is my bond, was accepted. Nobody would act on that nowadays I'm afraid, and that is a very bad sign. There has been a lowering of moral standards because of the intense competition and the desire to get rich quick which permeates our society nowadays.

What view did you take of Mrs Thatcher when she was in power?

I thought she was a very remarkable and able woman. I didn't by any means always agree with her policies, but I thought that she had a stronger personality probably than any prime minister I've known, and that she succeeded in dominating her cabinet probably more than any prime minister, even Churchill. This was not in itself a good thing, because the constitutional theory is that the prime minister is the first amongst equals, but this had ceased to be the case with her. Mr Major does not have the same dominant personality, but Mrs Thatcher on the whole was a woman who has had a considerable effect on the development of life in this country, and history will probably give a more favourable account of her than we're inclined to do at present.

Did you approve of her curbing the power of the unions?

Yes, entirely. I was the lawyer who was responsible for making the alternations in the law and introducing the Trades Disputes Bill in 1946, so I say with regret that Mrs Thatcher was right in restricting their powers. The trade union leadership had abused the powers given to them, and they had to be restricted. What she has done is not likely to be drastically altered by a labour government, so the position of the trade unions is now weaker but more responsible, and better from the point of view of the well-being of the country.

Although Mrs Thatcher was a tremendous force in politics she is not taken as seriously as before. Do you think this is the universal fate of those who lose high office – their charisma vanishes with their status?

No. It wasn't the case with Churchill who was defeated in 1945 by a very large majority, but his charisma and personality remained. Wherever he went, enormous crowds cheered him, and although I was a strong opponent of his, and very critical of him, I always said publicly that I would not have been there, able to criticize him and attack him, if it had not been for his leadership in the war. He had saved the country during the war, but he was not a good prime minister during the peace. Later on I became very friendly with him, and indeed acted in some minor cases as his legal adviser. Without a doubt he retained his charisma. Harold Macmillan also had a certain charm which remained after his defeat; Harold Wilson on the other hand went exactly the other way. I don't know if I agree that Mrs Thatcher has lost her charisma; she still attracts crowds, and I find her a very interesting and agreeable woman, but she has of course very strong opinions of her own with which I don't always agree.

Why do you think she was thrown out?

I wouldn't have believed it possible that a prime minister could be thrown out of the cabinet while she was actually abroad in Paris conducting the country's business. I had anticipated that there would be a tremendous outcry, but it all went off very quietly and calmly, and on the whole she behaved very well. She has deliberately remained rather quiet because she doesn't want to attack the conservatives in the run up to an election.

You were openly critical of Harold Wilson for what you saw as his reticence about the political motivation behind the strikes of the early 1970s. Were you generally critical of his premiership?

Yes. I was critical of him from the time that he left the labour government in 1951 when Attlee was in hospital; he followed Nye Bevan and resigned from the cabinet and produced something of a crisis. I didn't like him, and although I knew him fairly well, I was never a personal friend, and I was critical of his policies. He on the other hand was very fair towards me. I was unaware until quite recently that he regarded me as his main rival and competitor for the leadership of the Labour Party. I'd never really competed for the leadership, but Harold Wilson told another MP that I was his main danger, and if I'd wanted to be leader and prime minister that nothing could have stopped me. I never realized he felt that about me and in any case I never saw myself as prime minister. The only time I might have taken the first step in that direction was when Attlee resigned from the leadership after he'd ceased to be prime minister. Amongst the potential candidates was Herbert Morrison who had been a great friend and supporter of mine. He'd given me my first wartime job when he became home secretary. I had an interest in becoming foreign secretary, which was my one ambition in politics, but he felt he must take that job because it was the next in importance to the premiership. He was an honest man, but a Little Englander who knew nothing about foreign affairs and only took the job because he thought it was a step towards the leadership. When the time came for a leadership election I might have stood, but I didn't, and not having become leader of the Labour Party I would never have become prime minister. The rest of that story is too elaborate to go into now, but I was surprised at Harold Wilson's much more friendly attitude towards me than my own towards him.

Do you believe there was a dirty-tricks campaign against Harold Wilson?

I never had any reason to think there was any campaign of that kind. Anything is possible, but I would regard the idea that the secret service could have plotted against him as extremely unlikely. The heads of the secret service are appointed by the prime minister of the day, subject to an all-party degree of supervision. This is not regarded as a political appointment, so I cannot imagine that they would deliberately plot against the prime minister. It is conceivable that they might conclude from their own information that the prime minister himself was behaving in a way which was contrary to the interests of the country, that he was in league with the Soviets; there were suspicions of that kind undoubtedly, a general feeling that his association with the Russians was too close – that was certainly the political gossip. If the secret service had any concrete evidence that the prime minister of the day was behaving in a way which was treasonable, or seditious, the head of the service would have been in a very difficult position and he would have had to do something. But I don't think it possible that the secret service would engage in any secret and dishonest campaign against the prime minister. I think that is highly improbable.

Of all the labour elder statesmen Harold Wilson is the least talked about, the least respected perhaps. Why do you think that is?

It's partly the fact of his disappearance from public life, due to illness, and the very curious circumstances in which he resigned, quite unexpectedly, giving no reason at all, and even today we're still speculating about what the reasons were. Did he, for instance, know that he'd got a very grave illness coming on and decide that he would resign before it became obvious? That is a possible explanation, but I've no idea whether it is the correct one. The final honours list was regarded with great surprise and disfavour and his policies had not worked out very successfully. The country was in a mess at the end of his premiership. People also felt that he had a curious relationship with his secretary, that she had a very strange influence on him. I don't think they worried about any sexual relationship, but they thought she had a rather sinister influence on his political judgement, and they didn't like some of his friends.

But do you think history will be kinder to him?

No. I don't think that he's done anything that would earn much praise in the history books.

Do you think the press council really does any good at all? After all, it is rightly called a watchdog because it can't bite, it can only watch.

I was chairman of the press council and I wanted it to exercise much greater power, but the newspaper owners were always opposed to giving it real power and for a long time it consisted entirely of press people, without any independent element. It took some time before we got independent people on to it. It still is dominated by press people and it has always set its face against any really effective sanctions. There ought to be sanctions which involve dismissing a journalist who's transgressed, and even sacking an editor, but they won't do that. So it is a body without many teeth, but I don't think it's useless.

And it is incestuous . . .

Indeed it is. I'm afraid that there may have to be changes in the law. The worrying thing about the press now is the extent to which it is purveying trivialities, mostly sexual trivialities, but all the newspapers, even the quality ones, have deteriorated.

Are you in favour of a freedom of information act?

In America it is very fully observed and it is quite extraordinary that information which we should regard as confidential, the Americans are quite happy to have divulged. Here, government officials and members of government are perhaps too much inclined to think that everything they do is so important that it must be secret. On the other hand, as an executive officer of Asprey and Mappin and Webb, you could not allow your staff to talk to the newspapers whenever they found anything which they thought might be a nice little titbit. If they gave away your private correspondence, you'd sack them. You must have confidence that you can discuss things which will not be repeated, and in the case of a government, you must be able to discuss some matters in cabinet or reach some decisions which you can't publish. So I think some degree of secrecy is inevitable.

What about the Spycatcher *affair?*

Yes, the government did look foolish there. I think we overdo it, but I wouldn't go as far as the Americans go. I think the Americans have interfered with the efficiency of their government and made it sometimes reluctant to reach decisions because of the fact that they would be exposed to immediate publicity.

It is very fashionable these days to have voluntary codes of practice, but why should those controls that the government thinks necessary not be statutory? One can imagine the sort of attention a Robert Maxwell would give to a voluntary code of practice.

Some codes start as voluntary codes and are eventually incorporated in the law when a convenient opportunity arises, but one mustn't overload the law, and if matters can be dealt with by a voluntary code that's a good thing. What one needs as a condition of such codes is professionalism by those who are affected by them, a sense that it is their duty to themselves and to their profession to adhere to the code; and that doesn't always exist. You may get the code and find that people are only interested in seeing how close they can go to breaking it.

If you could do whatever you wanted, what aspect of the law would you change?

I would certainly change the criminal law about the defendant not being required to give evidence. That is the main obstacle to a great many people being convicted who ought to be convicted.

Apart from wishing to become foreign secretary, did you have other ambitions which you haven't attained?

I often wonder, looking back, whether I shirked public responsibilities in favour of a family life. I'm afraid I lacked ambition in the ordinary sense. I married very young, before I was qualified for the bar, a girl who turned out to be very ill. She was gravely ill at the time I married her, gravely and fatally ill.

Did you know then?

I didn't know at all; I discovered it within a day or two. But we had twenty

273

years of happy marriage – no sex, no children, but happiness, and though it ended in tragedy after twenty years, I look back on it with gratitude and remember it all very vividly. I married again very quickly having been advised by one particularly close friend not to observe the conventions. We had three children and we had a very happy married life. My main ambition was really to enjoy this, to have enough money to live reasonably comfortably and make provision for my family after I'd died. I had another thirty years of marriage before that too ended in tragedy. During that time I could have been chief justice. I was offered that position twice by Attlee, the first time because I was attorney-general, the tradition in those days being that if the lord chief justiceship fell vacant the attorney-general of the day was virtually automatically appointed. I thought that was absolutely wrong; I was a very young man, pretty well unknown to the public, I'd only been attorney-general for just over a year, and so I refused it. And Attlee was very pleased. Later on I was offered the position of master of the rolls, on the same basis, that it traditionally went to the attorney-general. I again refused it, and later still I had the possibility of becoming lord chancellor. I refused that too, and looking back on it, I wonder whether I was really being rather selfish, and concerned more with my own comfort and family life than I ought to have been. The same thing's true of the possibility of getting to the top in politics. The result is that I am nothing.

Are you disappointed in life?

My life has been content. I've had great sorrow, two tragedies . . . three really, because my younger brother, who was a QC also, died in an accident. But I was very close to my parents, and I'm very fond of my own family with whom I have an excellent relationship. I don't feel disappointed or embittered; I feel that I've had a happy life, not a very useful life, but a happy one.

BARBARA SKELTON

Barbara Skelton was born in England. During the war years she entered London's literary and social circles where she encountered Felix Topolski, Osbert Lancaster, Peter Quennell and Augustus John. In 1950 she married the writer Cyril Connolly and temporarily left London's high society for a rural retreat where their entourage included Evelyn Waugh, Lucian Freud, the Rothermeres, the Duff-Coopers and other leading lights of the day. In 1956 she married the publisher George Weidenfeld; they divorced in 1961. Her third marriage to millionaire physics professor Derek Jackson took her to France where she has lived ever since. She is the author of three novels and two volumes of autobiography, *Tears Before Bedtime* (1987) and *Weep No More* (1989).

When you write about your childhood it is not shrouded in the usual romanticism. The unhappinesses seems uppermost in your recollection. How far do you think these early years charted the course of your later life?

Quite a lot, because I was taught nothing at all by my parents, and I have inherited the rather weak characters of both of them. If there's an easy way of doing something, I always choose it, and I can always be talked into doing something even if I don't want to. I suppose one does it in order to be liked really. It's a desire to please, and rather stupid I think.

Which of your parents influenced you more?

Neither of them had any influence at all. I was actually a very difficult child and whenever I was reprimanded about anything I would fly into a fearful rage. I never liked being criticized. My father had a weak heart and I was always upsetting him because of my rages, so I was packed off to convent school. I was drawn more to my father, but although I felt affection for him, I also had a feeling of contempt. There was always a great distance between us, and we never had any conversations about anything.

You describe yourself as a difficult child, given to tantrums, wilfulness, bouts of jealousy . . . would you say that such things are decided largely genetically, i.e. in advance of upbringing, or are they more a result of family life and parental influence?

It's a result of family life, my parents' attitude . . . I never felt I was cared about at all. My mother was on the stage before I was born and I don't think she wanted to have a child at that point in her life. When my sister was born she was happier about it, but I was a sort of stumbling block for her.

Did the relationship with your mother improve later on?

No, never. We didn't argue, but I seldom saw her and in the end I felt pity for her. It wasn't the case that she was incapable of affection because she made a great fuss of my sister. At my age I've learned certain things about life which have compensated to some extent for that lack of early bonding, but I do think every child needs affection. If I had had love as a child my life would probably have taken a different course. As it is, I consider my life to have been an absolute mess quite honestly.

Your younger sister seems to have aroused jealous rages in you. The attention which she received from your parents led you to anorexia. Did you understand the reasons for your behaviour at that stage?

It's difficult to say. Obviously I was trying to draw attention to myself. It wasn't that I ever really disliked my sister; I just don't have anything in common with her. I was awful to her when she was born; the tantrums were terrible, but later on I got quite attached to her.

Your sister seems to have continued to haunt you as a kind of counterpart to your own life. She has been in the shadows as a symbol of the sort of life you could have had if you had wanted, although you present it as being intolerably dull. Have you despised, resented or perhaps even envied your sister's ordinariness?

Oh never, I hardly ever think of her, except when I get a letter from her. She aggravates me tremendously, she's so completely different from me, never reading a book, never interested in anything, knowing nothing. She's been a good mother, that's all. She's terribly dull, although she can be quite humorous, which redeems her a bit.

You had an abortion at a fairly early age. Women traditionally agonize over the decision to abort. Did you?

No. It was a decision I've always regretted having made, but it was a very common thing then for women to be having abortions . . . in fact, people were having abortions like crazy, all the time. And as soon as I realized I was pregnant I found an abortionist quickly and had it without any regrets at the time.

When did you start regretting it?

Later on, when I realized I couldn't have children. I'd had a bad abortion which made me incapable of having children.

Abortion often traumatizes women, did it traumatize you?

I can't remember that it did. I was working at the time, which helped. I don't think it tortured me particularly.

In your memoirs you recall saying to your doctor: 'If I can't have a child, I shall feel utterly useless to everyone.' How and when did you come to terms with it?

It's something that I go on regretting. I think it's very important, particularly when people get older. Not to have any children or grandchildren is very sad. I believe I was intended to have children, and I would probably then have had a more settled life.

Did you feel a biological need to have children?

Absolutely. This accounted for my promiscuity in a way. I had a great physical need.

Your marriage to Cyril Connolly struck most people as an unlikely match. He scarcely appeared to be the answer to a maiden's prayer . . .

It was the timing. Timing is very important in relationships, because you might become attached to somebody but had you met them three or four years later nothing would have come of it at all. Cyril wanted to have some new person in his life and I happened to be there at the time. I was very pretty then, and funny and lively, and Cyril was what I wanted for a husband. I wanted my marriage to last, but the problem was that I was always very obsessed with sex. Sex was extremely important, and when that abated between us I became very restless. I fell in love with that terrible man Weidenfeld just because I was seeking sex for satisfaction again.

Barbara Skelton

Do you think Weidenfeld and Connolly had anything in common?

No. I would describe them as totally different. They had nothing in common except books, one being a publisher and the other a writer.

Your relationship with Connolly seems to have been better before and after your marriage rather than during it. Is that a fair assessment?

No. I was extremely happy all the time, and I now consider it the happiest period of my life. Marriage suited me; the only difficulty was the obsession about my sex life the whole time. I obviously wasn't being satisfied sexually and he couldn't accept infidelity, so it broke up. Sex didn't mean as much to him as it did to me. He always had this idea that it was sapping his mental energy, that it was bad for him, and he didn't feel the inclination. Some people can do something about it, make an effort, but I didn't . . . I withdrew. Maybe if he'd been more outgoing and affectionate when I wanted sex, it might have worked.

You wrote of Weidenfeld in your diary: 'When I consider being married to him, it does not seem to be what I want at all. I'm simply obsessed with him sexually.' Was the sexual obsession something which disappeared with marriage?

Not on my part, but on his, because he was burdened with anxiety, and he never actually wanted to marry me.

But you were obsessed with him sexually?

Yes, absolutely.

Why was that?

Well, how can one know why one is obsessed with somebody sexually? But I was. He was very active and in those days I tended to be attracted to somebody who nauseated me at the same time, which, quite honestly, was the case with Weidenfeld. I had nothing in common with him whatsoever.

Once the divorce was through I never ever wished to see him again, and he never wished to see me again. And we never did.

So it wasn't a very friendly parting.

No, particularly as I felt he was responsible for the break-up of my marriage to Cyril, and I felt great resentment towards him. And I disapprove of Weidenfeld as a person; he's absolutely everything I disapprove of.

Your propensity for corpulent men, from King Farouk to Weidenfeld, was traced back by your psychiatrist to your relationship with your father, a strikingly thin man. But how do you explain it? Did you discover an eroticism in obesity?

Yes, but I can't explain why. I certainly don't think it's anything to do with my father – that's absolute nonsense. It's true that fat people are sort of cosier. They were probably my substitute for childhood teddy bears.

Are you still attracted to fat men?

Happily, I'm not attracted to any men now, whether fat or thin. When a woman has had a hysterectomy, which I have, the sexual urge really does go. I think that is the reason. I've no regrets; in fact it's a great relief to me.

Were you also dismissive of the psychiatrist's suggestion that you were father fixated?

No, I think he was absolutely right in that. When I was young I was always more attracted to somebody much older than myself. Even my women friends were much older. I suppose they were parental substitutes.

How do you explain your earliest sexual attraction to Sidney, your father's rich friend? Was that a way of getting at your father?

I don't think so at all. I was very lonely in London and he was a substitute father figure. He was an elderly man, and he helped me financially, which was very agreeable. I went on with it until I began to find him boring, and then that was that.

Referring to Cyril Connolly and Bernard Frank you said that they both were very difficult to live with. This is something you seem to look upon as a positive quality, a challenge perhaps . . . is that the way you saw it?

Obviously I do have a masochistic side to my nature and I suppose that because they were difficult it titillated me, whereas other women probably would not have put up with it. Bernard's present wife always says I must have been extremely masochistic to have endured life with him.

Cyril Connolly was quite dismissive of your own writing. Was that a source of tension in the marriage?

No. I myself never had a high opinion of my writing, quite honestly. What he really couldn't stand was the tap of the typewriter in a small house when he was in bed upstairs reading. I did see his point – it must have been very irritating. I never held it against him, and in fact when the marriage was breaking up he helped me with the proofs of the first book. I think he was trying to ingratiate himself with me.

Your marriage to Derek Jackson takes up barely six pages of your memoirs. Is that roughly the importance you accord him proportionately to the rest of your life?

Yes. He was a good man with a lot of very good qualities. Indeed he was a perfect husband, but I didn't want a perfect husband; and he was also not particularly literary. So again, I married somebody with whom I had very little in common and instead of sharing his interest in physics, which I would try to do now, I didn't take any interest in it at all. I also didn't care about going to race meetings which he liked doing, and it all became such a bore. He wasn't concerned about a home life . . . he wanted to eat in restaurants all the time and it's not ideal always to be going into restaurants since you have to make conversation, which I found irritating.

The happiest time in my life was when I was married to Cyril because with him I had a home and I would spend hours in the kitchen cooking luscious things. I'm absolutely one hundred per cent a homely person, without ever having stuck to a proper home.

Looking back would you say you experienced love – the haute passion *– more outside marriage than within?*

I can only say no to that question. I was passionately involved in my marriages. The physical aspect was always over-important to me for some inexplicable reason. I didn't feel well in myself if there wasn't sex going on.

Your attitude to men is well documented and much written about; your feeling towards women far less clear. Do you feel any great solidarity with your own sex? Were you affected by or at least sympathetic towards the feminist movement?

No. I'm not particularly in favour of the feminist movement because I think that a woman's function is to marry and have children. I'm very old fashioned I suppose, but there we are.

Did you ever feel at a disadvantage being a woman?

No, never. More than anything I thought of it as an advantage because I was blessed with good looks when I was young.

Have you ever had a passion for another woman?

Not a passion, no. I had one fleeting lesbian relationship which was shortlived and disappointing, and didn't interest me at all. There was no real passion – I just saw her as another man with breasts, that's all.

It strikes me that you present a great difficulty for feminists. On the one hand, allowing yourself to be flogged by King Farouk to gratify his sexual

283

desires, on the other hand maintaining a kind of self-sufficiency, almost a superiority over men. How do you see it?

I needed men to keep me, otherwise I would have had to earn my living since I never had any money of my own, but at the same time if I got bored with somebody I couldn't continue the relationship. At those times I had to be able to cope by myself. As far as King Farouk was concerned you can hardly call it flogging since it was a dressing-gown cord and it didn't hurt . . .

But it scarcely fits any known definition of feminism . . .

Perhaps not, but I was attracted to Farouk. He was a king after all, and it amused me to be with him. He was a big fat fellow and I was very keen on him. He had a schoolboy side which I found amusing. Of course, if he hadn't been a king I might have seen things differently since his jokes were rather infantile, but I enjoyed myself and felt very affectionate towards him.

He was sexually very active, wasn't he?

No. He was handicapped sexually, I'd say, though I'd rather not go into details.

But he wasn't the great lover he was made out to be?

Absolutely not. He was a very inanimate lover.

He also had the reputation of being very mean.

Yes, he was a great hoarder of everything. I did once receive a present when he made a lot of money gambling, but then he stole my rings, and I never saw them again. I had three eternity rings, one in sapphire, one in diamonds and one in emeralds which I always wore. He said he wanted to look at them, so I stupidly took them off, put them on the table, and he pocketed them.

Why did he do that?

I haven't the faintest idea. Probably he liked them. He was well known for taking things; he'd go to people's houses and say he liked something and they'd give him it. He liked collecting. I tried to reclaim my rings but he never gave them back.

But you still retain good memories of him?

Oh yes, I would love it if he walked into the room now. He is one of the few people I do feel I'd like to see again.

Your description of the war years in London evokes a picture of dancing and romancing while the bombs fell. Was your life then conscious escapism from the horrors of war?

The awful thing is, I never sensed the horrors of war; I was just so frivolous, I suppose, and too involved with what was going on in my life. I never really took notice of the war.

The social scene you describe among London post-war literati has all but vanished. Do you feel very nostalgic for those years?

No. I go on living very much in the present. When I was young I was always living in the future, thinking everything was going to be much better. But not now. If you mean, would I like to relive those times, then the answer is absolutely not. What a terrible idea.

Do you ever worry about the future?

Yes, I do. I worry about death and how I don't want to die. One thinks about death a great deal after a certain age. I'm not at all religious, so I don't believe in life after death or anything like that. I'm very worried about the manner in which I'm going to die. I'd like to be somebody with a weak heart and then I could simply have a heart attack. But alas, it won't be like that.

Barbara Skelton

When you view England now from France, does it strike you as terribly dull?

No. I don't think of England as being dull. I like the idea of going back, but I know that I couldn't. London has become so ugly, but there's much more going on there than here. I lead a very isolated life in France. Here one remains a foreigner always; one never becomes integrated in the country.

In your two volumes of memoirs you reveal the most intimate details of your relationships with men, be they husbands or lovers. Some would argue that such revelations are morally indefensible since people are inevitably damaged by them.

Well, I don't know about that, but if your autobiography isn't completely honest, there's no point in doing it. Anyway, who is damaged by it?

George Weidenfeld, for example, got very upset about the revelations.

Did he?

I know he did.

Well, I could have said much worse things than I did, quite honestly. I really didn't even know he was upset, but since I remain antipathetic to Weidenfeld, I'm not going to be particularly upset about his being upset. He's somebody I just wholeheartedly disapprove of.

Since the books contain explicit sexual details, and real people are involved, you surely run the risk of being accused of sensationalism for the sake of commercial gain.

It simply never entered my head to put things in to boost sales. You have to be outspoken, otherwise there's no point. In any case I didn't put myself in a very good light either. I treated myself like everybody else.

Frank Kermode in a review of Tears Before Bedtime *wrote, 'Sometimes she misbehaves merely to affirm her presence.' Is that something you accept about yourself?*

I wouldn't say that was true, but I thought he did a very good review. I even wrote and thanked him. I certainly didn't misbehave consciously; misbehaviour came quite naturally. I was indulging in what I wanted to do.

Did you care about what other people thought?

No, I've never cared about what other people think.

Seen from the outside your life has been one of emotional upheaval, to say the least. Now that you are of a certain age do you feel that a measure of serenity has entered your life?

Yes. I'd be very foolish not to be content with it, because it's extremely serene.

So you're not living a tortured life any more?

No. Once the whole sexual problem has been dispensed with one can lead a reasonable life. The sex thing has obviously been a great handicap in my life. It gave me great pleasure but to be dominated by the sexual drive is absolutely appalling; I wouldn't wish it on anybody.

Your memoirs are characterized by a discontent, a restlessness – emotions we associate with an unhappy state. Yet it is perhaps this very malcontent *which has led to all the excitement, the drama, the passion . . . has it been a price worth paying, do you think?*

Yes, because otherwise I might have been rather a dull person. One has obviously lived more intensely, which is better than my sister, doing nothing, thinking nothing.

Barbara Skelton

What wisdom has come your way from all the agony and the ecstasy? What strikes you as being the most enduring lesson?

Enduring lesson? To be more tolerant, I think, and less selfish.

If you were to choose one man as a lifelong companion from all the men you knew, who would it be?

It would be Cyril, there's just no question . . . oh yes, Cyril always. I have an undying love for him and a great deal of respect. As a friend I would choose Bernard Frank. In fact, that's why I live in this awful little suburb, because he and his wife are neighbours and I see them all the time. One of the most important things about these two men in my life is that they never told a lie; that's a very rare quality. The same could not be said of Weidenfeld.

If you were to live your life again, would you opt for a quieter, duller, more ordinary existence?

No. If I had to live my life again I would be determined to make a success of a marriage and to have children, that's all.

Do you consider yourself happy now?

No, I wouldn't say I'm very happy. At the age of eighty I don't think one can be terribly happy. But I'm resigned. I shall go on like this to the end.

LORD SOPER

Donald Oliver Soper was born in 1903 in Wandsworth, London of strict methodist parents. He read history at Cambridge and took his PhD at London University. As a methodist minister he was superintendent of the West London Mission from 1936–78 and is widely known for his open-air speaking on London's Tower Hill. He has written many books on Christianity and social questions, and particularly on international issues from the pacifist angle. He was chairman of Shelter from 1974–8, and he is president of the League against Cruel Sports. He was created a life peer in 1965.

If I were to ask you for a profession of religious faith, what would it include? And perhaps more interestingly, what would it exclude?

I am a professing Christian in the sense that for me Jesus Christ is the centre of my thinking and the dynamic power for the kind of life that I want to live. I find in the Christian faith centred upon Jesus, the expression of that which I find inarticulate in myself. Christianity for me is therefore the endeavour to copy and fulfil in my life those elements of truth and goodness which I have found in Jesus Christ, and in the Christian Church. This does not by any means exclude a devotion to the literature of Christianity but it's certainly not the same thing as an attitude of acceptance of the word of God, so to speak, because the word of God comes to us only through the very imperfect media of human beings. I'm therefore not a sabbatarian and I'm certainly not fundamentalist in the sense that I regard the Bible as the final authority. The final authority is a spiritual concept which is fragile but very real.

How orthodox do you think your religious views are? Do you think orthodoxy matters all that much?

I don't think that orthodoxy matters until you put it in its true context. Orthodoxy for the primitive church was a very important element in the continuing story of Christianity. If, however, we take orthodoxy in the sense of the various commitments in theological terms that the Christian Church has made from time to time, I find some of them disturbing, some of them impossible, and most of them fundamentally irrelevant.

Isn't there a case for saying that very liberal clergymen give scandal to the faithful? There appear, for example, to be clergymen who don't believe in God and yet they are supposed to have the fullness of the faith. You appear to think that God is a vindictive old man and to deny the divinity of Christ. Is there anything left beside a sort of kindly rationalism?

I do not deny the existence of God and I do not deny the divinity of Jesus, but I am conscious of the fragile nature of what is called the vocabulary of Christian thinking. Many of the greatest truths of the Christian faith go far beyond our capacity to put them into precise words; God is altogether too mighty and too profound. The very word conveys, or should convey, profundities which are better expressed in Pascal than in a great deal of the theological documents which I'm invited to read and to subscribe to. With regard to Jesus, I have always believed that if you can be sure of his humanity, his divinity will look after itself. But if you start with some concept of divinity you may never get down to the basic reality of his common humanity with us. It is for me a fundamental fact that if Jesus is divine, it may be impossible for me to follow in his steps, but if he is circumscribed within the humanities that I have to put up with, then I can look up to him as leader as well as lord.

But do you still believe that God is a vindictive old man?

Of course I don't. I believe that God is a word we use to describe all kinds of personal attitudes which have nothing to do with ultimate truth whatsoever. I have never tried to define God because I believe a definition is an impossibility. It's only when I find God in terms which I can understand, that is to say in the life of Jesus, that the reality of God comes home to me. Otherwise God is the ultimately mysterious entity. Pascal's final argument for God's existence was that there has to be a reason for there being anything at all, and I'm content with that. I have a very imperfect piece of machinery with which to make sense of the life all around me, but what I can do is see in a human person those qualities and elements in the nature of God which I think are real.

If your views are heterodox, what is it exactly that you preach? It can hardly be 'Christ crucified' in the traditional evangelical mode.

You're asking a question which depends on what we mean by evangelism. I do not believe that evangelism is the proclamation of some kind of completely faultless doctrine and offer of salvation. And therefore for me heterodoxy is the necessary care that I have to take to realize that everything that does come to me from God or through Jesus Christ comes through the very imperfect channel of human life. Jesus was not faultless but he was divine in the sense that he made a complete acceptance to God instead of what for everybody else is a partial and imperfect one.

There has been a good deal of controversy in recent years about the relationship between religion and politics. Mrs Thatcher's effort to convert the General Assembly to capitalism was one example. But should they not in some sense be distinct spheres? After all, Christ said: 'My kingdom is not of this world.'

But Jesus also said: 'Seek ye first the kingdom of God and its righteousness', which is very much in this world. His acceptance of leadership when he entered Jerusalem was a plain acceptance of the fact that for him the gospel was the good news of the fulfilment of God's purposes in so far as they can be fulfilled on this planet and in human affairs. For me the distinction between piety and politics is a very imperfect one. I am quite sure – and this comes from my experience of being a parson for so many years – that in ninety-nine cases out of every hundred our personal belief has a deep and clear relationship to our economic and political environment. And therefore the kingdom of God is far more important than the seeking of some personal identity when I die. The Christian Church time and time again has not been prepared to face the pacifism that is the essence of the teaching of Jesus, with the result that Christian propagandists have very largely concerned themselves with private piety, which is a very imperfect representation of what you can read in the Sermon on the Mount.

You once described your socialism as a logical consequence of your religious faith. Has your faith in socialism ever been shaken – Maxwell was a socialist after all. Socialist rhetoric can surely sound as hollow as the capitalist sort, in that they both seem to be endemically self-serving.

The sting is in the tail. Let me deal with the substance before I get to the tail. I have very frequently lost my faith in socialists, but I can say, without undue pride, that I have never lost my faith in socialism. It's not been tried and found wanting; it's been found difficult and not tried. So much of what passes for socialism today is in fact an acceptance of compromises which I feel are unworthy, and though I don't pretend to be looking for a martyr's crown, I'm quite sure that we haven't been prepared to pay the price for the socialism we've advocated. In that sense, the programme of our Christian faith increasingly has to be knitted together with the economic and political structure of society. I have never doubted that the second strongest thing in the universe is sin. That is to say, it doesn't surprise me when I find people not living up to the standards they profess, or not accepting the consequences of what they profess. That applies to me as much as to everyone else. It is a constant struggle. I wish I knew more about Maxwell – for one reason. I've been a prison chaplain and a practising parson, which has given me an increased and deepened sense that if you get to the bottom of things you'll find that people are better than their practice.

But do you ever think the problem might be original sin?

This is the ultimate question which I feel it's impossible to answer, but if I do get to heaven by a circuitous route, as I suppose is possible, then I want to ask God why he didn't give us a bit more information as to where original sin comes from. It is a problem, and in some cases it's a dilemma, because in the inscrutable wisdom of God we've got to find a place for the process of evolution in thinking and practice which is the background out of which we can think of ourselves as better than we were, or think of ourselves as striving for an ideal.

But are you yourself certain of going to heaven?

I am certain that if I fulfil certain conditions down here, heaven will be attainable and in the infinite mercy of God I think there's a chance of forgiveness on the other side. I don't claim to know much about it, however, and I'm a bit suspicious of those who seem to know more about heaven than they do about their next-door neighbours. 'In my Father's house,' said Jesus, 'there are many mansions; if it were not so I would have told you.' What I think Jesus was saying was, don't clutter up your mind with these impossible questions about the next world but believe that there is a continuity between this world and the next in which there is the same love and the same purpose and the same ultimate end.

You once said: 'I believe the principles of Toryism, enlightened self-interest, are incompatible with Christianity.'

I have never dared to say you cannot be a Christian and a Tory.

Do you nevertheless doubt that Tories can in practice be fully fledged Christians?

I'm quite sure they can't. One can't be a fully fledged Christian anyhow, but I think Tories are further off that attainment than other people. I get tired of denouncing other people as being unChristian, but what I'm prepared to say is this: the structure of Toryism – enlightened self-interest, market values and the concentration upon the individual – is not something that belongs to the Christian faith. Enlightened self-interest is in fact a rather kindly word for selfishness. Our involvement in the community is the essence of the Christian faith; individualistic emphases, in my judgement, are to be deprecated. The reason I have never been prepared to say that you can't be a Tory and a Christian is that it depends very much on one's definition of the terms, but I am absolutely certain that Toryism in principle is a contradiction of the Christian concept.

You reject the capitalist ethic totally. Yet you obviously believe very much in the practical application of Christianity, i.e. that the church should have relevance to modern life. Is it not unrealistic to expect to have an impact on the country at large without embracing some aspects of capitalism?

It all depends on what you mean by capitalism. I can accept the machinery of capitalism in some aspects of corporate living; I cannot accept the principle of capitalism as a worthy method whereby we conduct our public affairs. That could be regarded by some people as a bit specious, but you're asking a very difficult question. I do not believe that the capitalist is totally bereft of moral principle; it would be impudent and stupid of me to say so. One has to draw a distinction which is not easy to draw between capitalism as a working programme and capitalism as an ultimate principle. I totally reject the second but I think there are necessary ways in which in this very imperfect world we have to make use of the imperfect machinery until we can find a substitute for it.

Do you think we'll ever find a substitute for it?

Not on this planet, no. That's why I believe in eternal life.

Why is it so important for you to adhere to methodism, to serve under the banner of methodism, when you clearly are at odds with at least some of the methodist tenets and are not wholly approving of its founder John Wesley?

No one who took the precaution of reading John Wesley's life could totally approve of him. At the same time, he was a dynamic leader, and since I was brought up within the framework of methodism I see no reason to discard my background (even if I could). It doesn't seem to me to be very important which particular club you play for, providing you play the right game. In that regard there is a first-class argument for a multiplicity of churches with a common faith. One reason I've taken to the open air for the last sixty years is that John Wesley established the importance of open-air preaching, and in that respect I'm his dutiful son.

You have said that all statements to the effect that Jesus was the son of God are inexact, and that if only people could accept the humanity of Jesus the divinity would look after itself. This is something which doubters and agnostics would have no difficulty with, and certainly humanists have always emphasized the humanity of Jesus, but the idea seems rather strange coming from a man of God like yourself. In a different century you might have been burnt at the stake for saying such things.

I quite agree. You've only to read your history book to realize how tyrannical has been the attitude of official Christianity time and time again. Dostoevsky's *The Brothers Karamazov* is a perfect example of the way in which the official church has betrayed the gospel in the interests of the power which it was desirous of maintaining. Whenever there is an attempt to reconcile the kingdom of God with any particular regime, be it imperialism, or colonialism, or the capitalism of today, it simply doesn't work.

There was a proposal some years ago that you should be ordained as a priest in the Church of England. That was abandoned in the face of expected Anglican hostility. From your point of view could such a step have been anything other than a rather desperate attempt at Church unity, and given the divergence of beliefs, would this not have rendered the appointment purely symbolic?

The answer is conditioned by the fact that I didn't promote the enquiry. It was initiated by others, and I saw no reason to reject it in the light of what I believe to be the imperative need for church unity. I found a better way of expressing it later on in conversations we had with the Anglicans, but there was no reason why the methodists and the Anglicans shouldn't come together in one church. After all, John Wesley was an ordained Anglican priest. It is imperative to avoid the most damaging of all criticisms of the church, that we can't make up our own minds as to what we commonly believe and that we are separated at the point where the very concept of Christianity means unity. For me this is a desperate situation.

But do you think unity with the Catholic Church will ever be possible?

As things are at the moment, if unity means signing along the dotted line, that is out of the question. The hope of unity rests upon the ability of the Roman Catholic Church to abandon some of its cherished attitudes, and although there is some evidence of that already, it's highly unlikely in my time. I'm not being cynical when I say that unity can be more realistically conceived within the framework of the non-Catholic churches, there being a certain intransigence that is part of the absolutist concept of Rome. It is not nearly as rigid as it was, but until they change their attitude on, for example, the ordination of women priests, there's not much hope of progress. Female menstruation has been seen by the church as the time when a woman is impure, and you cannot have an impure priest. This is absolute rubbish, of course, and on this, as on so many sexual matters, the church is back in the middle ages.

From time to time you have spoken of your allegiance to the catholic church. I know that you use a small 'c' and that the word means universal, but in view of the fact that methodists do not approve of various doctrines about the Virgin, about the intercession of saints or about the real presence in the Eucharist, how is a universal church possible?

It is possible if the unity does not depend on a vocabulary which is assumed to be infallible. I'm not interested in the vocabulary of orthodoxy. With regard to the Virgin birth, for example, Mark didn't know anything about it, nor did Paul, nor the early Church, or the primitive Church. Jesus didn't know anything about it either. It seems to me to be a waste of time to ascribe to Jesus some kind of authority and divinity which is totally unnecessary. That is the way in which I would approach these problems.

Have you never felt tempted to move up to the high church, to graduate from the church hall to the church proper?

Yes. I am high chapel, if not high church; that is to say I have a firm belief that eucharistic worship is at the heart of the Christian practice of the faith. I should not feel able to go to Hyde Park on Sunday afternoon if I didn't receive the bread and wine on Sunday morning. Someone once said to me, 'I go to mass because it is the whole of Christianity in twenty-five minutes', and there's a very great deal of truth in that. Of course reality is far deeper than thought, far more than that which can be encapsulated within the framework of a doctrine. But I can honestly say that when I receive the bread and partake of the wine, that is a symbolic acceptance of my belief in the reality and the presence of Christ; unworthy as I am to receive it, I believe it to be the evangelical offer of salvation.

Can the Methodist Church or for that matter the Church of England survive?

They have already survived crises which would have destroyed other more rigid churches. There is an adaptability within the Anglican Church of which I very much approve. One thing I am certain of: the City of God remaineth and so long as we are in that city, there is a permanence which can defy the various vicissitudes and difficulties.

You had a crisis of faith when you were at Cambridge. Looking back, do you think the doubts presented a serious challenge in your life or were they merely a necessary path to the further consolidation of your faith?

Both. The doubts were very considerable, serious and hurtful. I had grown up within the close framework of a methodist tradition and when I went to Cambridge I was suddenly exposed. A friend gave me something to read about communism or rationalism, and it opened up a new world which was very disturbing. But it didn't last very long and the decisive factor was that the requirement of faith was a necessary filling of a gap which couldn't be filled elsewhere.

Your faith, and specifically your methodism, seems to be wholly a product of your parentage and background and upbringing. It was not something you came to by yourself or stumbled on by chance. In other words, it is very much an accident of birth. If you had been born a Catholic or a Moslem you might have embarked on a very different religious and moral crusade. Does that ever worry you?

It perplexes me in the sense that I can't put myself in a position of an entirely different environment. What I can say is that the changeover from the narrow methodism of my childhood to the socialist Christianity which I began to imbibe as a student was as fundamental a change as would have happened if I had started off as a Moslem and ended up as a Catholic. It was a radical and absolute difference.

Do you think that doubt is a necessary forerunner to the fullest kinds of faith?

Of course. You cannot believe unless you resolve doubt. Doubt is the precondition of questioning and enquiring. I have often been asked why I go to Tower Hill, why I go to Hyde Park on Sunday afternoon. It is because I believe in the fellowship of controversy. It is the only way in which we can deal with questions which otherwise accumulate in our minds or our make-up and are never resolved. There's no such thing as neutrality, and doubt is the first way in which you deal with that neutral presentation of brute fact.

The logic of your faith, besides leading you to socialism, also led you to pacifism. Doesn't the refusal to defend the right by arms if need be necessarily imply subjection to those who are prepared to use arms?

I believe we have yet to discover the power of non-violent resistance and indeed the power of self-sacrificing love. This is the only meaning I see of the Cross as distinct from the gun. The Cross of Jesus was his reliance upon the power of non-violent love, even when Pontius Pilate was perplexed by it, the disciples frustrated by it, and a great many ordinary people felt that Jesus was wasting his time and was no more than a lovable failure. Nobody can tell me that the way of non-violent love would not succeed, because as yet it hasn't been tried. The essence of the Christian faith today lies in finding an alternative force to the force of guns, and unless we find it I think that the prospect of the termination of this human race is as likely as that of the creatures that have disappeared already on this planet because they couldn't adapt themselves to the paramount need of living. We are in a very desperate position and in this instance I'm by no means a cheery optimist. I believe that there is a real prospect that we shall opt out of life by the use of an ever increasing destructive force. The emergence of the nuclear age has emphasized this as nothing previously could have done.

Is it not the case that pacifists trade on others' willingness to sacrifice themselves for the public good? Pacifists surely have a quiet conscience, but doesn't someone else just as surely pay the price?

I don't have a quiet conscience. In the cadet corps when I was a boy I was a bayonet-fighting instructor and loved it. I agree with you that if you regard pacifism as an easy option, it's discreditable, but I hope by the grace of God I should be prepared to pay the price of the pacifist case as soldiers pay the price of going to war.

Whatever good may accrue from pacifism in the long term, is it not true that in the short term individuals will suffer terribly for those ideals – and those individuals only have a short term?

This raises a fundamental question. I don't know very much about the long term, that is to say, I believe that the essence of the faith is that by doing things which are consonant with what is right, you release into the world forces which otherwise would be damned up. I think the man who stood in front of the tank in Tiananmen Square or those who decorate tanks with flowers and engage the tank commanders in argument are opening up a way. I have been asked what I would do if the Germans invaded Kingsway, and I said rather facetiously that we'd offer them a methodist tea; those who haven't appreciated the cathartic effects of a methodist tea shouldn't underrate it. Of course, this is regarded by most people as just silly nonsense, but I do believe that in one sense you can create an atmosphere of non-violence which is far more dynamic than the atmosphere of combat.

But who is to defend the old, the young, the vulnerable from the bully boy who is not open to rational argument? Are they to be sacrificed to a higher ideal?

The answer is that if you attempt to save people who are violently abused by the use of violence, the sum total of violence is not diminished. It's no good telling me that you fundamentally protect people by the use of war or violence; you don't. You can provide a temporary asylum for them but sooner or later that asylum turns into a fortress.

If conscience is a reliable guide to action, as you have often stated, what about those who in conscience believe that blacks are inferior or the Pope is the Antichrist . . . are their conscientious objections to be respected too?

It all depends on what you mean by the word conscience. When somebody says he believes he was justified in killing, or stealing something, I don't accept that as a conscientious attitude. That sort of conscience only records your condition at the moment you consult it, whereas the whole purpose of a conscience is to educate so that when the particular environment demands a response, it's an enlightened conscience which moves with the promotion of goodness and doesn't just lie fallow until it's called upon. When it's called upon in that fallow condition it isn't conscience at all; it's prejudice.

You have stated that it is more moral to risk the evil of somebody else than to apply that evil in order to prevent it. Would you really have had Britain submit to the Nazis in 1940 with all the consequences? It is hard to see how they could have been avoided without armed resistance.

The answer is if you chop up the film of life into a number of stills, you can provide yourself with insoluble problems. We could not have done anything other than what we did in 1940; but we could have done something very different in 1940 if we'd begun to do it in 1930. We very largely promoted the Hitlerism which afterwards we had to resist. I don't believe that you can at any moment, so to speak, isolate a situation; a situation is that which has developed from something that has gone before. We now have time to prevent the next war. We hadn't time in 1940 to avoid the war that happened.

It will surely seem extraordinary, perhaps even offensive to many people, that you should blame the British for the Nazi destruction of the Jews and others. You said that after we went in to defend the Jews they were massacred – they were merely persecuted before.

That is the first time I have objected to something you have quoted me as saying. I always take great care to say that I abominate the persecution of the Jews. The Christian Church should always make that humble apology since we have behaved disgracefully towards the Jews. But what I've tried to say again and again is this: that to go to the help of a persecuted people by fighting a war meant that many more of those persecuted people were in Auschwitz than if we hadn't fought a war. As a matter of fact, war exacerbates the very problem you go to try and solve. Let no one accuse me of saying that the Jews were getting on fairly well under Hitler; they weren't, they were in a condition of persecution which was an abomination, but the Auschwitz camps were the result of the war in the sense that Hitler was then able to isolate the problem from his own people.

The nuclear threat is certainly very real but it's difficult to understand how matters would be improved by having the Western democracies surrender their weapons while leaving others in the hands of terrorists or fanatics.

The risk of peacemaking is of course tremendous but we are so accustomed to accepting the risks of warmaking as to be the victims of very imperfect thinking. To me and to an increasing number of people, the emergence of a new situation in Europe demands the recognition that change is by no means limited to changes in the political field of power. There are radical changes now taking place in the culture of modern generations, and I take great comfort in watching the way in which new ideas are laying hold of communities who were previously immune from them. This isn't a complete answer, and I hope you don't think it's an evasion of the answer, but it's about time we realized that the traditional concepts of dealing with the evils in the community manifestly fail when they are linked to the requirement of violence.

But the question is, really, that if you were a man of power, would you do away with nuclear weapons at this point in time, knowing that others who are much more fanatical than you are, less democratic than you are, were retaining their weapons.

Yes. If I had the power then I should have been elected, and therefore there would have been behind my decision a community which was committed to it.

So you mean others would take the risk with you?

They would take the risk with me, and if that risk were generated within a community I believe it would spread like wildfire. The resistance to the communist regimes, which is the most remarkable thing to have happened in my lifetime, has come about because there has been a community which has taken a new road. I believe that is the hope of our survival.

You became a peer in 1965 and made the immortal remark that the House of Lords reaffirmed your belief in life after death. Is your seat in the House of Lords one you occupy easily and happily, or are you ill at ease with the power and the privilege which undoubtedly characterize the Lords?

In some ways the House of Lords can be a very useful instrument in the propagation of ideas which otherwise wouldn't see the light of day. I've had the opportunity of expressing my views on pacifism in the House of Lords and they've treated me with kindness. There is a value in the House of Lords, which is that it can be the occasion of an enquiry into matters which can take place one afternoon and can be reported in Hansard the next day. It isn't the same as a general enquiry but it is a way of fertilizing the intelligence of the other House on matters about which they may be less informed than they should be.

Although you sit on the labour benches, does it never seem to you as if you're supporting an institution which runs counter to the whole socialist ethic?

I have my temptations as of course many other people do, but I must be very careful not to assume a degree of piety with which I can look down on these sinners as if they're scoundrels. I have much to be thankful for in the steadfastness and the attitude of socialists whom I've loved and revered and who have been an example and an inspiration to me, and I'm not prepared to be cynical even if you wanted me to be. But I would say this: that sooner or later the House of Lords should be abolished. In the meantime I'm prepared to make use of instruments which sooner or later will be out of date.

On one occasion you spoke in the Lords about the way opposition to restricting homosexual propaganda had the whiff of fascism about it. Do you actually approve of sodomy?

Of course I don't. What I do approve of is the distinction between the condition of homosexuality for which you are not responsible, and the practice of homosexuality which can be bad. There is a prime case for saying that homosexuality is no more within the moral code than the colour of your hair or the size of your nose; what matters is what you do with it. The desecration of sex for the mere flippancy of enjoyment is one of the most dangerous and difficult of all issues, and at the same time I believe it's wrong. The prostitution of the body either in heterosexual or homosexual practice is to be regarded as a sin.

But where do you stand on the question of homosexuality? If we follow the argument that it is a natural human practice, because human beings do it, will we not logically have to count everything that human beings do as natural . . . murder, rape, slander, etc., etc.?

The distinction between the satisfaction of an appetite and the refusal to regard that satisfaction as right or wrong is a question which has to be faced. There are handicaps to the perfection of life. If, for example, you lose a leg or an eye, these are conditions which have to be accepted because they cannot be altered. In this sense one has to have profound sympathy for the homosexual because he is condemned to a world in which what is the creative and natural function of sex is to some extent changed by the fact that he is not heterosexual. In my judgement that involves a discipline which he is required to exercise which other people don't have to exercise. Far from blaming the homosexual who indulges in sodomy, I believe we have to have a great deal of sympathy with him; to condemn the thing that he does but to recognize that he has a much more difficult way of dealing with himself than those who are heterosexual. That's the sympathy. I do not believe that it is impossible for a future generation to find the answer to what is now the insuperable problem of how a homosexual changes into a heterosexual if he wants to. There are of course many relationships between homosexuals which are entirely right. Indeed in the lesbian field I can think of many women in the church who have been denied the opportunity of marriage or have lost their loved ones and who with other women have formed relationships which are of benefit to society. I can think of dozens and dozens of women who have in a very real sense loved one another but have avoided the cruder forms of sexual satisfaction. Of course this is easier for lesbians and not possible in the same way for the homosexual male. It's a very complex issue and when I criticize the church's attitude it is because I think we have to be much more charitable and to realize that some people have enormous problems which other people don't have to face, and that those problems are ineluctable in many respects. We're in a shocking mess over this whole question, and I believe only the grace of God is sufficient to meet these otherwise intransigent issues.

What are your views about allowing homosexuals within the church to give expression to their homosexual love?

It depends what you mean by giving expression to their homosexual love. I think it would be wrong to baptize, so to speak, the perversities of physical relationships; they are to be condemned as ugly. The consummation of the sexual act between a man and his wife can be regarded as a sacrament, it's beautiful. But in this very imperfect world one has to discipline oneself against misusing one's faculties in order to provide a satisfaction which is impossible in the same sense that a married couple can find that satisfaction.

Do you believe that in general sex is a gift of God to be enjoyed?

Yes, but to be enjoyed within the framework of a creative concept and not merely the idea of enjoyment for its own sake. It is important to remember that when, for example, it is said that the Moslem believes in that enjoyment, it results in the degradation of women. There's no doubt about that in my judgement; the woman is the instrument to provide the means of enjoyment for the man, and therefore the whole concept of the inferiority of women is part of that claim that sex is to be enjoyed.

Despite your own ardent teetotallism and belief in the monogamous purpose of marriage you are said to believe that heaven might just contain some light wines and that premarital sex might just be tolerated. What led you to this concession? Was it an attempt to take on board the reality of the times we live in or was it an unhappy recognition of falling standards of morality?

It was a further understanding of the spirit and teaching of Jesus. The evidence is increasingly obvious that Jesus had a relationship with Martha and Mary which was in part sexual. The essence of any relationship I've had with other people has always contained something of sexuality within it. The question is, at what point does the sexual behaviour pattern interfere with the real creative purpose of sexual relationships? I'm a teetotaller, but not because I believe there's something necessarily wrong in the ingestion of a particular liquid. I'm a teetotaller because of the social environment of drinking which I believe inhibits a great many people from leading a good life. The same holds true with regard to premarital sex. No one is suggesting that couples who kiss ought to wait till after they're married. We have to be a lot more healthy about this, and in my judgement it would be better, strangely enough, if we didn't think so much about it. I think there's an obsession with sex now. Sex in its right place is very important, but not too much of it. I'm eighty-nine now, so I can talk objectively about this, although I can very easily become a hypocrite unless I'm careful.

Do you still desire women at the age of eighty-nine?

Yes, of course, but it's rather different. In any case I'm blessed with a marvellous wife. But I see nothing wrong in admiring a pair of good legs. Why shouldn't I?

No, I think it's a very healthy attitude, I'm not opposed to it at all. You take a very liberal view of prison reform. But is there any real evidence that one can reform prisoners in any great numbers? Should public safety not be the first consideration?

I think the prison system is basically wrong, and can never be improved to the point at which it can be acceptable in a civilized society. That raises the question of what we do with the person who misbehaves, and unless we are prepared to think about that matter honestly we shall go on perpetuating the awful system we have at present; putting people away and forgetting about them. Very few people in my judgement are suitable for isolation.

You have suggested that prisoners should be treated well, be given holidays, and even be allowed sexual intercourse in prison. Would prison then be any deterrent? A lot of people might actually want to go to prison under these conditions . . .

Whatever you do, there are likely to be people who will abuse the system. But if you force me I would have to say I believe the evils of masturbation in prison to be greater than would be the dubious consequences of allowing prisoners who are married to have sexual intercourse. That on the whole would be better.

Are you totally against masturbation?

No. I think masturbation is an imperfect way of fulfilling a genuine impulse, and I'm not going to stand in judgement. It is a lack of self-discipline, but for people locked up for twenty years, I'm not going to say that masturbation is a crime or a sin.

You have practised open-air preaching for over sixty years now. It was forced on the first methodists, but what good do you actually think it does in a television age?

It offers a fellowship of controversy, and it remains the one free forum. I've enjoyed a lot of television, but I've suffered a good deal from it. That is to say, the necessary rules that govern television programmes do impair the kind of free for all which you can enjoy in Hyde Park. Open-air preaching provides a way to develop a particular argument in a real atmosphere in which there are no artificialities as there are in television programmes.

You have always pressed the need for man to be morally superior to his circumstances. In today's world, with all the modern pressures, isn't that just too daunting a task for most people?

Yes. That is why to ask them to do it on their own is an impudence. Most people are better able to face moral problems if they find that somebody else is trying to face them with them. That's the great virtue of the church, not so much the sermons preached, but the comradeship of effort.

Does it ever strike you that you are in a small dwindling church in an increasingly secular society. What is the point of your mission unless it is primarily a self-fulfilling one?

I can't distinguish between a self-fulfilling ministry and a public responsibility; to me they are both sides of the same medal. I believe that we are pack animals as distinct from isolated creatures who have no desire to run with the pack; at the same time we need fellowship, a word often misused. There's nothing so dangerous as the high-rise flat, the singularity and individualism of so much of modern life. One of the few real advantages of the mediaeval village was that everybody belonged; even the village idiot was a member of society.

Do you believe ultimately that faith is a gift of God?

Yes, but then I believe that everything worthwhile is the gift of God, though not something which God hands out as presents to certain people who are entitled to receive them. Faith is the way in which you deal with questions that you ask. Faith is a leap into the dark but only in so far as you have something firm enough underfoot to be able to make it. You can't leap out of a bog.

If faith is a gift of God do you think it is the duty of the minister to maintain a pious silence when it comes to something in which he cannot compel himself to believe even though he may wish to?

There is great value in preachers telling their congregations what they don't know as well as what they do. The preacher who gives the impression of knowing everything is going to lose his congregation; and he isn't worthy to retain it. There is a place for ignorance as well as the assertion of truth; a place for the confession that we're all sinners, doubters. Unless the preacher is like Jesus, a man among men, and unless he recognizes that there is a whole world in which we are all experimenting, I don't think he can do much good.

Do you ever consider that even the most honest, decent, and well-meaning men like yourself may be mistaken in their view of the world?

Yes. One of the advantages of speaking in the open air is that you're soon persuaded that you're not omniscient. I have any number of doubts, but one of the values of the Christian attitude embodied in the trilogy of faith, hope and love is this; my faith can be pretty slim and my love can be pretty imperfect, but there's nothing to prevent me hoping, since hope is a matter of the will. Faith is a matter of the intellect and the disposition, and love is the gift of God, but hope is something that you and I can do if we make up our minds. If you leave your mind to make itself up it's highly unlikely to do so, but hope is that solvent which brings the various facts into a focus of opportunity.

Have you ever been wrong in the sense that you believed in an idea, then changed your mind?

Oh yes, very often. For example, I was a teetotaler in the methodist form of regarding alcohol as the devil in solution. I don't hold that view any longer. Now I believe that temperance is required as a social responsibility.

Why has it been left to people like Mary Whitehouse to speak out on obscenity and related matters, do you think?

It hasn't. There have been a great many people who have spoken out just as clearly but, by accident or achievement, they haven't had the publicity. There's a great deal of the leaven of the Christian proclamation that proceeds only to make fairly small loaves. I admire Mary Whitehouse immensely, but, if I may say so, some of us have been saying the same thing for very much longer than she has.

Do you approve of all the things she says?

Not everything. But I approve of the intention she has and the general thrust of her argument which is that there's far too much dirt in the world of the media and the practice of people. My only criticism would be that in some cases there is a danger of doing more harm than good unless you can preserve an attitude of general charity. I'm not saying she doesn't, but she is a representative of some elements which are not as amenable to general understanding as others.

Now that you have reached the age of eighty-nine, are you concerned about the day of judgement?

I find it a waste of time to speculate as to how long I am going to last. I am more concerned with what I take with me to the next world than what my mansion in the sky or my hovel on the outskirts of the city of God will be in the next world. Most of my friends of my own generation are now dead. I'd like to see them again though I'm quite sure they've changed a good deal in the interim as probably I have. In my old age I'm beginning to learn about the virtue of living a day at a time, and believing that all things work together for good for those who love God. I hope at least that the next world will be as exciting in the sense of producing all kinds of issues and problems of which we know nothing now. I don't want it to be dull . . . sitting on a cloud and playing a harp.

Setting modesty aside, would you consider yourself to be a saint? If not, why not?

The answer is that a saint is somebody who is on the right road with his eyes persistently fixed on the horizon of the kingdom. If that is a saint, then by the grace of God I hope to be one. But it's a sheer waste of time to accord to oneself certain categories of goodness or badness; it is much more important to aim for what by the grace of God you can be. There is nothing so boring as people who feel that they have to be everlastingly telling you how good they are and how bad you are. Piety is a word which has fallen into disrepair, because true goodness is exuberant as well as faithful, and the exuberance is a part of goodness, and if you haven't got that you're about as useful as mutton.

The last question . . . have you any regrets?

An infinite number. At my age one's sense of failures in the past is an interesting and solemnizing experience. You haven't much time in which to put things right, which makes me say better prayers than I used to.